MAKING CHANGE HAPPEN

Shared Vision, No Limits

Bill Lamperes

ScarecrowEducation
Lanham, Maryland • Toronto • Oxford
2005

Published in the United States of America
by ScarecrowEducation
An imprint of The Rowman & Littlefield Publishing Group, Inc.
4501 Forbes Boulevard, Suite 200, Lanham, Maryland 20706
www.scarecroweducation.com

PO Box 317
Oxford
OX2 9RU, UK

British Library Cataloguing in Publication Information Available

Library of Congress Cataloging-in-Publication Data

Lamperes, Bill, 1943–
   Making change happen : shared vision, no limits / Bill Lamperes.
      p. cm.
   Includes bibliographical references and index.
   ISBN 1-57886-174-8 (pbk. : alk. paper)
   1. School improvement programs—United States—Case studies. 2. School
management and organization—United States—Case studies. 3. School
principals—United States. 4. Educational change—United States—Case
studies. I. Title.
LB2822.82.L35 2005
371.2'012—dc22

                                                        2004011668

∞™ The paper used in this publication meets the minimum requirements of
American National Standard for Information Sciences—Permanence of
Paper for Printed Library Materials, ANSI/NISO Z39.48-1992.
Manufactured in the United States of America.

To my sons, Mark and Bret . . .

may your lives be filled with passion and joy!

CONTENTS

FOREWORD

It's always inspiring to hear about school improvement success stories. Yet as educators, we can also feel intimidated by those successes because we often don't know *how* the changes came about. "How did they do it?" we wonder. "Would that work in my school?"

Part of what makes *Making Change Happen: Shared Vision, No Limits* such an outstanding example of school improvement is that it was written by a practitioner who lived the success story. Bill Lamperes accepted a temporary position as a brand new principal and planned to use it as a stepping-stone for his career. And while his career took an unexpected turn—he served as Centennial High School's principal for 12 years—it was Bill who turned out to be the stepping-stone for the school's road to success.

The timing of this book's publication is particularly appropriate because it so closely parallels the recommendations expressed in *Breaking Ranks II: Strategies for Leading High School Reform.* An acclaimed roadmap for school change, *Breaking Ranks II* outlines 31 recommendations for school leaders taking on the challenge of reforming their high schools. Each recommendation falls within the focus of three core areas:

- Collaborative leadership and professional learning communities
- Personalizing your school environment
- Curriculum, instruction, and assessment.

The success of Centennial High School, as you will discover in reading *Making Change Happen*, is based on strategies that fall under the same three core areas. And you'll likely find that you can put to rest any worries you may have about implementing the strategies in your school. The approaches are straightforward and applicable to sparking improvement in any school situation.

Making Change Happen not only encourages other school leaders to take up the challenge of improving their schools, but it explains in clear and simple language how to go about it. Because Lamperes was new to the principalship when he joined the staff at Centennial, his practical strategies for new and transitioning principals are especially valuable—and are appropriate for veteran principals as well.

Not too long ago, the term "school reform" was often said in a whisper because it could stir up fear and resentment. Today, improvement is something all principals should aspire to bring about in their schools—regardless of their current success level. There is *always* room for improvement, and what better way to motivate students than to teach them to always have a goal in sight?

I am confident that you will find inspiration in many of the strategies laid out in the pages that follow. Read them. Share them. By all means, *use them*, and your school will no doubt succeed in ways you have yet to imagine.

Gerald N. Tirozzi, Ph.D.
Executive Director
National Association of Secondary School Principals

ACKNOWLEDGMENTS

I used to think I was a word merchant until I started working with my friend and manuscript editor Frank Kaplan, who is a word master. I spent the better part of a year learning humility. Frank, a retired journalism professor from the University of Colorado, generously gave of his time and talent to edit each chapter of my manuscript. Every month I anticipated the return of the manuscript, marked with blue pencil and insightful suggestions related to word choice, punctuation, and sentence structure. I thank Frank for engaging me in a year-long English seminar that added life and polish to the work.

As I wrote each chapter, my friend Rebecca Reynolds carefully read each draft and asked difficult questions that required clarification. Rebecca offered me encouragement and support throughout the writing process. I also want to express my appreciation to the wait-staff at the Crown Pub in Fort Collins. They helped me nail down the details of the analogy I used to craft chapter 2 and kept me from getting rusty in my daily writing. The last bit of editing came from the pen of my administrative assistant, Cora Knies. Her perceptions, precision, and pen located the last remnants of grammar and punctuation mishaps that plagued the manuscript before I submitted it to the publisher.

I am grateful to Jane Nicolet, my former spouse. For more than a decade Jane provided support, counsel, patience, a listening ear, and professional advice as I shared daily events, stories, and dilemmas related to Centennial. She made it easier for me to return to school the next day, ready to accept the next challenge. I thank her for that partnership.

I am also grateful for the assistance of Paula Rogers, senior records technician for Poudre School District. Paula helped me locate Centennial graduates and checked the accuracy of my information related to school events. In similar fashion, I want to acknowledge the district's central office administrators who tolerated many unconventional practices that permitted Centennial to not only experiment with ideas but also to fail sometimes, and to achieve great outcomes most of the time. Specifically, the district administrators who championed Centennial's vision included James Sandoval, Monte Peterson, Joe Hendrickson, and Gary Bamford.

Centennial's success captured the community's imagination and earned respect and support from public leaders. Notable members of the Fort Collins Community who contributed to the success of the program include Sue Hammerton, nurse practitioner; Trudi Slater, private therapist; Terry Deniston, professional development, Colorado State University; Jerry Deffenbacher, psychology professor, Colorado State University; the Stryker-Short Foundation; the Bohemian Foundation; the Poudre Valley Hospital Foundation; Don Wilkerson, Golden K Kiwanis Club; The Belgian Brewing Company; Michael and Elaine Moravan Family Foundation; George and Louise Thornton Family Foundation; Joel Painter, director of the Jacob Center; members of the Building Trades Advisory Board; and Kathleen Tack, glass artist.

I want to acknowledge the hard work and collaboration of all the Centennial High School staff members who lived and worked with change for more than a decade. Centennial was never "my school." It was always "our school." We worked together as a team under a common set of beliefs and moved toward a common vision that guided our time together. We did not always agree on everything. In fact, we disagreed frequently and often talked issues to death in the process of achieving common ground. In every situation, those involved handled themselves as professionals. I always appreciated that fact.

A word of appreciation goes to the students and parents who were enrolled and participated in Centennial's program. They contributed time and energy to the school and became the beneficiaries of the staff's ability to make a difference in their lives. A special thanks goes to those parent leaders who guided the school's Parent Advisory Board and believed in the vision. They include Greg and Judie Evans, Karen Wiggins, Cheryl Yankowski, Doug Donaldson, Jake Udel, and Eileen Orme. I thank them all for participating with us, for believing in our process, and for working in the culture of learning we envisioned and achieved.

Finally, I want to express my thanks to Bob Farrace, the director of publications at the National Association of Secondary School Principals. He was one of the first professionals to read the manuscript, support the project, and direct me to potential publishers. This project has become a reality in part due to his encouragement and guidance.

INTRODUCTION

Making Change Happen is a book about an educational change that moved Centennial High School in Fort Collins, Colorado, from the cutting block and closure to exemplary status as a national model within the span of a little more than a decade. It is the story of a dedicated group of educators and a principal with leadership skills who embraced the challenges of change and relentlessly pursued a vision until they had created a program that addressed the specific needs of at-risk youth. Narrated by the school principal, the elements of passion, planning, motivation, conflict, and compromise unfold in a series of "how to" success strategies that are shared in each chapter. The strategies may inspire others with a sense of hope so that they too can guide their own organizations through the change process to the goal of success.

THE VOICE

I grew up in an era of change. As a ninth-grade student, I watched Sputnik streak across the night sky and I became a beneficiary of the massive changes that redesigned the country's educational landscape in a few years. What motivated me to become an educator was the call of "what

I could do for my country" as the wave of the New Frontier captured my imagination. I entered the education profession stimulated by hope and desire to make a difference, and I discovered abundant opportunities and federal grant dollars to experiment with new ideas. I taught through the radical and chaotic seventies and lived with its disappointments. Soon enough, I felt the condemnation and criticism of the 1983 *Nation at Risk* report and doubled my efforts to make the educational system responsive to society's needs. The nineties witnessed the advent of the charter school movement, corporate takeovers of schools, and renewed experiments with alternative education. Little did I realize my association with Centennial High School would become such an integral part of the change movement in public education.

I never wanted to be a school principal. Having earned a doctorate of arts in history at Carnegie-Mellon University in Pittsburgh, Pennsylvania, in 1985, I had every intention of becoming an assistant superintendent of curriculum and instruction in some school district in the country. I loved creating new instructional packets and possessed a real passion for assisting staff members in developing and delivering new curricula. Since 1980, I had served the Poudre School District in Fort Collins as its social studies curriculum coordinator and looked forward to the next logical step of becoming the district's director of curriculum. As fate would have it, this never materialized.

In my youth I had been a fairly brash, somewhat arrogant "young Turk" teacher who emerged from the mid-sixties with an attack-the-system attitude and a disdain for leaders who had lost touch with cultural changes impacting America and the needs of the new generation of students. Early in my career, I had sabotaged a couple of principals whom I considered managers and not leaders, individuals satisfied with keeping the lid on the program and controlling the inmates in the institution. These individuals conveyed neither a sense of vision nor mission. They wanted to make sure they did things the right way but failed to do what was right for the changing times that permeated the American culture.

So I attacked the system, created havoc, and became its critic, making fun of what I observed but lacking the power or authority to change the way things were. In schools where I worked, the staff never considered me a candidate for the teacher of the year award. In fact, many of my colleagues asked me why I didn't go back to where I came from and mustered me out of their building with great enthusiasm when I decided to change schools.

Over time, as I continued with my education, training, and life experiences, I learned how to temper irreverence for the system so that my professional beliefs could be translated into palatable ideas. I realized that hitting people over the head with perceived truths did not foster change, only resentment. So I took a less obtrusive track and began to model practices that worked more efficiently, both with adults and students. As experience and maturity began to modify my behaviors, I began to earn the respect of my colleagues and district leaders as an effective instructor. When the position of social studies coordinator was posted in 1980, the superintendent of schools reluctantly permitted me to step into the role on a trial basis.

Suddenly, my job was that of a middle manager rather than the outside critic. However, the position did not entitle me to use any real power to complete my responsibilities. I had to employ my people skills to work with all sorts of instructors' personalities, who, by the tradition of academic freedom and contractual agreement, exercised virtual autonomy in the area of instruction, discipline, and management. What a shock it was to be the "new suit" from the central office and to be viewed by my colleagues with suspicion and distrust.

My new challenge was to help instructors create a vision of a better and more engaging way to motivate students to participate in the learning process, and to share with others the most promising educational practices for success. During the decade I served the district in this capacity, I learned many lessons. I mastered the art of personal diplomacy, effective dialogue, and compromise. I learned how to negotiate from a win-win position instead of relying on power, dedicated myself to the progress and success of the work of others, and came to realize that personal humility is one of the most effective leadership traits when a larger and more distant goal is to be achieved. I practiced more patience with the system and expanded my capacity to tolerate ambiguity. I was able to delay decisions and took time to gather key bits of information that permitted analysis and direction for essential courses of action.

Most important, I began to develop the capacity to create visions of possible futures. I developed the skills and nurtured my intuitive capability to see the big picture, formulating plans and dreams that could be accomplished. I found the words to paint a picture of each vision and to capture the imaginative potential within my colleagues to achieve that vision.

My analytic side was activated to the extent that I could design implementation plans that made success possible. Furthermore, my attention to data gathering permitted me to create assessment instruments so that success could be measured and adjustments made to stay focused on stated goals. I exuded energy, passion, and charisma, and confidently became a leading force to motivate and create change in people and programs. For a decade, I immersed myself in a work of love, and one curriculum after another was successfully implemented by a cadre of teachers who took pride in what they did and how they interacted as an effective team. By the end of the 1980s, I was ready for new professional challenges.

At the same time, however, it became clear to me that the opportunity to become the assistant superintendent for curriculum and instruction would not come my way in the Fort Collins School District. Therefore, I dusted off my resume and began applying for positions throughout the country. After my fifth "runner-up" interview ended, I began asking questions: Was there something wrong with my resume, my training, my presentation, or my portfolio? Why was I always the runner-up and not the chosen candidate? One generous superintendent shared with me the insight that the selection committee's decision was based mainly on the fact that in all of my experience, I had never sat in the principal's chair. How could I be an effective director of a district's curriculum division if I had not experienced the challenges of being a building principal?

Now all of my previous disdain for principals came back to haunt me. Fate had dealt me an ugly blow. I could only think about the old phrase "What goes around, comes around." I was determined to dismiss that notion and to return to the job market without the principal leadership experience. However, in June 1990, another opportunity presented itself. My supervisor informed me that the principal of Centennial High School, the district's alternative high school program, had taken another job in the system and I could apply for this "one-year-only" interim position to get the needed experience to place on my resume. I balked at the idea at first but rationalized that anybody can do anything for one year, and the position could be used as a springboard to the post I really wanted. I entered the applicant pool and was selected as the temporary principal of Centennial High School.

Throughout this book, I tend to refer to myself in the third person. This is partly based on the personal humility that was drummed in to me while I developed my leadership style but it is also a way for you, the reader, to identify and interpret the strategies herein through your own personal lens. No two situations, schools, or principals are alike; each must be interpreted individually.

THE SCHOOL

Centennial High School occupies a two-acre space surrounded by an older neighborhood in downtown Fort Collins, Colorado. The school was constructed in 1906 and served the community as one of its original elementary school buildings. The building housed nine classrooms and an apartment for the custodian. Over time, other structures were added to the site. In the 1950s, a gym/cafeteria was built to the east of the main building, followed by a two-classroom building on the west side of campus that served as the program's kindergarten. A one-acre park separated the kindergarten from the other two buildings. It was a small site, and I felt it would be easy to supervise as a principal.

When I met with my supervisor to review the scope of the one-year-only job, I was greeted by another surprise. He informed me that my role as principal was: (1) to have a good year as they conducted a national search for a replacement, but more specifically, (2) to use my creativity and analytic skills to make the decision to "either fix it up or shut it down." It seemed the function of Centennial High School had changed over the previous decade. It had served a multitude of purposes for the district. It was both an alternative high school and an alternative junior high school. It had been the dropout prevention center, had housed the adult high school completion program, and still housed the G.E.D. program. It had been a vocational preparation center and a tutorial service. However, with the arrival of the city's community college in the late 1980s, all of these functions had slowly disappeared.

By 1990, Centennial High School was overstaffed, underutilized, and quite costly. During very difficult fiscal times, the district was challenged to examine its most costly programs and asked to cut those that failed to provide the services required by the educational community and by the taxpayers. Therefore, the one-year-only job that had been thrust upon me as a means to achieve a professional goal now turned me into a potential hatchet man. I would not be embraced with welcoming arms by a staff facing loss of jobs, receiving forced transfers, and watching the demise of a program that had existed for more than a decade.

As it turned out, my one-year-only job lasted a total of twelve years. During the years of my tenure as principal of Centennial, the staff successfully moved the school from a program fated to be closed and, in the process, created several educational models that have been replicated in many school districts across the country. To achieve this end, my staff and I worked through the change process, created two five-year visions, and used data and shared decision making to foster program changes. The program captured the imagination and pride of students and their parents, improved academic performance, and increased graduation rates and daily attendance. The school helped redefine the meaning of alternative education for the community and became a model for several charter schools. By the end of the 1990s, Centennial had become a school of choice rather than a last chance for kids who couldn't make it in traditional settings. With a great deal of pride and a clearly defined goal of meeting the needs of all students, the staff turned Centennial High School into the community's "golden child of education."

THE BOOK

The purpose of this book is to help the reader identify various aspects of the change process and for me to share how to create and achieve goals that will lead to a unifying vision. Such a vision must drive the actions of employees and clients served by the education system. The book is filled with strategies, ideas, suggestions, and processes that a leader could use to enhance the quality of any system, organization, or business. The Centennial High School experience provides the backdrop for each strategy used, but it could be modified and adjusted to meet the needs in any setting. The concepts and techniques discussed are powerful, effective, and simple to implement.

Chapter 1 focuses on strategies used to assess and analyze a system, to observe how it operates, and to foster credibility in a new leader so that a climate for change can be created. These techniques use data-gathering approaches as well as interpersonal activities to engage individual employees committed to the change.

Chapter 2 outlines the strategies needed to lay the foundation for change. The chapter's central theme is how to mobilize the staff and create the momentum to move from the status quo into an uncertain but planned future. Careful preparation for change is essential in order to successfully engage participants' heads and hearts in the change process.

Chapter 3 details the necessary steps to create an organization's vision. It is essential, first of all, that participants define and embrace a long-range, commonly shared vision. A clearly stated vision will guide and align the direction of all the arrows of those within the organization's culture. It is the glue that holds the organization together, and it becomes the centerpiece upon which yearly goals, both organizational and personal, are built. The vision drives the reason for existence and ignites the passion for activities in daily interactions. When the vision becomes the organization's driving force, attention will be given to strategies that engage all of its stakeholders.

Once the vision and mission of the organization are clarified, they must be translated into programs, policies, and actions that define the culture. In Centennial's case, a major shift in the program necessitated a retraining of the student population so that they could thrive and succeed in a new structure. Literally, the Centennial staff had to retrain students to modify their behavior so they could learn how to become part of the new vision. Chapter 4 identifies various program changes that were implemented to help students learn personal success.

Chapter 5 discusses the changes needed to refocus the program on academic success. Given the nature of high-risk students, the Centennial staff created programs that not only addressed district standards and expectations but also addressed the unique learning styles of its clientele.

Chapter 6 emphasizes the process of refining and creating a new five-year vision for the program. What happens to an organization when the original vision is achieved? This chapter outlines ways to move beyond celebration to embrace the next challenge. Using assessment tools, the findings of an outside evaluation team, and the knowledge and desires of employees, the discussion focuses on how to create a second five-year vision that refines the goals of a program that has successfully achieved its long-term vision for success.

Surprisingly, the "visioning" process cannot be recycled. With the addition of new staff members and their limited sense of the institution's history, the leader must use different strategies to create a new future. How does the leader help new staff members develop a sense of history and develop a passion for continued growth? How does the leader motivate veteran staff members to move from a position of comfort to seek greater levels of success? How does the leader help the staff redefine the boundaries of the new vision for the cultural expectations of the organization?

Chapter 7 invites readers to examine ways to engage various stakeholders in the process of creating an exemplary program. Parents may become discouraged with their students, lose hope, and give up their dreams of seeing their youngsters succeed in life. Specific strategies are outlined so other educational institutions can identify ways to build a better collaborative effort among the parents of students enrolled in school.

In addition, the district administration and community have legitimate reasons to commit to the success of a tax-supported educational program. Relationships with district officials, members of the school board, community service organizations, and individual citizens are reviewed in this chapter. When an organization undergoes immense changes, its members must be permitted to create and implement policies that radically depart from past patterns. The organizational leader must instill a sense of confidence in the system's supervisors and community observers so that the proposal for changes and ideas for improvement can be supported and implemented. It takes a deft hand and a strong will, coupled with effective communication strategies, to permit the organization to move forward unmolested by those mired in the concrete of organizational trappings and traditions.

Finally, chapter 8 is filled with reflections of how to court the central office, establish credibility as the organization's leader, lead and participate in the change process, and establish oneself as the community symbol of the school program. Since change is constant, how does an organization maintain tradition and embrace movement at the same time? How does an organization prepare for continuance and improvement necessitated by a changing population of clients and changing social and economic conditions in the community? This chapter summarizes many of the lessons mastered over a decade of change and insights related to moving the organization ahead in an exemplary fashion.

This book contains many leadership strategies forged and tempered over a period of twelve years by an administrator at one school. Some of them had immediate success and produced long-term results. Others had to be modified as conditions and situations changed, only to be resurrected and implemented again at a more propitious time. This list of ideas can, and has been, frequently modified to address changing situations—and for all of us, times continue to change.

1

FIX IT UP OR SHUT IT DOWN

The last thing the assistant superintendent told the new principal was: "You have one year. Either fix it up or shut it down. I'll live with your recommendation." The novice principal had no commitment to or passion for the school, its staff, or the students they served. Centennial High School was merely a stepping-stone to a future position as an assistant superintendent of curriculum and instruction. At the end of the year, Centennial High School would become a line item on a resume and part of larger career plans.

The administrator had no experience as a building principal or with Centennial High School, and only limited experience with the at-risk student population it served. The job began as a one-year-only interim placement and expanded into a twelve-year career that embraced not only the school and its students but also an intense passion about the program's potential and the staff and students who turned it into a national model for alternative programs.

How does one step into a job and earn the power granted by position? How does one earn the respect of authority inherited by the role? How does one get to know the nuances of the program and the dreams and concerns of employees who occupy spaces every day? How does one sense the needs of adolescents who may be reluctant participants in a system that may no longer be meeting their needs? How does one gather enough data and intuitive insights to help direct decisions for change? The five strategies identified in this chapter offer ways to address these questions and assist the novice principal in becoming an effective leader in a new setting.

STRATEGY #1: GETTING TO KNOW THE PLAYERS

Who were the people that worked at Centennial High School? Why were they there? What could they share about the previous decade of the organization's existence? What goals and visions did they have to justify their place in the big picture of things? What did they think of the institution or of its function, purpose, and success? With a new principal in place, what were their dreams, concerns, and suggestions for improvement? How did they feel about the students that Centennial served?

Usually the announcement for principal vacancies occurs in the spring of each year. This timeline provides a new principal with enough time to get to know the staff of the school, comprehend the school culture, and assess the program's progress toward meeting ongoing goals. One of the first tasks for the new principal of Centennial High School was to hold private conferences with each staff member who worked there. He proceeded to schedule breakfast, lunch, dinner, or coffee appointments with each one of them. This was easily accomplished, since the program had only fourteen staff members.

Note: If you are the first-year principal of a school with a much larger staff, the principal should meet individually with department supervisors and then groups of employees within each department. Department members should be invited to respond to the questions below in advance and to give them to the principal at the end of the group interview so they can be summarized and analyzed.

The purpose of this process is simple: to let employees get to know the new leader and to let them express concerns, anxieties, and dreams of what the future holds for the program. The previous principal at Centennial High School had been in place for the first ten years of the school's existence and had fostered many loyal followers as well as alienated some members of the staff. Based on this history, it was necessary to begin with one-on-one relationships before the business of running the organization began in September.

In an effort to get acquainted with the big picture of the program, each staff member was asked five basic questions:

1. Why do you like working at Centennial High School?
2. What is the vision or purpose of the program?
3. How have you contributed to this purpose or vision?
4. If you could change anything at all about the staff, program, or the business as it has been conducted, what would that look like?
5. What do you see as the long-range vision or goal of this program?

The scope of these questions permits a new principal to learn a great deal about each person's passion, commitment, and view of the program's potential. The individual meetings with staff members provide insights about how employees see their places in the hierarchy of the system, their perception of their own power within it, an overview of the building culture, and the degree of their commitment to it.

When interviews are complete, a new principal knows how the program works; who the key players are; what needs to be fixed immediately; and what long-range systems, policies, and structures require modification in order to accommodate the changing needs of students. In the interviews, participants often share many of their perceptions of the social nuances between and among staff. They reveal frictions and histories among employees so that more information about the past is shared than the new leader really needs to know. The individualized format, however, gives each person an opportunity to vent and express concerns, disappointments, and beliefs about the program and its future. This strategy provides the new principal with a big-picture view of the current employees as well as their personal strengths and limitations. This process can be used again in later years when it is time to create another program vision.

STRATEGY #2: STATING PERSONAL AND PROFESSIONAL BELIEFS

One of the first memos a new principal should distribute needs to be titled: "My beliefs about . . ." This document should clearly state what he or she believes about the profession, communication, decision making, students, and the change process. It is essential for the staff to get to know the beliefs behind the way the principal will conduct business, the core values that will drive decisions, and what he or she considers the most important priorities and outcomes.

This document needs to be designed to familiarize employees with the principal's personal passions and work ethic. It reveals a commitment and focus for accomplishing quality work. It sets the tone for establishing expectations of the way school business will be conducted. Even if the principal is in an interim role for a one-year experience, the school leader lives with personal values, cultural beliefs, and passions that guide his or her professional life. The school staff needs to know this information about their new leader.

After distributing this position paper, invite staff members to discuss individual items that need clarification and elaboration. Specifically emphasize the need to have staff members observe the correlation between words and actions in order to make sure that the leader "walks the talk"—or, in this case, the words put on paper. It is essential that the leader of an organization model, both publicly and privately, the beliefs and statements that guide and direct his or her actions. Modeling represents the passion one has for a position, the commitment one exhibits to accomplish stated goals, and the integrity level one must earn to lead effectively. In this way, the leader can assume power and gain the confidence of others to take the organization to the next level of success.

STRATEGY #3: ESTABLISHING CLEAR LINES OF COMMUNICATION

Effective communication is the centerpiece of an organization and is absolutely essential when changes and improvements are being implemented. The most important aspect of communication is to develop consistent, predictable patterns of behavior so that everyone in the organization can accurately receive and interpret clear messages. Communication patterns must also match the communication styles of each employee, so that no one in the organization feels left out or believes the boss has formed an inner circle of a privileged few that monopolizes his or her ear. One of the most frustrating barriers to the change process occurs when staff members, key players in the process of change, feel a sense of division based on perceptions of inconsistent communication. Since information *is* power, it is essential to make sure all involved are empowered with access to the same information at approximately the same time.

In order to accommodate the learning/communication styles of all employees and to provide easy access to information, the Centennial principal initiated a variety of procedures for information sharing. First, the administration announced a philosophy of the open-door policy, a common practice with leaders. However, the reality of the open door is more easily said than done in most organizations. A metal plate was secured to the principal's office door that read "OPEN." Unless instructed that a private meeting was in progress, the school secretary was instructed to permit walk-ins access to the office

The principal's office was furnished so that the desk would not be a barrier between any visitor and the administrator. The principal carefully rose from his desk and sat directly across from each person who visited his office. It was essential to maintain eye contact and establish appropriate physical touch, if necessary, in every conversation. Since time is a precious commodity, a small lava-lamp timer that flowed from top to bottom in a five-minute time period was purchased. If a staff member, student, or community member wanted "five minutes of conversation time," the lava lamp could easily be turned over to serve as a symbolic discussion guide. It was amusing to observe various behaviors of guests as time ran out during meetings. Several individuals either asked to turn the timer over for another five minutes or quickly indicated they had to leave.

Furniture placement also provides an effective means to enhance communication. Since the Centennial principal had a small, narrow office, he placed two chairs on one side of the room and a couch on the other. With the desk consuming space against the end wall, communication had to be conducted within a six-foot space. Carefully selected pictures and posters were mounted on the wall behind the chair and couch so they could impact the mood of the visitor who graced the office.

If a person had a concern to discuss, the visitor was positioned next to a picture of a mountain stream, with a quietly running water fountain sitting on the principal's desk providing the background sounds to ensure a calm setting. The principal sat across from the visitor, with various symbols of the school's vision and goals behind him, in order to keep the expressed concern or problem within the perspective of the school's "big picture." Whenever a community visitor dropped in, the administrator sat next to him or her so that each could focus on the symbols of the organization's culture and vision of success on an opposite wall. As conversations unfolded, the wall hangings begged individuals to ask more questions about the program.

When students dropped in or were sent to the principal's office for any reason, they were invited to sit next to the desk strewn with small manipulative toys and gadgets to play with as they nervously dialogued about their issues. This action minimized their stress level and made a visit to principal's office easier to handle. The administrator also kept a basket full of mints on the table between the chairs so that staff, students, and community members felt comfortable dropping into the office just to say hello or to grab a mint. Communication does not require long, in-depth sessions with every person. For some, a sweet tooth and a quick hello is all that may be necessary to feel connected to the organization's leader.

A second approach to establishing effective communication links with staff was the creation of a weekly communication form for staff members to submit on a volunteer basis. These forms were affectionately labeled the "weekly purple sheets." This one-page form was always printed on lavender paper so the staff would recognize its significance.

The first two sections of the communication form gave staff members a chance to express themselves about the kind of week they and their students had experienced. They provided the principal with a quick visual of how effective the week had been for the program. The third section addressed a communication link that began to change the way individuals interacted with each other. In most organizations there are countless daily acts of kindness and assistance provided by employees that go unheralded and often unnoticed—yet one or more of these actions could change the recipient's perspective on the day or week. This space gave the respondent an opportunity to acknowledge another who had made a difference that week.

Weekly Communication Network
Return to the principal before 3:00 P.M. on Friday

Staff member _____ (name optional)

1. For me, this week has been: (Please circle and comment)
   Excellent   Pretty Good   O.K.   Up and Down   Filled with Concerns
   Comment:

2. For students, this past week has been: (Please circle and comment)
   Excellent   Pretty Good   O.K.   Up and Down   Filled with Concerns
   Comment:

3. I'd like to pass on a compliment to _____ for . . .

4. I am particularly concerned with _____ because . . .

5. In regard to this matter, I consider it:
   _____ of high priority that needs to be handled quickly.
   _____ for information purposes to be shared with appropriate individuals.
   _____ low priority so let's talk about it in a future staff meeting.
   _____ really a "backburner" issue. Just thought you'd like to know.

6. When this issue is addressed:
   _____ I want to be a part of the decision-making process.
   _____ I want to be informed as the decision-making process evolves.
   _____ I think the principal and management team should handle it.
   _____ I'll handle it myself and let you know what happens.

Figure 1.1. Weekly Communication Network Form

The last three sections offered employees an opportunity to express a concern about something that occurred that week, how important it was, and how they wanted to see it resolved. The school secretary placed the purple sheets in every staff member's mailbox on Thursday morning of each week. By Friday at 4:00 P.M., the Centennial administrator usually received between 70 and 90 percent of the forms distributed. When all contributions were gathered, the principal could quickly look over the statements on the sheet and make a mental note of how successful the staff members felt about the school's operation that week. The cause of an employee's bad week could be quickly identified and an effective intervention process initiated.

A yellow "summary sheet" was easily created and placed in staff mailboxes, and greeted them on Monday morning when they reported to work for another week. Symbolically, the bright yellow sheet represented

---

Feedback from Last Week

For staff, last week was:
Excellent—6
Pretty Good—12
O.K.—7
Up and Down—0
Filled with Concerns—1

For students, the week was:
Excellent—7
Pretty Good—8
O.K.—7
Up and Down—4
Filled with Concerns—0

Compliments to:

Pamela, for being sensitive and skilled in working with students with special needs.
Sally, for her excellent job in work with a grieving student.
Leonard, for working so effectively with a student who had trouble with math.
Gayna, for her flexibility in scheduling students into the career center.
Kim, for the goodies she brought in to share.
Billy, for his passion for the Broncos.
Bill, for recognizing a staff member's stroke of genius.
Sylvia, for typing out grant proposals, letters, and for always having a friendly smile.
Steve, for the fine job he did in setting up the gym for our special event.
Caryl, for all the trouble she went through to arrange a volunteer placement for a student.
Dawn, for her idea of an equestrian program for students.
Tim, for his creative astronomy elective week class.
Carrie, for her ability to let students know that she cares.
Eric, for his insights and contributions to our staff meetings.
Volveriene, for her patience in helping me with my computer problems.
Kate, for her ability to help students write with quality.
Carolyn, for her commitment and passion for students with special learning needs.
Liskey, for setting up basketball games with other alternative schools.
John, for motivating students to do such excellent work with clock making.
Bryan, for his ability to touch students' hearts.
Mark, for adding so many new ideas to our program.
Susan, for making me laugh when I needed it most last week.

Figure 1.2. A Typical Monday Morning Feedback Sheet

the "Monday morning sun," greeting staff at the beginning of another week. This yellow form contained a tally of the responses of staff members who indicated they had an excellent week, pretty good week, and so on, and a list of compliments for people who gave others special gifts and courtesies the previous week.

This form proved to be an excellent culture barometer for staff members to observe. If a staff member had been the only one who indicated that the week was "filled with concerns" and 90 percent of the staff had an excellent week, it would convey the message that the individual's concerns from the previous week were more personal and not due to the decay of the organization's culture. However, the principal made a concerted effort to seek out staff members who had experienced a challenging week and attempted to provide assistance, counsel, or comfort as the case required.

Communication Memos

Just a word about the color coordinating of communication memos: Lavender was used for the weekly communicator forms, yellow for feedback to staff, a bright cherry red for emergency announcements or changes in schedule, and goldenrod for student information. Staff members were encouraged to use green paper for intra-staff messages—announcing field trips, for example. In this way, staff members could immediately identify the importance of various memos and papers that often packed their mailboxes. This format is very effective in the absence of a formal e-mail system.

The process also provided valuable information about specific members of the student body. If students were creating havoc in several classes, their names would appear in the concerns section on one or more of the feedback sheets. Early intervention by a counselor or member of the administrative staff quickly became a high priority by Monday morning.

The most enjoyable part of publishing the yellow sheets proved to be the compliments section of the page. Staff members took delight in finding their names printed in bold black letters for their specific gifts or courtesy to others. Compliments were often given for acts of kindness, professional assistance, and personal insights.

The staff purple feedback sheets and the Monday morning yellow response sheets became one of the most effective communication tools at Centennial High School. In over a decade, only two sarcastic attempts at humor caused friction that had to be resolved individually. This approach to communication speaks volumes for the need to foster more communication and collaboration among and between employees. This format provides a leader with an approach to address such a need. To achieve the same end electronically, a template of this form could be created, completed, and forwarded to the principal.

The last three sections of the form, dealing with weekly issues of concerns, provided valuable information about the program culture as it evolved. By identifying small problems or concerns on a weekly basis, the Centennial administration was able to keep a finger on the pulse of the program and its employees. The statement inviting staff members to express any concern in writing gave them ample opportunity to pinpoint small matters before they grew into large issues. The ensuing check-off sections let the principal know the level of concern an individual experienced and provided direction about the extent to which the individual wanted to be involved in the resolution of the expressed problem.

Inviting staff to identify negative aspects of working in the building lets employees know that the leader is not only interested in hearing the good news but is also open to listening and responding to areas of concern. This approach enhanced the staff's level of trust with the administration, because they were not only asked for this kind of feedback, but each issue received attention and a response as it arose.

A management team was organized and convened before school every Monday morning. The team consisted of two counselors, the office staff, the custodian, and the school resource officer as well as any interested instructional staff members. The agenda discussed the logistics of the upcoming week and the issues of concern listed on the purple sheets turned in the previous Friday. By 8:00 A.M. every Monday morning, issues brought to the administration's attention were delegated to the most appropriate management person for resolution. This team also provided a sounding board for upcoming decisions and actions and solicited advice to address issues that traditionally were reserved for the principal's arena of responsibility. Such collaboration invited others to participate in the decision-making process and helped resolve difficult issues that impacted the entire organization. The leader does not have to pretend that he or she must be the building's sole source of power and make all the decisions faced by the entire organization.

A third form of communication involved knowing the learning style/communication needs of individual staff members. Using an edited version of Anthony Gregoric's "Learning Style Indicator," the Centennial principal assessed the way each individual staff member perceived and processed information. After learning how they preferred to receive information, he used alternative methods to interact with each person. For example, several staff members were very concrete-sequential in their approach to communication and preferred not to develop a personal relationship with the administration in order to process information. Therefore, the principal only needed to put brief notes in their mailboxes, or articles with a quick note that said, "Read this and let's discuss it when you have the time" in order to effectively share information. These individuals required only what the *One-Minute Manager* called "one-legged" conversations, engaging them in a conversation for as long it took to steady oneself on one leg . . . about two minutes. Brief and concise messages provided the most effective way to communicate with them.

On the other hand, many other staff members processed information in a more random, holistic manner. They needed to process information in an extended dialogue with the administrator or, better yet, in a group setting. They needed to have a relationship with the person conveying the information and to relate to all aspects and implications of ideas being shared. For these individuals, the principal would go to great lengths to schedule additional time to discuss issues in depth. Because many of these staff members were "people persons," information sharing frequently required the principal to exercise more patience and spend time discussing personal issues, including family and weekend experiences, before launching into conversations related to business topics. With this approach, the administrator could easily communicate effectively with every staff member.

This approach to communication requires the principal to be aware of his or her own communication style in order to most effectively interact with others. The Centennial principal's communication style was a combination of an individual who is constantly creating new ideas and synthesizing a lot of previously gathered information, and one who is driven by data and analysis. Therefore, in Gregoric's terms, as concrete-random/abstract-sequential learner, the Centennial principal was often engaged in self-initiated, mental conversations as he carried out the day's activities.

Given this knowledge, he informed all staff members that they needed to "catch and hold his eyes" and make sure he was directly looking at them if they wanted to engage in an effective conversation. He also told them they needed to make some physical contact, such as a handshake or a touch on the arm or shoulder, to make sure he was focused on listening to their needs. Once the information about the leader's learning/communication style is identified, it provides staff members with information of the leader's strengths and limitations as a communicator and increases effective dialogue.

For the new Centennial principal, weekly status memos promoted communication. Through individual conferences with staff members, the principal learned how the system worked, the organizational norms, and the professional connections among and between staff members. He knew the program had to change in a variety of ways in order to become more effective. Therefore, he took the liberty of sharing his reflections of each week's activity in a one-page "status of the week" memo. This format provided the opportunity to express observations and feelings about how the school was functioning.

From the perspective of being the "new kid on the block," the leader expressed admiration for the way things were and surprise at what did and did not work. It proved to be an effective communication tool, because the staff liked to see what the new principal was learning as the weeks unfolded. Moreover, this format created an opportunity to honestly express thoughts and feelings in writing.

With the status of the week memo in place, the principal began outlining the strategies he wanted to initiate with the staff to bring about needed changes and improvements. The weekly status reports "dropped the seeds of change" on the minds of staff members. Concrete possibilities for program change emerged in the form of attached articles on teaching and evaluation strategies, found in journals like *Education Leadership* and *Phi Delta Kappan* magazine. The articles had great relevance to the Centennial program, its students, and education in general. Marginal notes and underlined paragraphs captured the leader's ideas of what could work at Centennial High School and began to lay the groundwork for future staff development opportunities.

In an effort to create a social forum for more informal communication, the principal started the Wednesday morning breakfast club. He invited all staff members to have breakfast together at a local restaurant about five blocks from school. The idea, greeted warmly at first by a few staff members, proved to be difficult to sustain. Most of the Centennial staff had child-care issues, were not morning people, or had other obligations. As a result, attendance dropped, causing the breakfast club idea to be shelved until a later time.

The format was revived years later when the special education program in the building grew to become a six-person department. This group frequently met before school for breakfast, so their professional dialogue encompassed a social-emotional connection as well. A great deal of essential communication can be accomplished in an informal social setting where people can relax over drinks or food and engage in conversation that may enhance the entire group's working relationship. Although the original breakfast club may have been initiated before its time, the idea provides another forum for all staff, regardless of position or authority, to break bread together and discover the personal side of their colleagues.

STRATEGY #4: CREATING THE VISION OF CAMELOT

Traditionally, a new leader of an organization has a brief honeymoon period before familiarity sets in and the mystique of freshness evaporates. A leader charged with being a change agent should develop strategies to extend the honeymoon period for as long as the mood can be sustained. Time is needed to become more familiar with the organization and employee patterns, and to lay the foundation for the vision and goals that will emerge from discussions and program assessment data.

John Steinbeck's *Travels with Charlie* suggests that the best way to get to know people is to claim that you are lost and need help. Steinbeck states that people usually go out of their way to help a stranger in need. By doing so, they reveal much of who they are and what they believe. The new Centennial principal employed the same kind of strategy in his

first few months as the school's leader. Although not actually lost, this
was his first job as a school principal. He had previously taught in a reform school, an elementary school, three junior high schools, and a high
school, and he served the previous ten years as a curriculum writer in
the school district. As principal, however, he was standing on unfamiliar
ground.

In spite of previous roles, the principal chose to posture a naive approach to his leadership position. This approach purchased more time
as colleagues made every attempt to help the novice principal understand the responsibilities of the job and unique needs of an alternative
educational program. This approach permitted the principal to enter
Centennial with humility and present himself to others as an interested,
enthusiastic, and inquisitive learner—but not an expert. This strategy
allowed the principal to minimize his role as a potential threat to the
status quo, and opinions and options he expressed in the process earned
a receptive audience.

As a result, the veteran staff went to great lengths to explain the way
the program operated, to clarify the traditions and procedures that had
been developed and implemented over the years, and to explain how to
deal with students who were enrolled in the school. The staff tolerated
constant questions and was not threatened by challenges in the form of
"what if" statements published in the status of the week memo. Staff
members were frequently complimented for their hard work, commitment to students, and their positive attitude and love for the alternative
students. In addition, printed statements such as "I have noticed a pattern that deals with. . . . I'm not sure what this means, but I would like
to invite you to help me understand this phenomenon from your perspective so that I can have more clarity about the program" invited more
dialogue and clarification.

Such an approach prompted many staff members to offer explana-
tions, write notes to help the "new guy" understand the concept, or begin dialogues among themselves to revisit the logic behind a specific
procedure or practice. The goal was to subtly challenge the way traditions and practices had led to policies that created the culture of the
school, without creating a defensive reaction from staff. One way to
move toward the creation of a new vision is to invite people to look at
traditions and ask if they are still applicable to the current situation, do-

ing it in a manner that is not threatening to the participants, who may have created the traditions in the first place.

This strategy created a forum for reflective thinking about the current organizational culture and a way to begin looking at the need for change. Based on the educational research published during the previous few years, some of the procedures and policies embedded in the culture of the Centennial program were not based on sound educational practice. Simply telling people they were out of touch with current research was inadequate. The power of asking questions and taking the humble stance of a person thrust into an unfamiliar leadership role proved more effective in stimulating change.

Information Sharing

Creating a climate where the truth is to be heard involves four basic practices:

1. Lead with questions, not answers.
2. Engage in dialogue and debate, not coercion.
3. Conduct autopsies, without blame.
4. Build red flag mechanisms that turn information into information that cannot be ignored.

—Jim Collins, *Good to Great* (2001), 74–79

Articles distributed weekly either challenged some operational idea currently being used in the program or introduced an idea that could eventually work in the building. Developing a new vision requires patience and careful planning, which supports the belief that one needs to move slowly at first in order to be able to move faster later.

For example, several staff members expressed the belief that at-risk students were not capable of succeeding in school because of their difficult home lives, alcohol and other drug addictions, out-of-school experiences, and lack of commitment. This attitude needed to change or the entire restructuring and improvement processes would be in jeopardy.

Therefore, research articles that focused on topics such as "Enabling Students Undermines Personal Responsibility," "Teaching Success to the Unsuccessful," or "How to Motivate At-Risk Students" were distributed throughout the first semester. The principal couched the invitation to read each article by stating that it reminded him of something he observed during the past week, a reflection from a previous experience with students, or an idea to share. By underlining specific passages, even the most disengaged staff member could be encouraged to glance at key elements in the article.

This strategy proved to be invaluable months later when the Centennial staff was in the thick of the debate over how the program should be restructured. On several occasions, a staff member announced that she or he had recently read an article about the topic and proceeded to quote information from one of the articles distributed much earlier in the year. One of the joys of leadership is the reward of watching the seeds planted early in the change process take root and become embedded in colleagues' belief systems.

By introducing a plethora of ideas on current educational standards, the principal began laying the foundation of a new vision for Centennial High School. Gently, the distributed articles began to challenge the traditional structures and practices that were not working, and started staff members thinking about how the practice or program could be improved. It became an invitation to dream of a better program, one that could capture the imagination of students and colleagues.

The vision of a Camelot must be modeled in order to become a reality. The modern principal is certainly not King Arthur, but the mythical kingdom most likely emerged through the perceived image of those who lived the dream. A modern poster proclaims, "If you can say it, you can see it, and if you can see it, you can believe it, and if you believe it, it will become real." A school administrator in Arizona puts it another way: "If you pretend something long enough and hard enough, it will become real."

The principal who embraces the change process is required to create and model an ideal image of an ideal school. The principal needs to help others see and believe in possible futures. Staff members needed to pretend that Centennial had the potential to become a great alternative high school. Such a hope must begin with the building leader and then be embraced by both the staff and students so that it will become real for everyone.

The use of symbols provides a leader focused on change with tools to model a passion of what the program could become. For example, on the first day of school, the Centennial principal held a pep rally with all the students and staff. At that rally, he introduced the phrase "Catch the Vision." He went to great lengths to role-play its meaning, dragging unsuspecting students out of the audience to play parts in mini-theatrical presentation.

In the mini-play, the principal instilled the concept of "the vision" in all the students and staff. The vision represented their purpose for being in school: to earn a diploma! Could they see their names printed on their own diploma? Did they have the vision for achieving the credits and grades necessary to earn the diploma? Did they have the commitment to attend school every day and to work hard in all of their classes? Did they see that the diploma could be used as a stepping-stone to the next phase of their lives? Did they know that the vision of earning a diploma represented a symbol of success to their family, friends, and the business community that would hire them?

The administrator held up a diploma, which would be carried daily, and asked students to imagine seeing their name embossed on it. They were asked to imagine walking across the stage at their graduation ceremony to the applause of an audience filled with relatives and friends. Students were asked to think about the vision of getting a diploma every time they walked through the front door of the school.

"Catch the Vision" become the symbolic centerpiece of the culture at Centennial High School. Eventually the phrase was embedded in concrete on the first step of the school's entrance. Thus, students and staff had a simple symbol to clearly represent the purpose of working and studying in the building every day.

To enhance the vision of earning a diploma, the Centennial staff created another symbolic ritual for the school. At the end of every six weeks, several students completed the necessary requirements to earn a diploma. This event was used as an opportunity to hold an interim graduation ceremony to celebrate the accomplishment of achieving the vision.

Centennial High School is a three-story building. Its "Quincy box" architectural design provides a broad stairway landing between the second and third floors. Each graduate dressed in traditional cap and gown in the basement while the entire student body formed a line to march through on both sides of the stairs and foyer. "Pomp and Circumstance" played from a CD and volunteer students provided a candlelight pathway as the newly graduated seniors ascended the various levels of stairs. As the graduates reached the second-floor landing to the sound of music, cheers, and applause, the principal talked to the assembled student body about what catching the vision meant for these particular students.

In turn, the microphone was passed to each graduate, who thanked the staff, their friends, and family for helping them graduate and said a few inspiring words to the assembled students below. They usually concluded their remarks by saying, "If I could do it, so can you . . . keep the vision!" and encouraged their peers to continue to work toward earning their own diploma. This was followed by sharing a giant sheet cake as the graduates stood in a receiving line to be congratulated by all of the students who witnessed the event. Each such ceremony proved to be an emotionally moving experience and helped set the stage for the next six-week academic term.

Centennial staff members posted enlarged copies of the diploma at strategic locations throughout the building. This symbol met students wherever they went and kept the focus on the reason for their being in school. Whenever the principal carried a copy of the Centennial diploma in hand, students would stop and ask to see it. Students affirmed they could see their name on it and had only one or two more academic terms to complete before they would earn it. The vision of earning a diploma began to have a defining impact on the school's culture.

The key to earning a diploma rested on school attendance. The daily attendance rate from the previous year measured a pitiful 70 percent. Consequently, students lost credit for nonattendance so that a traditional three-year program turned into four or five years. By that time, students who had started high school at age fifteen were now approaching nineteen or twenty, and in some cases even twenty-one, and were beginning to lose hope in ever earning a diploma. Consequently, many of these students dropped out of school.

In an effort to make daily attendance a significant part of students' lives, the administration created a symbolic goal of success for everyone. The state of Colorado mandated that all schools achieve a 95 percent daily attendance by the year 1995. Therefore, 95 percent daily attendance became a goal for all students who wanted to demonstrate they had the commitment to earn a diploma. A large daily attendance bulletin board was created and placed behind the receptionist's desk in the main lobby of the school. Daily attendance was calculated and the results posted as a daily barometer on the board. Attendance percent was also listed and discussed in building's daily announcements. Great attendance days received rave notice, including compliments for commitment. Students were encouraged to help their peers get to school as well.

The school purchased bicycles to loan students if they had a car problem and rented alarm clocks to help students wake up in the morning. Some students came in early and provided wake-up calls to anyone in need of such a service. Volunteer student drivers were paid one dollar per trip for gas money to pick up kids who called before first period and asked for a ride to school.

Slowly the daily attendance climbed into the 90 to 95 percent levels as the two hundred students began to take an interest in meeting the daily goal. By spring, students were challenged to achieve the impossible. If they could reach 95 percent daily attendance once in a while, why not achieve five straight days of 95 percent daily attendance? The students took on the challenge, organized calling trees and rides, and embraced the notion that they could accomplish a collective goal if they all worked together. In the third week of April, they recorded five consecutive days of 95 percent daily attendance, an amazing feat for students in an alternative school where daily attendance had been the major cause of student failure in previous academic settings. The visual symbol of the daily attendance goal kept the focus on what was necessary to ensure success as a learner: being in school every day. The symbol of achieving 95 percent daily attendance turned a goal into a pattern of behavior for most of the students.

Goals

When a person really desires something, all the universe conspires to help that person realize his dream.

—Paulo Coelho, *The Alchemist* (1994), 116

The principal's pizza forum provided another successful symbol for creating a positive learning environment at Centennial. The Centennial staff noted that students had little buy-in to the culture of the school. It was only a place to "hang" during the day. As an alternative high school, Centennial had no mascot, no teams, no clubs, and no dances. As a result, Centennial lacked a student culture, and students displayed little loyalty to their school. In general, students were ashamed of the school. They did not want to display Centennial bumper stickers on cars or admit they attended the school. It was important to invite the student voice into the culture of the building and to have students begin the process of creating the symbols of pride in their school.

Since it was important for staff and administration to know the individual personalities of the students served and to learn how their minds worked, the staff began holding pizza forums at lunch. Using food as a motivational tool, a dozen students and staff were randomly selected to have pizza once a week. During those lunches, students were asked to express why they liked the school, what could be improved, what the staff did well, and other similar questions. Staff members simply listened and took notes. As a result of these sessions, the staff created a student lounge, printed school shirts, ran an intramural sports program, distributed a monthly student feedback sheet similar to the one created for the staff, and held special events to celebrate student accomplishments. At the cost of a few hundred dollars in pizza, the process of getting students to design and endorse their learning culture at Centennial began.

Students who had attended the pizza forums took pride in seeing their ideas come to fruition. It would take another two years, a complete generation of students entering the three-year program, to completely change the student culture. However, dialogues with the staff and administration became the foundation for the Principal's Advisory Council and leadership class organizations, which would eventually emerge as a vehicle for the student voice to be heard and honored.

Another essential part of creating the magic of a Camelot begins with the leadership attitude one maintains as the "kingdom" begins to emerge. A change agent must view life and problem solving from an asset model rather than a deficit model. That is, every effort must be made to look at all the positive qualities each employee contributes to the organization and not look at the flaws and idiosyncrasies that cause drains on the organization's energy. In conventional wisdom and training, leaders who are charged with improving organizations often start by identifying what is wrong with the program and the apparent flaws in key employees. They then develop improvement plans, implement them, evaluate the results, and often replace people who cannot or will not follow orders.

Such an approach puts administrators and employees in an adversarial position that makes collaborative improvement an impossible task. In addition to the fact that teacher tenure laws make it challenging to quickly remove an ineffective instructor, this process may be a hatchet action that could eliminate some talented professional, who, with a little coaching and a renewed sense of focus, could have enhanced the organization's culture based on experience alone.

Most educators enter the field with the passion and commitment to make a difference. They have dreams and the desire to be an asset to the organization they worked for and to contribute something to either help improve it or help others to do so. That is the basic nature of the teaching profession. However, somewhere along the way, a few lose sight of the goals that motivate professional choices. The career becomes a job instead of an ideal and causes them to lose the energy it takes to remain focused on the goal. The individuals exhibiting such tendencies are not hopeless; it just takes more work to instill in them a renewed sense of hope, the belief that their role is essential and vital and that the program they work in is important for students and the future.

If some employees have become too comfortable or discouraged, lost their passion or focus, and chosen to settle for less rather than achieving dreams, no set of criticisms or reprimands will make a difference. Such a negative approach hardens people to change even more than does the threat of termination or transfer. It merely creates more barriers and saboteurs to any proposed improvement process.

Therefore, in order to promote a collaborative team approach to promote program changes, the Centennial administration used an asset model. The professional assets each staff member demonstrated in his or her respective role were noted and praised. The principal walked into classrooms and sat for fifteen minutes to thirty minutes and wrote extensive "I like" notes. These notes said things such as: "I like the way you gave Joe eye contact when he volunteered an answer." "I like the questions you asked when you changed topics." "I liked the way your room is arranged to promote student discussions." The notes also included questions that invited reflection and dialogue about something that needed attention. For example, a typical note would read: "Have you considered using a debate format to engage more students in the discussion I observed? Let's talk about other possible formats if you're interested."

The administration focused on the educationally sound strategies they used or the way they created a positive learning environment, and they temporarily ignored practices that were nonfunctional. This approach asked staff to consider different instructional strategies and to think about different ways of implementing classroom management. The notes never suggested a prescribed way of doing business. A spirit of curiosity and some increased level of concern ensued and motivated the discussion that followed. At each staff meeting, individual instructors who had been observed that day were publicly praised, and others were encouraged to talk with the instructor receiving the accolade about specific strategies used in class after the meeting. In this way, many of the most effective instructional techniques were replicated in other classrooms.

Employees began to feel they had not only contributed to the betterment of the whole program but also that they had something unique to offer others. When the principal visited classes a second or third time, staff members knew that he was looking for positive traits in their work and not trying to catch them doing something wrong. When questions or suggestions became more pointed, the instructors were not threatened by the presence or observation of the principal.

Several staff members began to invite the administrator into their classrooms to model a particular strategy suggested in conferences. After such demonstrations, the principal was invited to remain in the next class to observe and critique how the instructor delivered the same strategy. By working through an asset model with staff members, the groundwork was established for the major changes that would eventually take place in the entire school program. The administrator was viewed as a coach and guide, and not as a critical boss who was looking to fire the weakest link in the system. It was clear that trust and collaboration was an essential component at Centennial. If the staff was going to create a new inspirational vision, they needed to rely on each other's strengths to make it happen.

STRATEGY #5: GATHERING AND ANALYZING DATA

Good information leads to good decision making. The staff required solid data to drive decisions. Within the school district and the community, Centennial's image was that of a failing system that needed to be changed or closed. It was necessary to assess whether these perceptions were accurate or the product of myth and negative image. In an effort to gather all the pertinent information needed to make recommendations, data on every aspect of the program had to be collected in order to decide the next course of action.

The process of data collection begins by asking the correct questions about the topic being investigated. What was the original goal or purpose of establishing a specific program or activity? How did the creators of this program or activity envision being accountable for its results? How often was the program evaluated in the past, and what information did the initial assessment yield? What adjustments, if any, were made to the program based on the data generated by previous assessments?

In the case of Centennial High School, assessments and accountability measures were not part of the program. Programs and policies were developed to respond to immediate needs and problems as they arose. Many school policies and procedures in place at Centennial were based on the needs of individual teachers or the former principal, or for the convenience of the daily routine. Therefore, little was known about the success or productivity of school policies.

Since there was limited time to work with this system, the staff had to determine what data could be gathered in a short period of time, what data would be pertinent to analyze the culture of the program, and what data could best be used to drive decisions.

In an effort to streamline the data-gathering effort, the staff needed to know the following information:

1. What is the personal profile of the client (student) Centennial serves?
2. What motivates students to enroll in an alternative school?

3. What motivates students to attend school?
4. How do they perform in relationship to state standards of attendance, academic performance, and the completion of graduation requirements?
5. To what extent does the staff believe in the potential success of students to earn a diploma, meeting state standards?
6. What evidence is there that the policies, practices, and procedures already in place assist students to learn and practice the behavioral skills necessary to succeed at meeting program goals?

The staff began to track daily attendance, reasons for absences, office referrals for discipline, tardiness to class, dropout rate and reasons for leaving the program, academic performance in class, progress toward graduation, and graduation rate. The numbers spoke clearly to the problems facing the program. The school had a 70 percent daily attendance rate, a 44 percent dropout rate, and a 60 percent graduation rate. Students displayed the attitude that they were at Centennial only to put in their hours to earn a diploma and nothing more. Students demonstrated the belief "Don't bother us, and we won't bother you." They wanted to complete only minimum expectations to earn a diploma and did not care or want to be pushed to accomplish more. The learning culture described in Ted Sizer's *Horace's Compromise* was alive and well at Centennial High School.

The data-gathering process included both accumulating hard data as well as personal observations that fostered intuitive assessment and evaluation. In staff meetings, individuals listened and analyzed the statements staff members made about student behaviors, their nature as learners, and their potential for success in order to identify patterns related to the school's culture. Informally, staff members became more sensitive to interactions between adults and students in the halls and in the classrooms, and noted the attitudes and expectations expressed in nondirective interactions. Some staff members began to use their intuitive skills to begin constructing the undefined culture of the building and its inhabitants.

Many of the staff professed the belief that the students were somehow "damaged goods," based on past life experiences with drugs, alcohol, and disenfranchisement from nuclear family members. Consequently, they should not be expected to earn more than C grades. Many felt there was no reason to push them. Centennial could be a safe haven and a last resort for unhappy children. Teachers often expressed beliefs that proved to be more enabling rather then helping students grow into independent young adults.

An example of such enabling behavior can be seen in the analysis of how the Attendance Appeals Board operated. The previous year, the staff had created the attendance board. The purpose of this board was to make students become more responsible for their choices to violate the school's attendance policy. Many students were exceeding permitted absences as outlined in the school's attendance policy. There were few consequences in place to correct these behaviors.

The appeals board consisted of two staff members, three students, and the principal. The counselors represented students who violated the attendance policy. They functioned as the students' advocates. A student was given an opportunity to explain the reasons for excessive absences and to make a promise not to violate the policy again. With much discussion and stern reprimands by the board members, the student was placed on a contract and continued in the program. Board meetings were held weekly at 7:00 A.M. and lasted over an hour. The board heard three to five cases during each weekly meeting.

The staff began to collect data on this process and analyzed the results. From the findings it was discovered that no student had ever been dropped from the program or had "reformed" the pattern of attendance behaviors to remain in school. The board had never made a recommendation to drop a student for exceeding the attendance contract. Every student was given another chance to do better. However, 90 percent of those who appealed eventually dropped out of the program or violated their "second chances" and were automatically dropped.

Each attendance case often consumed eight man-hours and yielded only a 10 percent success rate, with little or no real change in general student body behaviors. Many of the students who appeared before the appeals board in one academic term appeared again in forthcoming terms. Even though the student board members had been empowered to make decisions about attendance, they were reluctant to require their peers to adhere to the clearly defined policy.

Informal discussions were held with students, who expressed the belief that the process was a joke. They knew they could get a second chance if they were liked by their counselor or by the students who sat on the board. With enough skill to elicit sympathy, they could beat the system and not face immediate consequences for their behavior. The appeals board proved to be an enabling device by which clever students could continually manipulate the system. By the end of the first academic term, this data had been presented to the staff in a document. The discussion that followed created enough awareness to terminate the attendance board.

Attendance problems became the sole responsibility of the principal, who handled each case on an individual basis and according to the best interests of each student. Manipulation was reduced, and both staff members and students could make better use of their time without being put in the uncomfortable position of judging peers or students enrolled in their classes. The data-collection process was simple and quickly led to an immediate and appreciated change in the school environment.

STRATEGIC SUMMARY

These five strategies were effectively used to establish the integrity of the principal as Centennial High School's new leader. The process of earning trust and credibility took almost three months. By that time, most staff members viewed the administrator as an individual who listened to their concerns and ideas, reserved judgment until enough information was gathered, and freely communicated and dialogued about ideas and the merits of procedures and policies that drove the system.

Those three months gave the principal an opportunity to learn the culture of the program, both defined and implied, from both logical and intuitive perspectives. The new outsider had the luxury, based on ignorance of the way things worked, to ask why and make "what if" statements to veteran employees without being greeted by rejection or a set of barriers. The "been there, done that" attitude did not surface, because the staff responded with politeness to this naïve person who expressed his beliefs with passion but, as rumor had it, would only be a short-time employee of the program. The stage had been successfully set for the change process to begin. Only strategic planning and empowerment of all of the stakeholders would permit Centennial to embark on a new vision for its success.

2

SETTING THE TABLE FOR A BANQUET OF CHANGE

In the spring of 1990, the state of Colorado reported a financial shortfall in its educational budget. As negotiations unfolded in the Poudre School District, each of its competing organizations wanted its fair share of the state funds allocated to the district. The negotiation package that year resulted in both staffing and program cutbacks for the district in general and drastic cuts for the high schools. The consensus-building facilitator hired by the district to resolve negotiations issues asked participants to identify the most expensive programs so cuts could be made the following year. Centennial High School's program claimed a prominent position near the top of the list.

The acting superintendent of schools, a former district principal, recalled how the three comprehensive high schools had each relinquished four staffing units to create the Centennial program in 1980. Was it time to reclaim those staffing units by absorbing Centennial's program, designed to work with at-risk students, into each comprehensive school and thus soften the current financial pressure? Had Centennial High School outlived its purpose? Could the comprehensive schools do a better job for at-risk students by creating programs within their own walls? Such a move would save the district thousands of dollars.

As the new principal began his one-year-only position in the fall of 1990, a committee of staff members in each of the three comprehensive high schools began identifying failures at Centennial High School in order to make cases for reclaiming staffing units. By January 1991, the superintendent formally asked if Centennial should remain a separate educational program or be closed and consolidated into at-risk programs within the comprehensive schools. The Centennial staff had four months prior to the initiation of the formal review process to demonstrate that the program had merit and should continue as a viable school.

This chapter focuses on strategies used to prepare the staff and community for the change process. One does not step into a status quo culture where the employees are comfortable and quickly or easily rally them to embrace change. The table of change must be set in a way that invites employees to sit down and consume a banquet of new ideas. However, before staff members take a place at the table of change, they must feel confident the host knows how to organize the dinner, bus the remnants of previous activities, and reset the table in an enticing manner. Attention to such detail earns the host the necessary trust to initiate the first step in the change process. Like the preparations for a fine banquet, this chapter prepares the table for the feast of change.

However, before setting a new table in anticipation of change, the staff had to see the clutter and disarray from previous meals (years) cleared and put in place. After listening to staff members during the summer interviews, the principal's first actions as Centennial's leader required some initial housecleaning and reorganizing. The following are strategies used to address that need.

STRATEGY #1: PROVIDING THE THREE Cs: CADILLACS, CUSHIONS, AND COMPUTERS

The building budget was examined, and a surplus of funds was located in the capital reserve budget. The choice was made to invest in several cosmetic improvements to create a more inviting atmosphere. First, all staff members were totally frustrated with the copy machine. It needed to be replaced rather than repaired. To improve efficiency, the "Cadillac" of copiers was purchased. It performed tasks that had never entered the minds of most staff members. It increased the speed of copy production, collated and stapled sets of papers at the touch of a button, and printed duplications back to back if required. The staff reacted with awe and bountiful appreciation. By signing a five-year lease on a copier, the main cause of frustration for both instructional and clerical staff had been expeditiously removed.

Second, the office staff redesigned their work area. They created a more inviting and professional atmosphere by hiring a workspace architect to review and redesign the limited office space. The consultant added soft-sided partitions and desktop shelves that changed the appearance from former handmade, temporary structures to ones that reflected professional pride. The change immediately improved employee attitude and promoted a more professional appearance around individuals who were the first to greet students, parents, and visitors.

Third, for students, the Centennial staff filled the large open spaces on each floor of the three-story school with soft, stuffed chairs, couches, and end tables and thus created student lounges. Students needed a place to congregate and feel welcome as invited members of the school's learning culture. The newly designed setting reinforced Centennial's family atmosphere that honored all students who attended.

Finally, it was apparent that computer access was limited to office staff and counselors. In an age of technology, it was surprising that instructors and students were still limited to hard-copy materials and textbooks. Students and educational staff had access to only five floppy-disc and stand-alone Mac computers with little or no software support. Keyboarding students were learning skills on twenty electric typewriters.

Therefore, a large portion of the unused capital reserve budget was allocated to initiate building a student computer lab. Staff members were also invited to consider adding computers to their classrooms, along with purchasing supporting computer software programs. This ongoing commitment proved to be an essential part of the vision of turning Centennial into a quality school. Each year that followed, the staff dedicated a portion of the budget to technology support or wrote various grant requests to add computers to the program. In 1990, the ratio of computers to students was 1:40. By 2002, computer to student ratio was 1:7, and the entire building was linked via a file server, with Internet access in every room.

Centennial High School had never had a media center within its walls; instead, Centennial obtained print materials from Colorado State University's main library and the public library, located within a five-block walking distance of the school. However, the financial support for expanding and enhancing computer technology spruced up the "dining area" around the table of change and impressed both the staff and students. Next, attention was given to clearing away the remnants of the past.

STRATEGY #2: HANG THE FORMER PRINCIPAL

The former Centennial principal had been its leader for the previous ten years and retained the loyalty of several staff members, who mourned his departure. Before the program could be moved in a new direction, former leadership and traditions needed to be celebrated and honored. Unless this occurred, any movement forward would be stifled by individuals who looked to the past and "the way things used to be" or "the good old days." A toast to the past was in order. A committee was established to create a celebration day for the former principal. Invitations were sent to graduates, parents, and former faculty members. The former principal's picture was mounted on a plaque and engraved with words of appreciation for his commitment to the program.

On the designated date, staff members and students assembled and took the opportunity to thank him for his leadership and wish him well in future endeavors. Participants shared cake and punch and, with all appropriate pomp and circumstance, dutifully hung his picture in a place of honor on the office wall. This celebration cost few dollars but made huge strides to bringing closure to his leadership era. In a short afternoon, the Centennial staff successfully cleared some of the past from the table and took another step closer to embracing change.

STRATEGY #3: WALKING THE TALK

Even though the principal had been hired for a one-year-only job as principal, it was necessary to establish credibility with the district office and site staff. This was accomplished in two ways. First, a copy of the principal's belief statements about education and initial vision statement for Centennial High School was sent to district administrators. Before the mandated yearly goal statements were required, a manifesto of beliefs and goals was sent to district supervisors outlining how business would be conducted on the one-year-only watch.

The action plan was separated into goals for students, staff, public image, and classroom instruction. By front-loading intentions, the principal took the initiative to announce his intentions of becoming an active change agent, dedicated to making the short tenure meaningful. Even though some of the goals listed on the three-page memo would take more than a year to accomplish, the intention was to get the process started. This strategy earned immediate credibility. An area supervisor sent the following memo: "After reviewing the contents of your vision and belief statement, I believe that there is no doubt that you were the right person to occupy the principal's office at Centennial High School. When your calendar permits, I would truly appreciate an opportunity to meet with you so I can learn about Centennial's programs. Please feel free to call upon me for any assistance that you may need." An appointment was immediately scheduled, and later in the improvement process, his generous offer to help became a key component of the restructuring process.

Creating an image of leadership permanence with the staff proved more challenging. As school started, the entire staff knew, through the grapevine, that the principal was a one-year placement, on his way to another position. Many staff members believed the principal had been placed at Centennial to gather information in order to judge the program's credibility and to play the role of the district's hatchet man, if necessary. To counter this belief, the staff was challenged to create building goals for the year that acknowledged the need for self-examination and that would lead to future improvements. The Centennial staff had to act as if it were the most important program in the district and would serve the needs of high-risk students no matter who sat in the principal's chair in the future. What the staff achieved during the year would lead either to the creation of a more efficient program or to its closure.

With little effort, the staff goals reflected an appropriate level of concern. They created the following goals for the year.

1. Drafting a set of graduation requirements that reflected the school's mission and philosophy.
2. Improving student achievement in reading, mathematics, and writing.
3. Lowering the dropout rate.
4. Identifying what was considered most essential for future change.
5. Collecting data that provided staff members with a better understanding of the makeup and needs of its students and the expectations of the school community.

This final goal required the staff to become more efficient data collectors and to keep a permanent written record of the current program and the progress being made throughout the year. The data were essential to the decisions made in the central office as the administrators debated Centennial's future. Even if several staff departed at the end of the year, the data gathered would assist the next principal to make more effective program decisions for the continuation and improvement of the school's programs. This goal ushered in the age of accountability at Centennial, which was required to validate the program's importance to the district and its students.

STRATEGY #4: WHO'S IN CHARGE OF WHAT AROUND HERE?

In many organizations, power and authority tend to be held by a few key players, leaving many employees feeling like outsiders. In previous years, the two counselors and the principal's secretary had been empowered to take care of most of the business decisions in the building. The two school counselors enrolled students, placed them in classes, disciplined students, took care of attendance issues, dropped truant students if needed, and made many decisions related to class offerings and school policy. They had inherited this authority from the former principal, because his professional interests frequently took him elsewhere.

The authority to allocate building budget dollars belonged to the office manager by virtue of her job description. The principal authorized her to spend money from predetermined codes. Most staff members complained about their lack of voice in the daily operation of the building, how policies were implemented, how students were handled, and how the budget was spent. If change as a way of life was to be successfully introduced in the building, it had to be modeled so that both power and authority were distributed among all staff members.

Shared decision making and shared responsibility are key ingredients in creating an atmosphere for change and program improvement. In order to encourage people to take risks, create new futures, and produce quality results, they must be empowered and enjoy a sense of autonomy and authority. A clear understanding of responsibility, lines of communication, and decision making must be established in order to increase employee satisfaction and involvement. The staff must develop the feeling that they control their part of the successful functioning of the organization and must be held accountable for their actions.

Given this reality, the following improvements were implemented to make the table of change more inviting. The modifications cleared away most of the clutter of previous business practices and established an atmosphere that invited restructuring.

Who's on First?

An authority/responsibility flow chart was created and published for all staff members. This chart delineated the authority and responsibilities held by counselors and the office staff, and what responsibility remained in the principal's hands. In essence, roles and responsibilities were clarified. The role of the counselors was to counsel students, and the role of the principal was to handle all disciplinary and behavioral issues. Each office employee also had a new job description. To support their work, the flowchart identified time lines and forms the staff was required to use to make their jobs easier and more efficient. By redesigning job and role descriptions, communication and attitudes were improved immediately.

All in Favor, Say . . . Aye!

A major key to success is shared decision making. Top-down decision making promotes intentional or unintentional rebellion and sabotage.

Nobody enjoys being told what to do. All want to have a voice in determining their own destiny. Controlling one's destiny begins with clarifying an organization's decision-making process. The players must have a clear understanding of what decisions belong exclusively to the administrator, what decisions fall into the shared category, and what decisions are reached by group consensus.

During the first few staff meetings of the year at Centennial, personal interactions and behaviors were appalling. People shouted over others, made snide side comments, and denigrated each other's ideas. Such negative interactions created an atmosphere of distrust and suspicion that permeated the meeting room. At one meeting, a staff member became so angry that she yelled at the entire group and stomped out of the room. Clearly, changes had to be introduced in the way people interacted, or no program improvements could occur.

To ameliorate the observed communication barrier, the staff was introduced to a communication model. The art of effective listening was implemented with the group by requiring anyone who wanted to speak to hold a "talking stick." The next speaker had to summarize what the previous speaker had said before sharing new thoughts or responses. It was an arduous shift in expectations, but it demonstrated the need to be more professional in professional conversations.

New meeting norms were created that established a polite and efficient way to interact with each other. Co-facilitators were identified to keep participants within the boundaries of discussion etiquette. Staff members sat in a circle, and each person had the right to speak his or her position while the rest of the group listened. Like a good family, each person in the circle had the floor and got their "first helping of time" before anyone could get "seconds." With everyone having the opportunity to speak in a courteous, professional atmosphere, the business of running the school began to move more smoothly.

Everyone felt empowered by having a voice in setting policy, commenting on the status of the school culture, and making suggestions for improvement. It took most of the fall to teach and practice this process, but it made a significant difference as the staff members began to feel more professional sitting at the table of change together. This approach to empowerment improved the attitude toward courtesy, respect, and dignity in the building culture.

Key Attributes of Effective Teams

1. Commitment (a willingness to put group goals above personal goals)
2. Trust (a feeling of confidence and support on the part of group members for each other)
3. Purpose (understanding of what the team's mission is)
4. Communication (the ability to handle conflict, decision making, and day-to-day interactions)
5. Involvement (partnership and ownership in the team's mission)
6. Process orientation (tools, activities, processes, structures for dealing with day-to-day operation of the team)

—Elaine McEwan, *Leading Your Team to Excellence* (1997), 35

Brother, Can You Spare a Dime?

In previous years, the building budget had been the sole responsibility of the principal and office manager. Individuals were given allocations of money for the year, but the principal was always available to dole out supplemental funds upon request or at the principal's discretion. Only the principal and office manager knew how the budget process worked. Staff members, as adults, should be empowered to run their own budgets. Since Centennial was not large enough to create department budgets, the process was changed to hold all staff members accountable for their own funds.

A shared decision-making process was used to reach consensus on how the building budget would be allocated. The process was delightful to observe as each employee used all of her or his communication/listening skills to determine how the allocation of the meager building funds would occur. Collaboratively, they created a formula to disperse funds for individual copy budgets, materials budgets, staff development budgets, office/business budgets, and the building contingency funds. This process proved to be the watershed experience that forged a collaborative problem-solving team among staff members.

For the first time, staff members shared a total understanding of the financial structure and limitations placed on the program. They had the foresight to identify funds specifically marked for program innovation. If a staff member created a marvelous instructional idea late in the year but ran out of allocated dollars, the staff formulated a process by which the individual could secure additional funds without having to beg from the principal. The budget allocation process effectively expanded the concept of shared decision making.

Getting All the Diners to the Table

In response to the need to structure school business efficiently, three working committees were organized and empowered. These committees were called the PITS, the POTS, and the PANS, simply due to the novelty of alliteration. The committee labels stuck and were accepted by the staff. The most powerful committee was the PITS (Program Improvement Team Staff), because it had access to additional staff and curriculum development dollars. These classified and certified committee members took their jobs very seriously, because they believed the school's future was in their hands.

The PITS committee created a series of staff request forms to be used to attend conferences or to purchase materials that exceeded individual budget allocations. The committee members asked their colleagues to justify requests based on individual professional goals and building goals. They analyzed how an individual's budget had been managed prior to a request. The committee members interviewed the individual requesting additional funds with great solemnity and interest.

This process effectively eliminated the long-standing belief that the principal rewarded a chosen few within his inner circle. When staff members went to the principal's office to ask for money to attend a conference, they received a PITS financial request form, verbal support, and encouragement. Such empowerment not only demanded that staff members practice good fiscal stewardship but helped committee members to get a broader picture of the entire school program.

This committee also reviewed all grant possibilities and encouraged their colleagues to seek these sources of funding when opportunities arose. During the year, Centennial received several hundred dollars to establish an alcohol and drug intervention program and, later, secured a large grant to establish a service-learning program. As Centennial began its staff development activities and the program restructuring that followed, this committee's insight and knowledge became an invaluable asset to the process.

The POTS committee (Policy, Operations Team Staff) was the Monday morning management committee that assisted the principal with troubleshooting issues, people, and problems before a negative impact occurred. (See chapter 1 for further discussion of this committee.)

The PANS committee (Personnel and Needs Staff) consisted mostly of individuals who planned social events for both students and staff. For example, they organized the mini-graduation ceremonies, school picnics, Thanksgiving Feast Day, and student pancake breakfasts, to name a few activities. They dabbled with organizing faculty parties and end-of-the-week gatherings at local restaurants. The committee provided creativity, as its members planned and implemented traditional events and designed new ideas to enhance the school's learning culture.

By December, the principal was no longer the sole authority in the school. Power had successfully been distributed to all staff members who wanted to accept that responsibility. The act of empowering others, clarifying lines of communication, and sharing authority helped set the table for the more pressing work that lay before the school. In order to host the forthcoming change process, the staff had to reorganize the table and set out "appetizers" of shared power as an invitation to participate in the rest of the banquet.

STRATEGY #5: POLISHING THE PLATES AND SILVERWARE

As the fall months passed, the shared decision-making process was used to refine and clarify policies that drove the program. The Centennial staff clarified and reached a common agreement on the school's purpose and the types of students it served. The staff created written documents that outlined the student orientation process, admission requirements, requirements for junior high school student placements, enrollment of students with special needs, the student selection process, and other expectations. Policies related to ethics in journalism, unexcused tardiness, attendance requirements, and art displays were also drafted or revised.

Centennial's curriculum offerings were reviewed, and a service-learning program for students was added. In collaboration with the social work department at a local university, a tutorial program was designed to support instructional staff with student achievement. Instructional strategies, used to teach students with special learning needs, were analyzed and adjustments made to help instructors become more effective.

As the staff began to work together, assessment data was more effectively used to drive the shared decision-making process. The need for data led to measuring student opinions with surveys about course offerings, attitudes related to school culture, and suggested improvements. The staff analyzed the success of students in classes and examined for the causes of student failure. They also looked for creative ways to help students deal with smoking issues and alcohol/drug use that prevented them from succeeding in school. Centennial became more accountable and gathered information that gave staff an explanation of programs, policies, and issues facing the school and its students. By refining the information-gathering process and practicing shared decision making, the staff at Centennial polished their skills and were positioned to respond to the call for change.

STRATEGY #6: CREATING A NEW PUBLIC IMAGE

The image of Centennial High School was either tarnished or nonexistent. When people thought of Centennial, they imagined troubled youth, gangsters, drug users, and dropouts. For most people, Centennial's name recognition spawned a vision of youth who were academic losers. If students couldn't succeed in comprehensive high schools, they attended Centennial, a second-rate school. In general, the majority of the Fort Collins community had little knowledge of the program's existence. It had no sports program, no academic superstars, and virtually no local press coverage.

Ninety percent of an administrator's job demands exceptional public relations skills. With that focus in mind, a marketing plan needed to be developed to help the community recognize Centennial's existence and also become aware of the essential niche its program filled. This goal was accomplished in several ways. First, Centennial was consistently and frequently referred to in public as the "fourth high school." School district employees and the local community continually referred to "the three high schools in town." Staff used every opportunity to interrupt speakers and say, "You mean the four high schools, don't you?" Finally, by midyear, people recognized the message and began self-correcting their references to the city's three high schools. Centennial became an authentic entity as a program, at least in name, which helped elevate its status and legitimize the authenticity of its program.

Secondly, Centennial created a student speaker's bureau. Various service clubs throughout the community were contacted and asked if they would like to hear student success stories, shared by actual young people. These clubs were delighted to have such a topic for their respective meetings and eagerly accepted the offer. As time passed, Centennial's students were invited on a regular basis to speak at local clubs.

Each student was assisted in the preparation of what the staff called "the public speech." Students started their talk with a "thought for the day" borrowed from one of several books of quotes located in the front office. They explained what this thought meant to them and how it applied to their lives. This introduction was followed by an autobiographical account of events that had occurred prior to their arrival at Centennial High School. Next, students explained in great detail how Centennial had helped turn their lives around and gave them a vision for future success. They outlined possible futures for themselves and thanked the audience for inviting them to speak. In conclusion, they revisited the thought for the day and drove home its meaning.

These short messages were filled with hope and recognition that a program existed to help them succeed. The message was not lost on audiences, which praised each student speaker with applause and often tears. Audience members personally congratulated the youths for their individual triumphs. Organizations anticipated Centennial students' speeches and embraced each student who provided an educational version of the Horatio Alger story.

This strategy later paid dividends for many student speakers. Seniors used the speakers' bureau to introduce themselves to organizations that offered college scholarships in the spring of each year. Personal knowledge of students, who were competing with others for a scholarship, improved their position immensely. Additionally, the Fort Collins Breakfast Rotary Club, impressed with Centennial's students, created two annual $1,000 scholarships exclusively for its student applicants. Centennial students had earned respect from the community by telling their personal stories in public.

In addition to students, staff members also hit the speaker's trail. As a program in transition, various staff made appearances at services clubs, churches, and other local organizations that had an interest in hearing views on education in general and the new vision for Centennial in particular. They made presentations in university classrooms, where the merits of alternative education were discussed along with the characteristics of students who needed to be served. Several staff members took students into college classes or to other organizations to speak about their programs or student success in an alternative educational setting. Letters of thanks arrived on a weekly basis. Centennial's public image slowly changed as the school year passed.

Third, the local newspaper was contacted and a working relationship with the educational reporter developed. The Centennial administrator asked to have a story about the school published at least once a month. The staff and the newspaper worked together to create ideas for human-interest stories about the program, staff, and students. The local paper was quite generous and followed the school's change process over the next few years with keen interest and understanding.

Next, Centennial was featured on a local television show that discussed ways to reduce student dropouts. This program aired throughout the city for a full month. Finally, the high school newspapers began to take an interest in their sister school. In a January article featured in Rocky Mountain High School's *Highlighter,* a student reporter generously reviewed Centennial's program and discussed the personal touch found at the city's fourth high school.

Finally, a special effort was initiated to encourage staff to share only positive things about Centennial when in the public arena. Experience proves that negative stories—shared in the grocery store, for instance—multiply tenfold in a short time and that each retelling often embellishes the story for added impact. Before long, the story and the reputation that follows become bigger than life. When people invite gossip about a program, the grapevine effect exaggerates the message and stories often grow lives of their own.

Therefore, an informal agreement was struck among the staff to keep their differences and disagreements in-house and make a concerted effort to say only positive things in public. Even if the staff had a terrible day, it was essential to remain positive about the overall program. So, the word went out into the community how "things were great at Centennial," "the program was simply wonderful," and "students were doing well." Before long, people stopped staff members on the street and said, "I hear Centennial is doing quite well these days." If you repeat something long enough, it becomes real, and Centennial began to attract positive energy from the larger community.

By spring, the perception of Centennial had shifted. Organizations, school officials, and students saw Centennial and its program as essential but needing to be updated and improved. The community began to recognize that an urgency existed to work with students and their unique needs in a program specifically designed to teach them how to succeed.

Both the Fort Collins Breakfast Optimist Club and the Golden K Kiwanis Club approached the school with financial offers to help students. Many of the students lived on their own and often quit school because they ran out of money before the end of the month. These organizations offered Centennial seed money to initiate an expendable trust fund for students to use as "loans" for personal emergencies to get through the month. The objective was to assist students in financial crisis so they would remain in school. Each organization contributed $500, and Centennial set up an application process to make funds available to students for short-term loans. For twelve years, the $1,000 expendable trust fund created loans that exceeded $10,000. The fund lost only $132 to students who failed to honor their financial contracts. By demonstrating fiscal responsibility to donating organizations, Centennial and its students earned more community respect.

Through this process, Centennial also earned the loyalty of a local resident and member of the Golden K Kiwanis Club. He became a community advocate for the school and supported the program at every opportunity. He encouraged his club to send one Centennial student to the Hugh O'Brian Leadership Conference every year. He was an active voice in supporting the program with state and local politicians. He proved to be a one-man cheerleader for everything Centennial attempted to do.

Such advocates are heroes, difficult to find but essential to promote the vision of a quality program. It is vital to nurture and embrace such nonschool community activists who believe in the dream. This local citizen was among the initial group to see the potential of Centennial's vision, and he continued to support the program over the years. Every school needs to nurture the support of such individuals in the community to add value and credibility to improvement efforts.

STRATEGY #7: TEACHING OLD DOGS NEW TRICKS

The new centerpiece for the table of change appeared in the form of Centennial's fall staff development plan. One staff member proposed that the entire staff read William Glasser's *The Quality School*. She indicated that many ideas for school improvement were to be found there. The idea soared, and most of the certified and classified staff enrolled in the reading seminar. The class, attached to college credit, provided a forum to discuss educational philosophies and interact with the new principal and each other in an informal setting.

Discussions that followed were both inspiring and unifying. Staff members had ample time to express beliefs about how students learn, how to establish effective learning environments, and how to approach the unique needs of learners. The reading seminar proved to be the philosophical catalyst that united the staff in a common vision about a program that could be created for students. The class created a practical foundation that led to program and professional changes. It provided a common, shared experience and reflection time to reach a professional understanding among colleagues.

Throughout this staff development time, many educational approaches were proposed, and as staff members continued to be exposed to shared decision making and empowerment, they wanted to create a similar opportunity to empower their students. They wanted students to develop the skills and desire to complete quality work and direct their own destiny. Many staff members endorsed the ideas expressed in

Glasser's book and began to implement them in their classrooms. Coupled with the barrage of current educational articles, presented to staff members on a weekly basis, "what if" thoughts began to permeate active minds throughout the semester as the reading seminar progressed.

Although the staff did not become part of Glasser's Quality Schools Coalition, they endorsed the best ideas and implemented the most appealing aspects of the philosophy. For example, Glasser postulates that the problem with schools revolves around coercive management. He suggests that students would increase performance if they were empowered with participatory skills to succeed. The Centennial staff incorporated this philosophy into its new Discovery program and the modifications and policies that evolved.

Centennial staff development meetings created a desire for more team-building activities. This need culminated in early December, with unanimous participation in an all-day ropes-course experience. Utilizing a designated district staff-development day, the staff met at school for breakfast, moved to the ropes course, and engaged in a variety of low- and high-ropes course activities. This team-building event created an opportunity for individual and group challenges that encouraged collaboration. The day was electrifying and unifying for all. Staff members were ready to take on any challenge that tested their professional resolve and ability to work together as a team. After this activity, the Centennial staff was ready to be seated at the table of change, which was now fully set.

STRATEGY #8: YOUR NUMBER, PLEASE!

Throughout all efforts to prepare the staff to sit at the table of change, the pulse of the school and the culture of the staff and students were constantly monitored. Was the pace of change too fast, too slow, or just right? Were the principal's leadership strategies accepted by the staff as a positive contribution to school improvement? Did they trust the organizational and communication procedures that were being implemented? What adjustments needed to occur in order to keep the herd generally moving west? To answer these questions, a short survey was created to gather information. In November, the staff was requested to respond to a survey with a satisfaction range from 1 (low) to 5 (high). Some of the responses that encouraged the change process to continue at the current pace are listed below. The number to the right of each question is the average score of that question.

1. To what extent are we achieving the goal of participatory management . . . 4.22
2. To what extent does the principal support you and your program . . . 4.9
3. To what extent do you feel the principal is available for individual discussions . . . 4.6
4. The pace of change at Centennial is about what I expected from a new principal . . . 4.4
5. The pace of change in this building is appropriate to meet our needs . . . 4.0
6. The reading seminar on quality schools introduced an interesting model to pursue . . . 4.2
7. After the first quarter, my energy level is high, based on the potential of taking the school in a new direction . . . 4

This survey was followed by a midyear evaluation of the principal, which was distributed the week before the holiday break in December. The survey responses, using the previous high–low scale, encouraged the administration to continue with the change process. The school was moving in the right direction. Examples of indicators of professional support for the principal included the following items. Averages using a scale of 1 (low) to 5 (high) are tabulated to the right of each question.

1. Protects instructional time . . . 4.42
2. Translates program goals into practice . . . 4.20
3. Monitors work of teachers/students to ensure alignment of efforts to school goals . . . 4.21
4. Effectively delegates authority for school improvement . . . 4.33
5. Treats staff equally and fairly . . . 4.06
6. Demonstrates understanding, timing, and patience with the change process . . . 3.80

YOU MAY BE SEATED

After analyzing the results of these surveys, the staff felt confident and prepared for the difficult task awaiting them upon returning from the holiday break. The staff believed that the first steps in the change process had empowered them to communicate more effectively, to make better decisions, and to begin dreaming of possible different futures for the program. All the steps necessary to set the table for the forthcoming banquet of change were complete. The Centennial staff had been challenged to change or die, and now they were primed to take their places at the table. The task was simple: create a vision of excellence for the new Centennial High School and convince others that it would prove effective for students.

3

TO SHAPE A VISION:
IMAGINE IF YOU WILL

On December 12, 1990, a conversation at the high school principals'
meeting surrounding the fate of Centennial High School created anticipation and discomfort for Centennial's principal. The leaders of the district's three comprehensive high schools prepared a list of concerns related to Centennial's shortcomings and accused the program of no
longer being "user-friendly." The Centennial principal carefully listened
to each item and asked questions to make sure he understood his colleagues' positions. The principal's honeymoon period had officially
ended, and the challenge of responding to district needs became a reality. The upcoming holiday break provided the necessary planning time
to develop a strategy to mobilize the staff and embrace the difficult work
of program restructuring.

The Centennial staff had learned and practiced the foundational work
needed to position themselves for the change process. The next step was
to implement strategies to successfully improve the program. What
strategies were needed to motivate employees from within and keep
outside critics at bay until the team had its act together? Several
emerged as the year progressed.

STRATEGY #1: LONG LIVE THE KING

Occasionally, time works in one's best interest; often, it does not. Upon returning from holiday break, bad timing eliminated the luxury of reflective thinking. The assistant superintendent informed the Centennial staff that the Centennial High School's principal position would be posted in February and asked the interim principal if he was interested in applying for the job. The principal used this invitation to assess the staff's attitude about the potential of becoming their future leader.

A memo asking for feedback on whether he should "apply for the job, go back to the administration building, or just go" was distributed among the staff. The results indicated that 99 percent of the staff favored his candidacy; only one staff member recommended that he "just go!" This person felt the principal was too demanding, too critical, and too threatening. This person indicated it was time for a rest and that the school needed a principal who would lead with a calming hand and not be obsessed with change all the time; perhaps this individual found comfort in living in the past and did not recognize the immense task that lay before the staff. With broad support, the interim principal dismissed the one negative feedback and applied for the permanent position.

Testing one's viability as a candidate for the position proves to be an excellent leadership barometer. The task of leading the staff through the change process is not easy. Too often, ego and territoriality create barriers to the change process. When discussions and actions reach obstacles, the leader must cast the deciding vote to move people beyond roadblocks. In the process, the leader loses support and draws ire and criticism from those who feel they are on the losing end of the decision. Knowing that a principal enjoys a significant approval level before the change process begins boosts his or her confidence and permits the luxury of taking bold steps at the onset of a restructuring effort.

STRATEGY #2: PAINTING THE BIG PICTURE

When an organization is on the verge of making large-scale changes, the leader must become an artist with a broad brush. He or she must have the ability to sense, intuit, and synthesize all the big-picture ideas that have permeated the thinking and discussion of the group and to paint them in words that capture the imagination of employees. Participants in the change process must successfully visualize the "what if" possibilities postulated by the leader's broad-brush strokes. Employees must imagine themselves as participants in the picture created by the leader. The broad strokes of change do not require great detail, only inspiring statements that describe a compelling dream of a possible future. The vision must articulate and create hopes and expectations that evoke passion within the group. Such a vision will motivate others to engage in the process of creating a plan that reflects their commitment to excellence.

The Need to Dream Bigger and Better Visions

Reinventing our public schools could provide an exciting opportunity to use our often forgotten power to create imaginary worlds, share theories, and act out possibilities. . . . Schools embody the dreams we have for our children . . . all of them.

—Deborah Meier, *The Power of Their Ideas* (1995), 110

Shortly after the "go for it" memo, another unexpected event changed the school's improvement time frame. The assistant superintendent handed the principal another broad paintbrush. He requested that the principal create a position paper for the superintendent's cabinet that outlined recommendations about the status of Centennial High School. Did the interim principal see a future in the program, or, based on the myriad of identified concerns, did he recommend its closure?

Just prior to this request, Centennial's leader had been invited to return as the school's interim principal for the following year, yet now he was authorized to become the school's pallbearer. Confused by the mixed messages from the district, the principal vacillated between feeling used as a pawn to do the administration's bidding and having professional integrity to complete a job with passion. In spite of confusion, the principal took brush in hand and created a vision for the future.

The vision memo, dated January 24, 1991, outlined the history of Centennial's program and listed the seven major criticisms expressed by the comprehensive high school principals in December. The second part of the memo created a vivid picture of what Centennial could become. It suggested specific ways to restructure the program and resolve the concerns expressed by members of the three comprehensive high schools. The memo invited the cabinet to imagine a different future for an alternative-learning center by proposing a future in which Centennial would become a quality alternative educational setting for the entire school district. Centennial could become a laboratory school where creative and innovative ideas could be developed and tested; a center to work with students with special needs who were unsuccessful at other high schools; a transitional placement for students who transferred into the district late in the semester and could not be enrolled at comprehensive schools; and a "service broker" for the school district. In this capacity, the district would monitor high school students enrolled in both college and high school classes; become the clearinghouse for all student volunteer work in the community; evolve into a training ground for teachers who needed additional instructional or classroom management skills; be identified as the district's grant-writing center for innovative instructional ideas, pilot-tested with its high-risk student population; expand its role as the summer school learning center for the district; and be structured into a parent training center, offering suggestions of how to more effectively work with reluctant learners.

The vision memo was filled with hope. It outlined possibilities for a program that previously had only provided an outlet for unsuccessful students. Centennial had the potential of becoming the district's centerpiece, a place where educational innovation would thrive and prosper. The broad strokes painted in the memo were bigger than life but could be accomplished if the district leadership wanted to move in that direction and give the staff time to create such a possibility.

The superintendent's cabinet endorsed the entire concept, asked the current principal to continue serving as the interim principal for the 1991–1992 school year, charged with chairing a study committee to ameliorate the concerns related to the current Centennial program, and to create an umbrella structure to solidify all of the district's alternative programs. Consequently, the large paintbrush was put down and the process of motivating the staff to add substance and detail to the image of what Centennial could become was initiated.

STRATEGY #3: SITTING IN THE HOT SEAT

By the end of January, decisions had been made at the superintendent level to give Centennial the necessary time to remain open for another school year. The cabinet had given the staff an opportunity to restructure and create a program that would address the district's needs. The big-picture marketing strategy had given Centennial's team permission to dream and imagine a different future for its program and students. However, emotional turmoil emerged and temporarily slowed the change process. The Centennial staff felt angry, manipulated, betrayed, and used by the district authorities, and by its administrator.

The speedy time line that drove the "what if" proposal and decisions reached by the superintendent's cabinet made it impossible to use the shared decision-making process with the Centennial staff. In early January, Centennial's principal asked if he should apply for the principal's position. Now, within a five-day period, he was named principal for the upcoming year and had a vision plan approved without consulting the staff. The staff believed that all the training in shared decision making had been abandoned and that the old top-down process was still operating.

Staff members felt betrayed and believed they were being set up for failure, that the principal was the "administrative lackey" charged with leading them into a futile exercise that would end in the school's closure. Distrust of the superintendent, his cabinet, the assistant superintendent, and the principal spawned a barrage of parking-lot conversations that erupted into rumors, fears, and general animosity. Morale plummeted, and the best opportunity to control Centennial's own destiny began slipping away.

In response to staff member concerns, the principal scheduled two meetings. The first meeting was facilitated by Centennial's custodian, the most trusted member of the staff. She had graduated from Centennial a decade before, loved the program and its potential, and had chosen to work in the building as an employee after graduation. This meeting was scheduled on the day before the assistant superintendent was to meet with the staff and formally charge them with the task of program restructuring. Students were dismissed early, and the staff met for three hours.

During the meeting, the staff sat in a circle, and each person had an opportunity to express concerns, anger, and fears about the decisions made without input. All of their comments were directed at the principal. He was in the hot seat and the recipient of every volley.

In situations like this, the best strategy to follow is to become a good listener and not defend actions taken by yourself or the central office administration. When staff members are angry, hurt, or fearful, one cannot afford the luxury of personalizing any comment. Even when integrity is questioned, it is best to swallow hard and accept the feedback. In Centennial's case, the timing of decisions at the district level had subverted the decision-making process initiated and formalized in the first semester, and the principal had to pay the price for the district's violation of the school's organizational norms.

When all staff members were finished offering their viewpoints, the principal's response was measured and clear. He tried not to expose any hint of personalized emotion and apologized for not engaging the entire staff in the decisions made for them. He explained the short time line had not been his to choose and apologized for abandoning the school's process. However, he indicated that the ideas stated in the vision memo were thoughts and scenarios that had emerged in the school's staff development process and weekly meetings throughout the first semester.

Staff members were invited to find the seeds of their ideas embedded in the multitiered vision statement submitted in the memo. The staff was also thanked for their honest communication that revealed underlying fears and concerns. Once openly expressed, such concerns provided a healthy, public exchange of ideas and set the agenda for the meeting scheduled with the assistant superintendent the next day. By the time the staff met with the assistant superintendent, emotions had been neutralized and the staff was primed to accept his charge to create a new program.

The hot-seat experience proved to be a necessary component in the change process. The Centennial leader had earned a vote of confidence in December and by January represented a visible and personalized threat. Terry Deal, an expert on school culture, has suggested that organizational reform requires a collective renegotiation of historically anchored myths and meanings. A crisis necessitates letting go of old values and beliefs and creating new forms that represent stability.

This process stimulates fear and anxiety in staff members. Finding someone to blame for the crisis and the feelings of loss that follow are part of the grief process that emerges as the inevitability of change occurs. In order to move the group forward, an emotional venting event must occur to permit staff members to "dump" on the symbol of the authority that caused such disequilibrium. Effective leadership requires one to absorb professional wrath without ego involvement from time to time so that the business of change can proceed, clear of unresolved issues.

STRATEGY #4: INVITING LIONS INTO THE DEN

After twenty-four hours to get emotionally refocused, the meeting with the assistant superintendent went smoothly. The Centennial staff accepted the challenge to restructure the program in order to meet district needs. A districtwide Centennial High School Study Committee was formed. Six volunteer staff members from Centennial were selected. The principal of each comprehensive high school chose four staff members from their schools to join this committee as well. Their teams were composed of administrators, counselors, and teachers who had expressed the most concern with Centennial's program.

Members of the Centennial team were advised to be effective listeners, take copious notes, and refrain from defending or explaining any part of its program to the critics during the first meeting. It was important that they heard all the criticisms so that the team could adequately respond with program changes as required. The meeting, held in late February, was cordial, professional, and enlightening to the Centennial staff members. For the first time, the staff learned how others in the school system perceived Centennial's program, teachers, students, and learning expectations. It proved to be a sobering experience.

Some of the criticisms of the Centennial program were petty, but major concerns were reduced to several issues that required immediate attention. Centennial was labeled "non-user-friendly" because:

1. The program structure was outdated and focused on vocational students and not high school dropouts. Centennial had originally been designed to be a work-study program. Students who enrolled at Centennial were required to be sixteen years old and employed

in the community. According to the school's original instructional plan, students attended academic classes in the morning and reported to work in the afternoon. If they lost their jobs or quit without notice, they were dropped from the academic program. The critics complained that their fifteen-year-old sophomores were dropping out of school in large numbers and could not qualify for admission to Centennial because they were too young to hold a job. The program, considered a safety net for the district, failed to prevent comprehensive high school dropouts from leaving the educational system.

2. Seniors seeking enrollment at Centennial were given priority over sophomores. Frequently, seniors who realized they would not graduate in the comprehensive school program by year's end would choose to transfer to Centennial, a program that required fewer credits to earn a diploma and contained less rigorous academic standards. By permitting seniors to fill available openings, the needs of sophomore and junior students in need of an alternative placement were ignored.

3. Centennial High School had become a mini–high school, with courses that did not correlate with current district curriculum offerings, lacked academic rigor, and graduated students with diplomas filled with "fluff and stuff."

4. The nine-week-quarter system created a long waiting period for students who wanted to enroll in the Centennial program and fostered negative public relations in the community. Parents of students who were dropped from the comprehensive high school for lack of attendance complained to high school principals, the superintendent, and school board members that the alternative school was not available for their students, whereas, by law, they were entitled to an education. Fear of potential lawsuits made the district administration uneasy with the school's admission procedures.

5. Centennial High School had not successfully transitioned students back into the comprehensive high schools and had failed to communicate with key staff members when students transferred from Centennial to their comprehensive high school. As a result, Centennial had become too isolated in the school community and

lacked respect as a legitimate educational institution. Centennial might have outlived its purpose.

By the third meeting in March, the accepting attitude of the Centennial team began to tame the critical lions. Meetings were transformed into brainstorming sessions to help plan a new program. Former critics began to play the "what if" game with the Centennial representatives. What would the ideal alternative school look like? How could it accommodate the needs of the district and sophomore students who required more guidance and structure? How should the program transition students back into the comprehensive high schools? How could Centennial align its curriculum with the rest of the district so that its diploma would gain merit and respectability? How could Centennial become user-friendly?

The critics engaged in the planning process and created a list of suggestions that proved to be impressive and helpful. By the final meeting, all members of the Centennial study committee confirmed the need to have an alternative school like Centennial in place if program modifications were designed and implemented by the following year. The lions roared approval, and the strategy earned Centennial two months within which to create a vision for a new alternative program.

STRATEGY #5: BECOMING EXPERT PROFILERS

The Centennial staff began the process of restructuring by identifying the profile of its student population. Staff needed to know what kinds of students chose to attend the alternative high school and what types of programs they needed. An analysis of enrollment information provided by the study committee revealed that the typical Centennial student was approximately seventeen years old at the time of enrollment and that many remained enrolled until they reached the age of twenty or twenty-one. Almost one-third of them lived on their own or with friends, and fewer than one-third had two parents living at home. They were also systems-toxic—they did not have the necessary social skills to deal with the structure, authority, and power exercised inside systems. They rebelled against all systems—family, school, and community. Their "social skills tool bag" contained two negative tools. One was the "hammer of anger," which was used on anyone who represented authority or did not respond to an immediate need for gratification. They used the hammer on anyone and anything that did not respond to their needs. These students hammered their parents for getting divorced and for using them as pawns in the family power game. They struck at peers because they did not find acceptance by playing sports, joining clubs, or becoming a part of the socially correct clique. They hit at principals, teachers, and police because these groups had bigger hammers and used them to uphold the status quo. Anarchy was an expressed belief, and they took pride in being labeled "Goths" and malcontents. As self-esteem and self-worth eroded, they eventually turned the hammer of anger on themselves. When this action created the pain of self-loathing, these young people turned to alcohol and other drugs to sooth their discomfort, creating chemical dependency issues in their lives as well.

The screwdriver of manipulation was the second tool in their social skills tool bag. These young people had the ability to locate every "enabling button" on people they knew and turned each screw tight enough to exercise control over them. Parents, not knowing how to handle adolescents effectively, were manipulated to excuse ignored curfews, misbehaviors, and minor criminal offenses. Teachers who tended to exhibit enabling behaviors to help students succeed became easy prey to the silver-tongued children who talked their way out of homework, classroom performance, and rigorous academic expectations. The "poor me" performance permitted these students to coast in their classes and in the community. Manipulation became a finely honed way of life and paid excellent dividends. Further analysis of student profiles revealed that

- Almost 75 percent of Centennial's students tested at or above grade level but failed to produce. They were bright but lacked motivation, academic structure, clearly defined expectations, and few, if any, suffered consequences for their choice not to comply with directives.
- Such behavior fostered a need for immediate gratification. The semester's academic structure, or even a nine-week term, proved too much of a challenge for them. Their lives were riddled with

constant episodes of personal crises that set them on a roller coaster of perpetual high-drama behavior.

- Once a crisis occurred, they used this high-drama approach to create havoc and chaos in their lives and the lives of those around them. These young people lacked the problem-solving skills to establish any sense of emotional consistency or stability.

- At-risk students tended to be loners who lacked emotional connections with adults who modeled appropriate ways of handling life issues. Students who enrolled at Centennial quickly discovered that one of the program's strengths revolved around relationship, relationship, and relationship. Any student who remained at Centennial for more than three weeks developed a close relationship with at least one staff member and began to view the school as a welcoming family environment.

By clearly identifying the profile of its students, the staff began to examine those aspects of the program that successfully addressed student needs and the gaps that begged to be filled. Next, the staff turned its attention to developing a clear understanding of the program's mission.

STRATEGY #6: MISSION IMPOSSIBLE

Did the words of Centennial's mission statement convey understanding, meaning, and purpose? Did the programs and policies support the mission? Did the staff endorse the intent and essence of the school's mission?

Centennial's mission statement was articulated in one sentence: "The purpose of Centennial High School is to create a nurturing, intimate environment in order to promote personal, academic, and vocational success." A careful review of the mission statement helped solidify a common understanding of the school's purpose. Since a school cannot be all things to all people and a mark of a solid organization revolves around clarity of purpose, the Centennial staff needed to identify exactly what it did best and develop programs and strategies to ensure quality performance.

One of the major problems with educational organizations today is lack of clarity. In order to please everyone in the community, the organization yields to the pressure of special-interest groups and adds more and more to its program with fewer and fewer resources. In the process, the organization loses sight of its purpose. School personnel, parents, students, and the community must have a common understanding of what the institution is dedicated to accomplish. In essence, each school should clearly state its purpose and accomplish it with quality and passion.

Since Centennial High School had a special goal of serving the personal, academic, and vocational needs of high-risk students, it needed to become the best possible program to accomplish this end. Ancient Greeks called this *Tar'apieta*, or "those things that are best." Essentially, Centennial's mission statement clearly articulated its core purpose and justified its existence to provide the best program it could.

After an extensive discussion about the mission statement and its meaning, the staff made one small modification. They substituted the word "career" for "vocational," because the staff wanted to emphasize that the new vision and program needed to assist students in making lifelong career choices rather than focus on more temporary vocational placements that provided hourly jobs.

STRATEGY #7: WALLPAPERING THE WAR ROOM

As the staff prepared for creating a new program vision, they established a war room, a planning area where all ideas and thoughts were visually displayed on butcher paper hung on every inch of available wall space. One chart displayed the characteristics of the "student profile," while another listed program criticisms. The revised mission statement filled another section of the wall. Some sheets reviewed aspects of the program that were working, while others contained statistics showing problem areas. Finally, several sheets were crammed with scrawled ideas and "what if" statements posted by staff members. These ideas emerged from discussions, the *Quality School* reading seminar, and odds and ends found in various articles distributed weekly to the staff. During planning periods, staff members ventured into the war room to add an idea or to reread charts. The room became the social and professional focal point of the building.

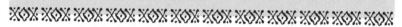

Leading in a Culture of Change

Leading in a culture of change means creating a culture (not just a structure) of change. It does not mean adapting innovations, one after another; it does mean producing the capacity to seek, critically access, and selectively incorporate new ideas and practices—all the time, inside the organization as well as outside of it.

—Michael Fullan, *Leading in a Culture of Change* (2001), 44

With a planning room filled with bold visuals of its task, the challenge of creating the new vision and restructuring the program became the dominant activity in the building. The staff had two months to create something new, and all its attention was directed toward that goal. However, they were still functioning in a vacuum and needed to experience practical insights of colleagues who were implementing successful programs at other school sites. Staff skeptics had to see what ideas were actually working.

STRATEGY #8: TICKETS FOR OFF-BROADWAY PRODUCTIONS

In early March, Centennial's principal reminded his supervisor of the invitation to seek help if needed. The principal explained that the staff was ready to create a new vision and restructure the program but needed some firsthand experiences at schools they had read about in various articles. A proposed staff development schedule was identified so that various staff members could visit selected schools throughout the country and return with information to share. The assistant superintendent endorsed the idea and supported Centennial with an additional $4,000 in staff-development money.

The staff was divided into two- to four-person teams, allocated per diem funds, and completed twenty-five school visits in March and April.

One group visited the Apollo School in Simi, California, a quality-school model mentioned in Glasser's book. At the recommendation of the assistant superintendent, another group visited Bostrom Alternative School in Phoenix, Arizona. Many of the other schools were located within driving distance of Fort Collins and cost little to visit.

As each group returned from the road, the staff gathered in the war room and added sheets of paper to the wall. Each group reported on the program ideas that could be adapted at Centennial and addressed one or more of the areas that needed improvement. Groups who returned from site visits added to the staff excitement, thus creating an infectious attitude of anticipation and importance to the task being undertaken. Staff members had intellectualized educational theories and programs, but the reality of actually seeing and experiencing ideas in practice completed the picture for them.

Individuals charged with making huge changes in their lives must accept the necessity for change in their hearts, minds, and souls in order for change to occur. If they neglect any of these areas, they will only give tacit commitment to the process. Passion must percolate from within each participant so that the experience of creating change permits one to let go of the old and to grab on to the new. Each individual must believe conditions can be improved.

When sharing insights, experiences, and ideas as a group starts, an infectious attitude of empowerment overtakes all participants. They begin to encourage each other to dream and contribute to the big picture of the future. By displaying ideas on butcher paper, the best aspects of brainstorming can be visualized. No idea is rejected at face value. Even if an "ah-ha" is not considered a major idea at first, others may incorporate these thoughts into a different, more interesting concept at a later time in the planning process.

STRATEGY #9: LAYING THE CARDS ON THE TABLE

By the end of April, the Centennial staff was ready to put their cards on the table and create a vision for the future. They had practiced the skills of shared decision making in meetings for eight months. They also had been humbled by criticisms expressed by colleagues at comprehensive high schools and, as a collective whole, had embraced the need for change. Every employee had been primed with reading seminar ideas and educational articles for weeks. They had participated in a Centennial study committee and reviewed identified recommendations.

Staff members had spent hours agonizing over the language that best captured their common beliefs about the students served and the school's purpose. Instructors had examined Centennial's student assessment data, developed a profile of the student population, and experienced firsthand successful programs at more than twenty school sites. The Centennial team had slightly over six weeks to create a new program for the school or lose its status as a legitimate educational institution. They were ready.

On April 23, 1991, the principal distributed a memo and designated three full staff-development days for the redesign project. The memo challenged staff to design a five-year model that took the program "from here to there" in incremental steps, planned, evaluated, and flexible enough to reach intended goals. Participants were encouraged to expose any "sacred cows" that were still lurking on the school grounds. It was glibly suggested that the best thing about cows is that they would make the best barbeque for an end-of-the-year celebration.

The memo also included several structured work forms to assist staff members in planning and imparting a common understanding for their colleagues. The forms asked participants to clarify each new proposed idea, explain how it supported the school's mission, and identify possible impacts the change would have on student performance and behavior, school policies, daily schedule, staff needs, and procedures related to school culture. A change in one area often has a domino effect on other policies, programs, and procedures, so staff members were asked to think globally when considering program modifications.

In the three days dedicated to program imagining, visioning, and planning, the sixteen staff members who participated displayed exemplary professional skills and behaviors. The staff was proud of the way they put personal differences aside and listened and debated with integrity, sensitivity, and respect for each other. They demonstrated exceptional insight as they addressed the school's immediate needs as well as the long-range vision of the program. In approximately thirty hours of work, the Centennial staff restructured the entire program and built a vision for the future. It proved to be an honorable endeavor. The major program changes are noted below:

- *Problem*: High-risk students drop out of school at a younger age and cannot enroll in Centennial without a job.
  New Plan: Redesign the work-related program to emphasize career options, eliminate job requirement for admission, create a service-learning component to emphasize internships and professional shadowing experiences instead of job placements. The Centennial staff changed the admissions policy so that up to 40 percent of its population would include sophomore students who dropped out of comprehensive high schools. Lines of communications with designated members of the comprehensive schools' staffs were proposed so that students could transition from one school to another with greater success.
- *Problem*: Students have a toxic relationship with systems and do not have the necessary skills or positive attitude to cope with a school structure.
  New Plan: Create a six-week, all-day orientation program that teaches students the specific behavior expectations of the school. The staff named this program "Discovery," and it became the school's flagship program. Designed and refined by one of the Centennial teachers, the Discovery structure was borrowed and extensively modified from a prototype orientation program the staff had observed at Bostrom Alternative School in Phoenix, Arizona, which a small team visited. The program, discussed in detail in the next chapter, provided students and staff with a foundation that became a training ground to establish the expectations of the school's culture.
- *Problem*: Students have frequent crises in their lives and could not delay gratification related to earning grades and credits for an eighteen-week semester or a nine-week quarter.
  New Plan: Create the "no fail schedule." In order to design this schedule, the staff combined ideas contained in two articles distributed earlier in the year. The Copernican plan (*Phi Delta Kappan*, January 1990) and the Dalton plan (*Phi Delta Kappan*, Janu-

ary 1991) helped the staff create a plan that organized academic terms into six-week hexters. (Note: "hexter" is a word created for internal use. It identifies a six-week academic term.)

Copernican Plan Creates More Learning Time

The Copernican Plan is predicated on the assumption that, if the schedule for students and teachers is completely reoriented to provide conditions that will accommodate better instructional practice, then many practices identified with more effective instruction can be implemented.

—Joseph Carroll, "The Copernican Plan: Restructuring the American High School," *Phi Delta Kappan*, 361

The daily schedule included five seventy-minute periods for four days a week and five forty-five-minute periods on Fridays. The Friday schedule added a ninety-minute zero-period that preceded the daily schedule. During zero period, students worked with teachers in one-on-one relationships to make up missed assignments, retake tests, get individual help, get ahead, or enhance their personal student-teacher relationships. Attendance was mandatory for students who had missed any day or period during the week. Staff members personally invited individual students who needed help. In this way, Centennial created a schedule that kept students on-task and up to speed on their academic work on a week to week basis. Hence, students had little chance to fall behind in their work or fail at the end of the term.

Students liked this format very much. They recognized that all their teachers wanted to help them succeed, and they thrived on the personalized attention. They also saw the schedule as a reward for meeting academic expectations. If students had perfect attendance all week and did not require individual help, they earned a bonus of an additional hour of sleep, because first period began at 9:30 A.M. on Fridays.

The Dalton Plan Promotes Individualized Learning Packets

Central to the Dalton plan were teacher-designed contracts that outline activities geared not only to learning basic skills and concepts, but also to independent thinking and creativity. . . . Students learn responsibility, can work slowly and thoroughly, work rapidly and advance quickly, [stay] actively involved, and request individual help when needed.

Teachers are friends and counselors, work with students who are motivated and self-reliant and work cooperatively with colleagues and so feel less isolated.

—June Edwards, "To Teach Responsibility,
Bring Back the Dalton Plan," *Phi Delta Kappan*, 399–401

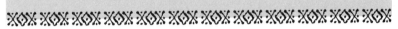

- *Problem*: High-risk students needed individual attention and staff needed preparation time built into the new schedule.
  New Plan: One of the Centennial mathematics teachers, who designed the master schedule, carefully calculated the required number of instructional minutes dictated by the state. He discovered the new schedule provided instructional time that far exceeded state requirements. Therefore, the teacher suggested Centennial alter its elective week (discussed in detail in chapter 5) to meet with students only during the mornings of the last three days of each hexter and use the afternoons for designated staff planning time.

  The staff enthusiastically endorsed this proposal. As a result, students had more instructional time per class than their peers at comprehensive high schools and enjoyed additional elective class time for special events created by individual staff members. The staff also benefited from this schedule, because they had more time to correct and grade papers, record academic grades, prepare materials for the next academic term, meet with colleagues, or attend staff development activities.

- *Problem*: High-risk students need more structure in their lives.
  New Plan: Create a closed campus for Centennial High School. In the most controversial discussion of the planning process, the concept of open versus closed campus offered a healthy debate. Many staff members believed students should receive "natural consequences" for poor attendance, being dropped from the program. Others felt students had been dropped from the comprehensive high schools because they did not have the self-discipline to return to campus after lunch. They believed Centennial's program needed to provide these students with the structure of a closed environment to help them learn to change behaviors.

  After reviewing data related to afternoon attendance issues at Centennial and recognizing that the program had to teach students how to develop an internal locus of self-control, the staff unanimously agreed to create a closed campus. This single policy change created an amazing difference in the student population. For years, students thanked the staff profusely for having the courage to run a school with a closed campus. Most claimed it helped them stay focused on schoolwork and not be distracted by off-campus social life.

- *Problem*: Curriculum and academic requirements did not correlate with district requirements.
  New Plan: Each staff member committed to redesign his or her course objectives to meet district and state standards so that expectations for earning a diploma paralleled district requirements. Computer keyboarding was added to Centennial's list of requirements as a prerequisite to earning a diploma. Although course content and skills were enhanced, the staff reserved the right to continue to implement hands-on, experiential instructional strategies used to teach high-risk students. They believed this delivery system was the most effective way to teach alternative learners.

By the last week in May, Centennial's vision was complete. The proposal was submitted to the administration and welcomed with praise and admiration. The assistant superintendent visited Centennial and personally congratulated individuals for their hard work. With all of its norming, storming, and reforming, the staff had restructured a program that not only met the present district needs but created a model that altered the face of alternative education in the district. Most importantly, the vision, filled with hope and potential, captured the support and enthusiasm of the individuals who planned to implement it in the following year.

As the staff was about to celebrate its successful work, the administration made a political move that altered their outlook. The assistant superintendent informed the principal that the district administration planned to move him back to a central office as the district's social studies coordinator and replace him as principal with an administrator who would be transferred to Centennial. The decision, driven by district personnel issues, required a change in administrative placement. It was explained that Centennial's interim position provided the most flexible way to accommodate the district's need.

The decision shocked the Centennial staff. Again the staff felt betrayed. How could someone who knew nothing about the staff's hard work and planning process have the necessary passion and commitment to implement the newly designed program? A letter to the central administration, signed by a majority of Centennial staff, stated, "Many hours and considerable effort were invested in the development of plans for next year, based on the assumption that the interim principal would be in the leadership position. Changing leadership would invalidate that process and those plans, since we see the current principal as critical to the implementation and refinement of planned program changes."

This letter of support, private meetings, and individual dialogue caused the district administration to reconsider its position, and the Centennial principal was reinstated to implement the proposed changes during the forthcoming school year. If the restructuring plan were to work, it would take the leadership of one who had been engaged in the passion of staff members committed to the planning process.

STRATEGY #10: STEPPING INTO THE CIRCLE

With the temporary distraction of district politics resolved, the final step in creating the vision took place. Before the end of the school year, a staff meeting was called to ask a question that would guide the program for the next five years. During the meeting, the principal drew a large circle on the chalkboard and labeled the circle "Centennial High School culture." On the edges he wrote, "New program components," "New policies and procedures," "New belief statements," and "New mission statement." These statements defined the boundaries of the new Centennial culture and outlined the edges of the circle that represented the program. The principal asked the staff to think about what they wanted to accomplish in the next five years. He asked them to identify words that described what the new vision of Centennial High School would look like. After some discussion, the five-year vision of Centennial High School emerged with unanimous support. The vision the staff wanted to attain was "to earn a national reputation as an exemplary alternative high school."

Next, the administrator asked the staff to identify benchmarks that indicated successful completion of such a vision statement. They rattled off the following indicators of attainment: students maintaining a 95 percent daily attendance rate; students achieving a 90 percent graduation rate; reducing Centennial's dropout rate to less than 5 percent; earning 90 percent school satisfaction rate on the annual student survey; 90 percent of the staff publishing materials and/or sharing successful instructional strategies at the local, state, or national levels; parents seeking enrollment for their students in the school; receiving grant money and financial contributions to provide additional support for the programs; and numerous visitors and educators from around the nation making site visits to see the program in operation and implementing Centennial's ideas.

The principal returned to the chalkboard and drew a huge arrow that led from the circle to the vision statement written at the top of the board. Then, horizontal lines were drawn across the arrow to represent each of the next five years. It was proposed that Centennial would achieve its vision if the staff divided the next five years into incremental steps, written into goal statements for each year. In this way, Centennial could measure its progress and stay focused on achieving the long-range vision.

During the meeting, staff created the following annual goals for each yearly division:

- 1991–1992 school year: Implement the new programs, modify them as needed to guarantee success, and build and refine a solid, supportive student culture.

- 1992–1993 school year: Redesign and align all curriculum offerings to match the district's core academic requirements.
- 1993–1994 school year: Create program and instructional assessments to measure the success of each aspect of program and course goals.
- 1994–1995 school year: Invite a team from the North Central Evaluation program to Centennial to conduct an external audit of our school and make further recommendations for program improvement.
- 1995–1996 school year: Implement North Central Evaluation team's recommendations that will help Centennial reach its vision, celebrate achievement, and recycle the vision process.

After the staff agreed with the yearly goals, the principal called attention to the circle on the chalkboard and placed a triangle in the circle's center. Staff members were told that the triangle represented the role of Centennial's principal as instructional leader. It was his responsibility to carry the vision torch. He needed to model the vision, promote it to create images related to the vision, motivate parents and students to believe in the vision, and create a public awareness and endorsement of the vision. His main responsibility was to move the school's staff in steady, incremental steps toward realizing the vision. Their first responsibility was to make sure the principal walked his talk and that all actions matched a commitment to the school's vision and mission statement.

The staff was also charged with a second responsibility. The principal then placed a series of three Xs on the board. One X was placed near the triangle, one on the edge of the circle, and the other outside the circle. Staff members were informed that each X represented an individual's personal commitment to the new vision and program structure recently created. Staff members were asked to determine which X best represented their place in the Centennial program. The X closest to the triangle represented the staff members who totally endorsed all the proposed changes in the restructuring process. These people had leadership responsibility in the building. They needed to model the new culture for both their colleagues and the students being served. They needed to reach out to other, less-committed staff members and help them become more comfortable with the changes and new behaviors required in the program.

Vision:
To earn a national reputation as an exemplary alternative high school

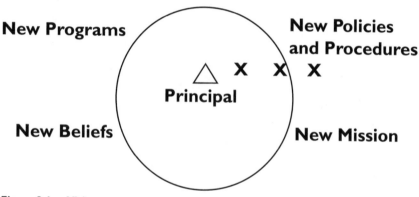

1995–1996   Implement North Central recommendations as needed

1994–1995   North Central visitation team

1993–1994   Create program assessments

1992–1993   Align all program curriculum to district expectations

1991–1992   Implement program, make modifications,
            and build student culture

New Programs   **New Policies
                                    and Procedures**

△ X   X X
Principal

New Beliefs   **New Mission**

Figure 3.1.   Vision

The X closest to the edge of the circle symbolized staff members who endorsed most of what the new program had to offer but did not feel completely comfortable with all of the changes. They were encouraged to move closer to the center of the circle by developing partnerships with individuals who already embraced the culture in the middle of the circle. The importance and strength exhibited by a unified constituency, especially when dealing with students who have thrived on the divide-and-conquer manipulative mentality, was discussed and emphasized.

Centennial staff who lived on the edge of a culture could unintentionally or covertly sabotage the culture, because they were uncomfortable with the nuances of the changes being made. Staff members who saw themselves on the edge of the circle were encouraged to use shared decision-making forums to express their concerns as changes occurred. It is essential that all staff members be aware of issues that emerge as program changes are implemented. It is not professionally healthy to express discontent in parking-lot conversations that undermine progress. Such awareness requires some risk and a safe environment in which to express views but ensures a professional approach to enhancing the school culture and making improvements in programs and policies.

To the people who saw themselves as the Xs on the outside of the circle, stepping inside the circle of the new Centennial culture might not have been an option. For whatever reason, they did not feel personally or professionally comfortable with the shift in programs and policies, nor did they have the necessary commitment to achieve the common vision designed by the group. The principal explained there was no shame or blame attached to being in this position. The restructuring process may have grown beyond the comfort zone of those who believed they might no longer fit into the new Centennial culture.

These people might be more comfortable in an educational setting that more closely matched their professional and personal beliefs, one in which they saw themselves closer to the center of the circle. Therefore, anyone who felt outside the circle was invited to talk with the principal privately so that he could help individuals address their feelings, work with a colleague to embrace the new culture, transfer, or exchange with another teacher in a different building if desired.

The ultimate success of the vision required everyone to be involved and committed to the grunt work of implementing the restructured program. Such a commitment made it essential to take a giant step into the circle of the new Centennial culture. When restructuring takes place, the attitude of the least committed staff member often plays a vital role as a predictor of success. This person is frequently the first to complain and spread a negative response when plans don't unfold smoothly. If program implementation produces only mild, unenthusiastic participation by several staff members, all the planning time and visionary hope is wasted and sabotaged by neglect—more so than would occur with outright insurrection. Therefore, the message of stepping into the circle provides a symbolic way of asking people for their professional commitment to work hard at making the vision become a reality.

The staff accepted the invitation to step into the circle as a time for personal soul-searching. In time, three staff members expressed various reasons why they felt uncomfortable with the direction the school was heading. Each request to move was handled in a different way but was eventually successful in matching individual desires. One teacher was committed to early retirement and used the upcoming year as a transition out of the profession. Another moved into a curriculum leadership position in the administration building. A third person negotiated a one-year exchange with a staff member at a comprehensive high school. By the end of the year, the staff members who exchanged for one year expressed the desire, and received approval, to make the temporary exchange a permanent one.

This strategy of accommodation is essential as change occurs, because it continues to recognize, honor, and support the needs of professionals. It also reduces the number of adversarial relationships that emerge as a building leader guides the change process. Major change presents an unwanted crisis for many people, and the leader must continue to be sensitive to the grief and loss that individuals experience when links to comfortable historical patterns are severed.

Some people feel more comfortable withdrawing from the reordering process rather than coping with involuntary changes in beliefs and behaviors. The leader must include opportunities for individuals to retain a level of personal comfort in a respectful, professional manner. If not, the leader encourages unwanted dissension and creates a force that could undermine and distract others from achieving the vision. Passion for both the preservation of old values and implementation of the new can be powerful forces to deal with as the implementation phase of a new vision is initiated.

STRATEGY #11: READY OR NOT, HERE WE COME

The phrase "when all is said and done, more is said than done" haunted the principal throughout the summer of 1991 as plans for implementing the new vision unfolded. To what extent did the staff endorse the restructured plan, since they had just had several relaxing summer weeks to rethink and possibly reconsider the completed work? Had the high energy, passion, and hope for all the staff evaporated under the warm summer sun? Were they ready to invest in the difficult task of putting marvelous, often complex, ideas into practice? It was necessary to know to what extent the staff was ready to implement the new vision so that appropriate strategies could be developed.

In August, staff members received the traditional "welcome back to school" letter, which also included a copy of the CBAM questionnaire. The CBAM, or Concerns-Based Adoption Model, is an instrument created by the Research and Development Center for Teacher Education at the University of Texas at Austin (1974). It had been successfully used several times in the district to determine program implementation strategies. The form includes thirty-five statements related to the respondent's level of involvement or potential involvement with a specific program or change. Response choices range from "irrelevant," "not true of me now," "somewhat true of me now," to "very true of me now." Sample statements include

- I am concerned about students' attitude toward this innovation.
- I am concerned about conflict between my interests and my responsibilities.
- I am concerned about my inability to manage all the innovation requires.
- I would like to revise the innovation's instructional approach.

The total score of all the statements in this instrument revealed various stages of concern felt by Centennial staff members. The results provided indicators of the kind of staff development strategies that had to be planned in order to successfully implement the proposed program changes. The stages of concern found in the scoring include

- Awareness: I am not concerned about the innovation.
- Informational: I would like to know more about it.
- Personal: How will using it affect me?

- Management: I seem to be spending all of my time in getting material ready.
- Consequence: How is my use affecting students?
- Collaboration: I am concerned about relating what I am doing with what other instructors are doing.
- Refocusing: I have some ideas about something that would work even better.

After reviewing the returned surveys, the results showed that almost every staff member expressed a personal (stage c) or an informational (stage b) level of concern for implementing program changes. To the staff's satisfaction, this stage was appropriate—where they needed to be in order to begin the process of transforming a vision statement into an effective reality. The staff was empowered to "flesh out" ideas and create policies and procedures that reflected the needs of the restructured program. In addition, the staff had to answer the question: Did program changes make a difference for Centennial students? Assessment tools were created to gather data and measure the success of program changes.

ONWARD TO THE FUTURE

The staff seemed ready and anxious to begin working on the first phase of its plan. They were ready to pilot-test all of their ideas and to assist students in modifying their behaviors to the new Centennial culture. Students knew that instructors had spent a great deal of time in staff development meetings, provided them with input along the way, and enjoyed the early release days the previous year. So students had an inkling of the forthcoming program changes. However, they were not prepared for the major shift in the Centennial learning culture that became fully operational by the middle of the 1991–1992 school year. Much effort, planning, and teaching had to occur in order to help these young people make the adjustment to a different Centennial High School. Therefore, a plan to court students to become integral parts of the new program had to be developed.

4

RELATIONSHIP, RELATIONSHIP, RELATIONSHIP

Motivating people to create a vision of success is one thing, but putting plans and ideas into practice presents a greater challenge. The implementation year began with a lot of enthusiasm and high energy. The Centennial staff believed it could, with some minor adjustments along the way, create a marvelous learning environment for at-risk students. The real challenge presented itself in the form of two hundred students who were not prepared for the major shift in thinking. School as they knew it no longer existed, and their comfort level had to adjust to a different daily culture. Perspective, patience, time, and the influx of new students would be the most effective change agents as the new structure and program took shape.

The staff had nine months to teach its students how to embrace the new program and to earn their loyalty. In spite of a marvelous plan and vision, however, Centennial continued to find itself a primary candidate for the financial cutting block. The district was still seeking solutions to its financial shortfall for the 1991–1992 school year, and it was widely reported that the closing of Centennial High School could save the district $189,000 per year. The staff was under pressure to produce or perish as an alternative high school program. Only a culture driven by high relationships could effectively make Centennial's ideas work.

Relationships are based on trust, clarity of expectations, honest communications, consistency of actions, and a shared vision. In order to nurture and refine these characteristics, the following student strategies were initiated. Most of the strategies listed below were implemented during the 1991–1992 school year. Those marked with an asterisk (°) were designed and added within the five-year period following the initial plan. They are included in this chapter as examples of continuous efforts to enhance positive student-adult relationships.

STRATEGY #1: GREETINGS FROM UNCLE SAM

Once the schedule was moved to the hexter system, the counselors and administration held orientations for interested new students on the third Tuesday of each hexter. The orientation, held in the school gym, began by locking the doors precisely at 1:00 P.M. No late arrivals were allowed. Promptness was a key component of the new culture, and every action had to model behavioral expectations. Parents and students who arrived late were told the meeting had already begun and were not admitted. A counselor informed them that the next orientation would be held at 1:00 P.M. sharp in six weeks.

Some disgruntled parents called the central office to complain, but Centennial was attempting to establish clear expectations and sent a message to the community and students that it was going to be doing business in a different way. Centennial no longer enabled stragglers to wander into the program. As a result, the word spread, and parents and students began to appear in the school's gym as early as noon for the 1:00 P.M. orientation.

At the orientation, chairs were arranged in two circles, with candidates for admission sitting on the inside circle and parents and friends occupying the outside circle. Centennial's two counselors sat in the inner circle and took copious notes as the principal interviewed each candidate. The circle symbolized Centennial's learning culture. Sitting in the circle represented the first step each student made to enter the program. As the meeting began, the principal emphasized the importance of everyone in the room being heard. The administration needed to hear why each candidate wanted to enroll at Centennial and why he or she should be selected for admission to the program.

The staff stressed that admission to Centennial was a privilege and not an automatic process as it had been in the past. Students were asked to give their names and reasons why they wanted to attend Centennial. As each student around the circle began to speak, the principal asked questions and counselors recorded answers, observed behaviors, and assessed attitudes.

A typical interview would unfold like this:

Principal: Tell me your name, your home school, and why you want to come to Centennial.

Student: My name is Joe, and I got kicked out of Fort Collins High School.

Principal: How did you get kicked out of Fort Collins High School?

Student: The assistant principal kicked me out.

Principal: You mean to tell me that the assistant principal saw you in the hall one day and told you to leave the school?

Student: Yes.

Principal: Why did she do that?

Student: Well, I missed a few classes.

Principal: A few classes? How many is a few classes?

Student: Well, maybe forty or fifty . . . I don't remember.

Principal: So, you missed forty classes and don't know why you got kicked out?

Student: Yeah.

Principal: So, who really kicked you out of school? Was it the assistant principal or you?

Student: Well, I guess it was me.

Principal: Good response! From this point forward, you must take responsibility for all of your actions at Centennial and accept the consequences for each behavior you choose. Are you ready to do that?

Student: Yes, I am.

Principal: Good.

The dialogue continued, with the principal asking students to identify what had changed in their life so such past behaviors would not be repeated at Centennial. Each interchange was individually tailored to discover the reasons given for seeking admission to the school. Whether students talked about drug use, violence, misdemeanors, alienation from parents, isolation from peers, or trouble with the law, or were simply seeking a smaller learning community, the principal's inquisition challenged each student to justify why he or she felt ready to be admitted into the school.

After all the students were interviewed, they were introduced to the new vision. They were told that the purpose of attending any high school was to earn a diploma. A copy of the Centennial diploma was shown, and the principal moved around the circle asking students if they could really "see" their name, printed in the appropriate blank space, on the diploma. When they said "Yes," they were asked to point to it. Even though the space was empty, students were told that the vision they needed to embrace was that of themselves walking across the stage at the graduation ceremony and receiving their high school diploma.

In reality, it was shared, a person could get married many times and earn lots of advanced college degrees but would receive only one high school diploma in his or her lifetime. Employers often look at a high school diploma as demonstrated evidence that the job applicant is capable of completing a task and worthy of a long-term commitment as an employee. According to the Department of Labor statistics, the completion of a high school diploma represented potential earning power of approximately $175,000 dollars more over a lifetime, which translated to about $75 for each hour the student spent in a high school program. Earning a high school diploma might be the easiest thing an individual can do in life. At Centennial, however, in order to earn a diploma, one had to adhere to the expectations printed on its pledge card. (See strategy #2 for specifics.) Each statement was reviewed, and students were asked to make a commitment to each expectation printed on the pledge card.

After the principal completed his part of the orientation, each counselor said a few words about his or her role and various aspects of the program. Students took a locator pretest for the TABE (Test of Adult Basic Skills) and left with a number of forms they had to fill out before attending a formal testing session, scheduled for Friday of the same week. The forms consisted of various legal and registration papers required of parents, plus a request for a letter of recommendation to be completed by an independent party who recognized the student's potential. Additionally, each student had to write a personal essay explaining why he or she should be selected for admission to the program.

Completed forms, the personal essay, and a recommendation letter were the student's ticket to the Friday testing session. Those without all completed papers in hand were told to attend the next orientation session. This hard-nosed approach placed the responsibility of admission on the student's shoulders. During the testing session, candidates were asked to schedule a one-hour appointment with the counselor of their choice and a fifteen-minute meeting with a student panel for another interview. Keeping appointments on time provided another test of student's responsibility and maturity. If candidates could not make an appointment or were running late, it was their responsibility to call and reschedule. If they didn't show up or arrived late, the admission process ceased, and they were invited to the next orientation.

The counselors reviewed TABE test results with candidates, looked at their life experience and emotional stability, and evaluated their intellectual readiness for Centennial's program. The student panel, composed of veteran students who had a clear vision of success, asked more personal questions about alcohol and drug use, conflicts with other students, and other similar questions to determine if the new candidate would fit into the new Centennial vision and culture.

When the final list of potential candidates was handed to the principal, he had recommendations and observations from the test monitor, the student panel, and the counselors, who had observed candidates at the orientation and had spent an hour with each candidate. Every six weeks, twenty-five new students were selected to be enrolled in the Discovery program (see strategy #3), and the others were placed on a wait list that required the completion of certain academic and/or behavioral requirements before consideration for admission at the beginning of the next term.

The orientation process engaged several Centennial staff members and students, and consumed three to five hours. Consequently, Centennial earned the reputation of being a school that required commitment and passion from those who wanted to attend. Such a process also sent the message to the community that Centennial consisted of a caring group of adults and peers who planned to guide and coach candidates to success by establishing a supportive relationship.

STRATEGY #2: TAKING THE PLEDGE

Too often, organizations embrace new members with initial enthusiasm and then abandon them to figure out the innuendoes and subtle norms of the culture on their own. The Centennial staff clearly stated that the vision was designed to help new students earn a diploma but, in order to achieve that goal, each student had to conform to very specific expectations. These expectations, listed on a pledge card, were signed and dated by the student upon enrollment. Not only were the expectations clearly delineated, but the Discovery program, required of all new students, also provided students with an opportunity to learn and practice each behavior. In addition, these expectations were included in every teacher's classroom norms and posted throughout the school in strategic locations. Once learned, the norms left no room for abhorrent behavior.

Student pledge cards were kept on file in the principal's office for easy access if a student needed a reminder conference with the administrator or counselor. The first week in the Discovery program was devoted to helping students learn and understand the pledge card expectations, and students spent the next five weeks practicing behavioral expectations to support each pledge statement.

Students who graduated from the Discovery program and matriculated into academic classes were occasionally sent to or asked to come to the principal's office for discipline issues or other matters of appropriate behavior or patterns of attendance. When students appeared in the office for any of these reasons, the administrator reached for their pledge card to review the expectations instead of reprimanding them.

The administrator used the pledge card as a teaching tool to help students make choices to improve their success. The principal and student reviewed the statements on the card to reach a common understanding of what each pledge statement meant. The principal then asked the student to identify when and why a particular statement was difficult to achieve. They discussed each behavior and dialogued about the choices

I, _____, pledge to work toward my success as a student at Centennial High School. In order to accomplish my goal of earning my diploma I promise I will:

- Maintain 95 percent daily attendance, knowing I lose credit after two absences in any class each hexter and may be dropped after my third absence.
- Stay clean, sober, and tobacco-free on campus and come to school free of alcohol and other drugs or submit to the drug or smoking cessation intervention program.
- Resolve conflicts in a responsible manner by using the school's peer mediation program and accepting the school's no-fighting norm.
- Apply the six Ps (Prompt, Polite, Prepared, Participate, Positive Mental Attitude, and Produce) to all I do at school.
- Accept and support the general norms at Centennial High School.
- Treat others and myself with courtesy, respect, and dignity.

Figure 4.1. Pledge Card

the student made and the consequences of each choice. Collaboratively, the two of them designed an intervention plan to improve behavior, attitude, or attendance issues related to the pledge statements printed on the card.

These new behavioral plans were shared with the teachers or counselors who had recommended the student for a formal meeting with the principal. Often, during business meetings that focused on student issues, staff members were encouraged to identify other students who struggled with specific pledge card promises. The staff shared insights about these specific students and offered ideas, both academic and behavioral, that worked in their classes. Staff members who enjoyed a solid personal relationship with certain students were encouraged to discuss these topics and potential corrective strategies with the student. Such one-on-one conversations with a meaningful adult helped perpetuate the staff's philosophy that personal relationship was one of the central core beliefs of the program. Such attention was appreciated by the student.

The pledge card provided students with a clear set of behavioral guidelines in the form of a simple checklist. This list distilled the basic beliefs of the program and provided staff and students with clear expectations. When a student violated any of the pledges, the collaboration between the staff/principal and students helped the students work through the consequences of actions to develop an intervention strategy to get back on track. The connection between staff and students assisted these emerging adults view the staff as a helping guide that was not based on power, shame, or guilt. Students realized that failure was a teacher and not an undertaker. Centennial became a training ground for successful adult behaviors.

STRATEGY #3: DISCOVERING THE REAL YOU

The Discovery program became the flagship of the Centennial learning culture. Designed and taught by a Centennial language arts teacher, the program provided students with a sabbatical leave from academics in order to learn the appropriate interaction skills necessary to work effectively within systems.

Mark Twain is credited with suggesting that the best thing to do with adolescents is to put them in a barrel and feed them through the bunghole for a year. At the end of the year, all you need to do is to put a stopper in the hole. Adults often forget adolescents are mere glandular interlopers between childhood and adulthood. Teachers observe adultlike bodies and childlike behaviors. Parents and teachers want adolescents to act like adults; however, little time is dedicated to train youngsters to act that way. Worse yet, the culture often models actions that perpetuate the worst kinds of adult behaviors, which teenagers quickly learn and repeat.

As the staff examined the common characteristics of the typical at-risk student, they recognized the need to create an appropriate training ground for behaviors that would help these young people change their toxic relationships with systems and authoritative adults. This approach necessitated the creation of an introductory program that fostered positive adult-student relationships, increased self-esteem, emphasized the acquisition of new skill strategies, and provided time to practice. The staff believed it was important for students to master these skills in an environment separate from the academic arena so that skill acquisition would be the dominant theme and not be confused with intellectual performance or content acquisition.

The Discovery teacher had the passion, heart, and insight to respond to the needs of the most disenfranchised young person. He worked tireless hours to create a program that taught students the prosocial skills

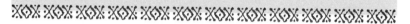

Model Behaviors to Eliminate Enabling Students

Students can be successful if "We [adults] model first-rate standards of performance and reinforce the idea that significant learning and personal growth come only from hard work and persistence. Good teachers don't give a good education to students; they provide experiences that facilitate and motivate youngsters to educate themselves through trial and error, success and failure."

—Steven E. Landfried, "Enabling Undermines Responsibility in Students," *Educational Leadership*, 80

necessary to cope with the adult world. Using William Glasser's philosophy as a starting point, the teacher quickly added and adapted Thomas Harris's *I'm O.K., You're O.K.* transactional analysis concepts as a communication model for the program. He borrowed ideas from Arnold Goldstein's *Prepare Curriculum* and incorporated strategies for prosocial skill competencies. He solicited the help of a psychology professor at Colorado State University and developed an effective unit on anger-management strategies.

The Discovery instructor used his years of classroom experience to develop other learning strategies to add to the program. Finally, he applied his intuitive insights about adolescents to create a safe environment in which students, previously alienated from adults, began to trust him, their peers, and eventually, the Centennial culture in which they would learn and function.

The Discovery program created an exemplary social skills–based model and is currently being used in more than 150 school districts in sixteen states. In addition to teaching the program at Centennial High School, the instructor became a facilitator for the Sopris West Educational Services, an educational company that purchased the training rights to the program. The program effectively changes students' behavior by empowering them with the necessary skills required to succeed in the school and community.

The Discovery program at Centennial is a self-contained six-week program, meeting five hours per day. Twenty-five students learn and practice the skills and concepts taught in the following curriculum.

Week One

Effective group skills and learning culture expectations are taught. Students, normally loners, learn the power of group synergy, school and classroom expectations, how to incorporate the pledge card statements into behaviors, and how to collaborate with and trust peers. The teacher emphasized the concept of attending skills especially: giving the speaker eye contact, demonstrating engaged body language, asking clarifying questions, and staying focused and "in the moment."

The most powerful part of the first week is introducing students to the quality communication-sharing circle. This is a whole-group dialogue where the goals of trust building, personal sharing, and risk taking occur. Students are asked to place their desks in a tight circle, and the teacher gives them prompts to respond as the conversation unfolds. Students are asked to give their name, state a feeling they are experiencing, rank their day from a 1 (low) to a 10 (great day), and then respond to the prompt. The prompts range from easy topics such as, "If you were a car, what would you be and why?" to more personal issues like, "Which of the skills learned in this class has made the biggest impact on your behavior in the last week?"

This approach helps students to recognize the importance of relationships with peers, discover similar issues of concern related to growing up, and recognize the power of group synergy, which can foster friendship, trust, and assistance from others who share the same emotions and experiences. The teacher, acting as a guiding facilitator, uses professional insight and experience to help students overcome personal rough spots so that each student recognizes his or her individual capacity to use newly acquired skills effectively.

Week Two

Students who enroll at Centennial are often angry. Their anger is frequently displayed in unproductive ways that lead to social alienation.

The second Discovery unit helps students recognize sources of anger and offers a variety of strategies to handle anger differently. The program teaches students that anger can be viewed on a scale from one to one hundred. One to twenty reflects daily stresses we all experience, while eighty to one hundred indicates out-of-control behavior—veins sticking out in the neck and striking out with fists. The teacher emphasizes that people can all recognize the increase in anger from twenty to eighty, yet can also do effective personal work to "keep our cool." The course teaches students how to use "water words" (calming self-talk) instead of "fire words" (that increase anger). Students identify triggers that cause anger and learn other effective intervention strategies.

Weeks Three and Four

The Discovery teacher considers this unit to be the core of the program. Harris's classic model of the critical/nurturing parent, the angry/playful child, and the adult mode of communicating are easily grasped and understood by adolescents. Students recognize the characteristics of each model, because most of them have personally experienced every behavior. Students are required to create role-playing scenarios that use the adult-mode of front-loading information, negotiating agreements and commitments, and reaching win-win conclusions. After practicing these skills, students are usually amazed that such simple adjustments in communication can change relationships with parents, teachers, and others.

Weeks Five and Six

These weeks are devoted to teaching students Centennial's conflict mediation model, assertiveness training (getting what you want without being aggressive or intimidating), and a simple five-step problem-solving model. By the end of the six-week hexter, students are required to demonstrate all skills learned in Discovery by creating and acting a role-playing scenario, passing written tests on each skill, participating in a class-scheduled ropes course designed to solidify team building and relationships, and completing an autobiography.

In addition, the program includes an art project. Discovery students spend one hour per day creating a quilt that represents their class. The quilt is eventually displayed at an all-school assembly and formally presented to the school. The quilt is a symbolic representation of a group of twenty-five individuals who, by the end of Discovery, became a team and completed a project together. The quilt, presented before the assembly, permits every Discovery student to introduce himself or herself, talk about the meaning of his or her quilt square, and say something about the effort the team made to complete the project.

Centennial's art teacher used the quilt-making activity as an opportunity for students to develop personal relationships with their classmates and to reinforce the school's norms and expectations in an informal setting. Each presentation was an emotional and rewarding experience for both students and staff. The finished quilt hangs in a place of honor for six weeks until the next Discovery class presents its unique quilt.

Centennial: A Safe, Consistent Haven

Centennial is a place where students choose to go, either to graduate on time or even early, to gain support, and be in a safe learning environment. Centennial teaches important skills and enforces rules that are made so everyone here is equal, producing quality work, and is safe. They have strict attendance rules and teach you effective people skills to succeed.

Discovery, a six-week required course, teaches you how to maintain a positive mental attitude, essential for success in life, and other important skills such as anger management, effective communication skills, conflict mediation, problem solving, and decision-making. The goal is to pass this class and use these skills throughout your years at Centennial. It works because students feel safe to learn and like the consistency of the program.

—Jasmine Bean, excerpt from a class assignment (2001)
—Cathina Gregory, 1994–1995 Centennial High School year book

Discovery students participate in a formal completion ceremony at the end of the hexter, and as they receive their certificate of completion, they recognize their readiness to reenter the system and succeed. They are empowered with a new set of skills that have been practiced and added to their invisible social skills tool bag. The students know they will be held accountable for these newly acquired aptitudes by teachers who have learned to employ the same skills through ongoing staff development workshops and staff meetings.

STRATEGY #4: SPARE THE ROD . . . EMPOWER THE CHILD

The consistent implementation of a clearly defined discipline system may be one of the central keys to running an effective educational program. If behavioral expectations are universally known by staff and students and the consequences of infringements are quickly and fairly applied, the learning culture will thrive. There is nothing more irritating and unsettling to students than observing the inconsistent application of agreed-upon norms and rules of behavior. They equate fairness with consistency. The learning culture is undermined and denigrated when students are unsure of who will invoke which rule when, and what consequence under which circumstance.

In many cases, students purposely test the system or sabotage classroom and school rules out of boredom, retribution, or the sheer challenge of manipulating the system to see what can be achieved. In order to promote student and staff consistency and respect for school discipline, the Centennial staff created a four-step behavior protocol that was easy to implement and clearly understood by students and staff. The system provided "teachable moments" and empowered students to self-correct behaviors with a minimal disruption to classroom instruction.

The system consisted of a four-step format for staff to follow. Prior to implementing the process, the instructors collaborated with students on the first day of each academic term to identify class expectations that would create the most positive learning environment possible. Using a sheet of butcher paper, students and teachers listed nonnegotiable classroom norms and expectations desired to help the class run smoothly. Since all students had previously attended the Discovery program, these norms were based on familiar classroom expectations. The list usually consisted of phrases like "follow the six Ps, practice attending skills, listen to the speaker, no put-downs," and other housekeeping rules. Students signed the butcher paper as a symbol of initial understanding and buy-in. The list was posted in a prominent place in the room for easy reference. After the list was created, the discipline—"redirect" behavior—protocol was implemented.

Step One: The Question

If a student is causing any sort of minor disruption, the teacher asks the student a question—for example, "Judy, how are your attending skills?" (being in the moment, eye contact, listening, asking clarifying questions, and engaged body language). Realizing that her behavior was off-task, the student's response is usually, "Not so good." The teacher's follow-up statement ends the redirect process with a quick, "Please take care of that. Thank you."

Step Two: The Directive

After a second infringement of classroom norms, the teacher takes a more assertive stance with the student. "Judy, this is what I see you doing (disrupting your neighbor) and this is what you need to be doing (working independently on the assignment). Please take care of that. This is your second redirect."

Step Three: The Conference in the Hall

After Judy's third infringement, the teacher asks the student to step into the hall for a private conference. At the beginning of the conference, the instructor begins the dialogue by asking Judy a series of clarifying questions. "Do you still have the vision of earning a diploma? Is there anything troubling you that is getting in the way of your success in this class? Do you need to visit with a counselor or another adult in the building to help you get refocused on learning?"

Depending on the answers given, the instructor then outlines the list of behaviors that have taken Judy off-task and requests Judy to explain why this behavior persists after two previous redirects. Listening carefully to the explanation, the teacher continues the dialogue so that both the student and teacher understand the situation. Finally, the instructor requests that Judy develop a plan to solve the problem herself. The plan becomes her ticket to return to class. The teacher empowers the student, in a teachable moment, to redirect her own behavior. At the conclusion of the conference, the teacher adds one final encouraging word and a caution. The teacher summarizes the conversation by stating, "I have every confidence that you can implement your plan. However, if you can't, the next step in the protocol is to be sent to the principal."

Step Four: Visit to the Principal

Upon the fourth violation of classroom norms, the student is sent to the principal. The principal begins the visit with the following question: "Why are you here instead of being in class?" If the student was sent to the office for discipline, the principal follows with these questions: "Did you have your first and second redirect? Did you have a conference in the hall? How effective was the plan?"

After a brief conversation, the principal hands the student a "success contract" and suspends the student by stating, "You have chosen to step outside of the learning circle. As a result, you will be sent home today with this success contract to complete. It is your ticket to return to school tomorrow. You must complete the form, have your parents sign it, review the contents with your instructor, and have it on my desk before going to any of your classes tomorrow. Have a nice day."

If the student protests and inquires if the principal wants to hear her side of the story, the principal responds by stating that this suspension is the result of four redirects in behavior. Since the principal was not in the classroom, he is simply following the school's discipline protocol. The behavioral issues concern only those people directly involved and must be settled by the two parties. The principal may express sympathy for the situation or agree to mediate if a resolution cannot be found, but he assures the student that he or she must follow the agreed-upon procedures to correct the situation and to guarantee that the learning environment has the least amount of disruption.

The success contract follows a problem-solving format that empowers the student to be reflective about the situation and offer ways to correct it. The student must

- Define the problem.
- List possible ways to solve the problem.
- Choose one of the solutions from the list.
- Identify what the student wants the instructor to do to assist the student achieve the chosen solution.
- Determine what consequence will follow if the contract is broken.

The next day, the student and instructor meet before school to review the student's perception of the problem and solution. The language in the contract can be negotiated and rewritten. Once the conference ends, the student returns the form to the principal and reenters the program without further concern. If the contract is broken, the principal will review it with the student and enforce the consequence stated in the signed contract.

This process permits the teacher, parent, principal, and student to successfully collaborate to solve behavior problems. It empowers students to engage in the dialogue with teachers and parents and to plan self-corrective actions. The protocol minimizes the use of instructional time for behavioral issues.

The staff is also held accountable to follow protocol. If a staff member sends a student to the office without following all of the steps in the process, the principal leaves the student in the office, goes to the classroom, reminds the teacher of the protocol, takes over the class, and asks the staff member to deal with his or her problem in the office. Once the teacher and student resolve the issue, both return to class, and the principal goes back to the front office.

On rare occasions, a student can abruptly short-circuit the process and be sent to the principal without following protocol. For example, if a teacher asks, "How are your attending skills?" and the student responds, "F**k the attending skills!" the student is immediately sent to visit with the principal. The instructor alerts the principal with a phone call so the administrator is prepared for the student's arrival.

The principal greets the student with his pledge card in hand. After confirming the student signed the card, the principal asks key questions: "Please help me understand how the phrase 'F**k the attending skills' meets the criteria for being polite, and treating others with courtesy, respect, and dignity?" Of course, the student is left with no response except, "It doesn't."

The principal then tells the student that the remark placed him out-side the circle of the learning culture, resulting in two possible options. The principal can immediately suspend the student, or the student can identify a way to repair the damage. Almost always, the student chooses to repair the damage. The student designs a plan to correct the infrac-tion, and the principal role-plays the anticipated dialogue between stu-dent and teacher. The entire staff is aware of this intervention strategy and knows that the return of the student is the result of being primed by the principal. The principal uses the incident as another teachable moment to help an adolescent use appropriate methods to repair a hu-man mistake.

This strategy not only establishes a consistent way to handle discipline issues but it permits the entire staff to empower students to practice ap-propriate skills and expectations for the learning culture. When any of the classroom or school norms are broken, the student is not shamed, blamed, or made to feel guilty for the infraction. The student is given choices and is "coached" to repair the damage and return to the learn-ing mode.

STRATEGY #5: WHERE THERE'S A WILL, THERE'S A WEED*

As the staff reviewed the profile of its students and the district's annual drug and alcohol survey results, it became obvious most of Centennial's students were frequent marijuana users and heavy party drinkers. They believed their use of the "weed" and alcohol were part of the social scene and that "recreational use" was harmless and played no part in their inability to succeed in school.

To gather more information on students, school counselors adminis-tered the S.A.S.S.I. survey (Substance Abuse Subtle Screening Inven-tory) to all students who enrolled in the Discovery program. The staff was surprised by the results. The surveys indicated that more than 60 percent of the students were chemically dependent and used alcohol and other drugs as a form of relaxation to reduce stresses produced by their unful-filling lifestyles. The staff recognized that alcohol and other drug use were not compatible with promoting a focused learning culture. There-fore, a drug and alcohol intervention strategy needed to be developed to help students get clean so they could reach their learning potential.

Centennial approached the substance abuse issue as if it were a health problem and not a discipline issue. The administration formed a partnership with the Jacob Center, a private, state-licensed foster care and treatment center located two blocks from the school. The Jacob Center program director worked with the Centennial counseling staff to develop an intervention program called "Joel and Company." The company made periodic information presentations to students in Discovery, administered the S.A.S.S.I. survey, and shared results with students in a confidential meeting. The presence of the center's director on the campus encouraged students to develop a relationship with a community-based adult who cared about their well-being. This relationship proved to be vital to the enforcement of the school's drug policy as several students were sent to the Jacob Center throughout the year.

Using the pledge card statement related to drug use as a starting point, the school's policy was designed to assist students in beating the drug habit. The initial step in the process was recognizing that a problem existed. If at least three staff members, students, and/or parents recognized a change in a student's attitude, attendance, behavior, or performance, the youth was recommended to the principal as a candidate for a drug screening (urine analysis). After the third recommendation, the principal reviewed the student's pledge card and engaged in an informal discussion with the student related to the frequency and amount of drugs used. Observations related to changes in behavior were shared, and the student was informed that his or her parents had already been contacted to get permission to send the student to the Jacob Center for a urinalysis (U.A.). The student was assured that the Centennial staff was concerned about his or her health and not interested in catching him or her doing the wrong thing. Since the Jacob Center was five minutes away, its receptionist was alerted by phone and requested to report if the student went AWOL.

The center's director played a wonderful "good cop" role. As he administered the urine screening, he asked students if they suspected it might be "hot." Since students were familiar with the director through his classroom presentations and trusted his sincerity, they often admitted using various substances. He encouraged them to return to school and inform the principal in order to work with him to get help. This strategy frequently worked, and the battle to deal with student's substance issues began on a positive note.

The results of the urine test reached school within two days, and another meeting was scheduled with the student to review the findings. Even though the principal was not an expert on drug use, a simple format was used to help the student understand what his or her drug use meant. A test results reading of zero indicated the student was clean, 1–50 revealed the student had used marijuana in the last month, 50–200 showed use in the last two weeks, and 200–400+ proved he or she had used marijuana within the last twenty-four to forty-eight hours.

The student sat in amazement as test results, often ranging from a low of 450 to over 2,000, were reviewed. Students reasoned they did not use any more or less than their friends did. Recreational use, however, often translated to mean daily use, which was a common practice among these young people. Students were quick to emphasize they never came to school high and saved drug use for after school or weekends.

Again, the principal invoked his prerogative to create a unique definition of drug use with Centennial students. The administration maintained there was a significant difference between being "high" and being "stoned." Students often did not show any outward physical signs of being high. However, the physical characteristics of THC, the main ingredient in marijuana, acted like honey in their system. THC is sticky and accumulates in the fatty parts of the brain. It slowly coats the dendrites responsible for mental and creative brain functions, thereby altering the student's capacity to process information rapidly and, more importantly, transferring short-term learning into long-term memory. So, in effect, the student was stoned, which still created a barrier to academic success at Centennial. This reasoning made sense to most students, and they agreed to address the problem.

Given this understanding and the commitment to empower students with choices, they were offered two alternatives. They could choose to be dropped from the program, based on the violation of their pledge card commitment to stay clean, or they could stay in school, work through Centennial's drug intervention process, and get clean and healthy again. In more than a decade, only two students chose to leave the school.

The district's comprehensive schools suspended students for three days for drug violation and had an elaborate process to follow after each infringement. At Centennial, working with high-risk students required

that the staff identify the problem immediately and begin an intervention process to solve it. This process proved to be effective by empowering students, and it continued to reinforce the school's commitment to
maintain a positive, personal relationship.

The drug intervention process was simple and extremely effective.
Students who agreed to participate in the school's drug intervention
process were scheduled for another appointment at the Jacob Center.
The director, a certified addictions counselor, conducted a clinical interview and administered a series of written surveys to determine why
the student chose to use the drugs of choice and how willing the student
was to change behaviors. His findings were summarized in a report that
included a number of free or low-cost recommendations for the student
to follow.

A meeting with the student, his or her parents, and the counselor was
scheduled at the earliest convenience of all participants. The report was
read aloud, and the director of the Jacob Center interpreted the meaning of every finding. The group reviewed the recommendations and set
up a time line to monitor progress. One recommendation always included the student's agreeing to random urine screenings to check
progress. The student was not expected to get clean immediately, because changing behaviors is challenging. However, the administrator
had to see that each urine screen score was lower than the previous one.
This was the student's ticket to stay in school. If the urine reading
jumped higher than the previous score, the student would be given an
automatic leave of absence until he or she was totally clean.

This process treated students with courtesy, respect, and dignity.
Students understood that school officials, community members, and
parents wanted them to succeed, that they did not want to punish them
for behaviors driven by chemical dependency. Counselors frequently
met with these students to offer alternative ways to handle stress or to
engage them with peers in a drug and alcohol support group. The student's closest friends were often interviewed and asked to help the student get clean by keeping him or her off drugs when socializing away
from school.

The process worked. Every year Centennial identified approximately
seventeen to twenty students who tested positive for drug use, and every
year approximately fifteen to seventeen students were clean by the end

of the school year. Counselors held private celebrations of success, and several students went public, thanked the adults who helped them get healthy, and sometimes led in-school classes and seminars or became drug counselors for peers who were still struggling with chemical dependency issues.

This policy provided another way to promote high relationship with students and to empower them with skills and strategies to apply to their lives. Parents, students, and staff appreciated the way Centennial handled drug issues. A prime example of an effective substance abuse intervention involves a student named Lee C. Prior to enrolling at Centennial, she had attended two other comprehensive high schools in the city, become involved with drug use, and dropped out of both schools. After enrolling at Centennial, she graduated from the Discovery program, successfully masked her drug dependency issues, and began participating in academic classes.

Within a short period of time, staff members began to notice a change in her attitude, behavior, attendance, and academic performance, and reported their observation in a student-oriented staff meeting. It was recommended that Lee C. submit to a U.A. test at the Jacob Center. The results revealed a reading of 700+. The counseling staff reviewed the results with Lee C. and explained that her steady use of marijuana represented a sizable barrier to success in school. In complete denial, she chose to withdraw from Centennial rather than deal with the issue.

A couple of months later, however, she appeared, requesting readmission and help with her drug issues. In collaboration with her mother's insurance company, counselors secured a bed at a treatment facility before admitting her to academic classes at Centennial. After spending thirty-eight days in treatment, Lee C. returned to Centennial clean and sober. She undertook random U.A. tests for the next ninety days; all were clean. She participated in school counseling sessions and became a member of Centennial's peer drug support group to help her with recovery. A year later, as a clean, healthy, grateful, twenty-year-old, she graduated from Centennial High School.

In an attempt to earn an academic scholarship to college, Lee C. accepted an invitation to share her success story with the Fort Collins Noon Rotary Club. She invited her mother and offered the following remarks.

My name is Lee C. I'm a senior at Centennial High School and we have a tradition at Centennial involving thoughts for the day. So, here is one I found in the principal's office that kind of fits the story I'm going to share: "If all the cars in the country were lined up bumper to bumper, some idiot would try to pass them." I was that idiot before I got to Centennial; to always take the hard road, ignoring every sign of logic, every piece of advice, and, not to mention, just making everyone you pass very angry.

I started high school at Fort Collins High School in 1991 and had every aspiration and hope of graduating in the usual amount of time, having tons of friends, being on a sports team, and doing typical, normal, healthy high school things. It took me until the end of my first week to realize something wasn't exactly right with me. I would walk down the halls of school every day, sit in class all hour, and not have a teacher look at me. I knew people, but I wasn't close enough to any of them to have a conversation. The most help I got from them was assistance on assignments or a "Hey, can I have your parking space?" In a school of that size, it wasn't enough. I felt invisible and I didn't know or understand why.

I gave it time, tried to fit in and meet people, but I ended up with thirty-some absences in each class and only one friend, who happened to be a big fan of cocaine. Slowly I started my gradual descent into what most people call hell. I continued to hang out with the only group that seemed to accept me and participated in every area of their drug use. My parents, whom I've always been close to and loved very much, had recently divorced and were oblivious to my struggles. I became an expert at lying and stealing and used both to my full advantage until I had racked up a total of sixty-four absences and was dropped from high school for nonattendance. All that time, my parents thought I was doing just fine in school and it became painfully obvious I wasn't.

I tried Rocky Mountain High School, but it was worse than my first try. I think I went to a total of three periods a week for an entire quarter and found myself unable to handle anything. I dropped out again, left home, and moved in with some very unmotivated and nonintelligent people. In the span of one year, my life was completely opposite of what I had known or visualized. As a seventeen-year-old, I was addicted to every kind of drug, living with others who weren't the best of people, and the hardest thing for me to admit, I had nothing to do with the family that loved me more than I loved myself.

I finally got homesick and eventually physically sick. I was tired of being treated badly by friends and finding myself in situations I had no control over. I was lost, totally lost, and I knew it. I returned home, always welcomed by my mom. One day an adult friend suggested I might give Centennial a try. "I don't know much about it, but I hear they work miracles on brats like you." So I attended orientation and to this day, I don't exactly know why.

When I entered Centennial, I had a job but still no positive feelings about myself, no liveliness, and hated every kind of adult authority. However, once I arrived at Centennial, I realized that most of the other students, my new friends, were a lot like me. The teachers at Centennial not only helped you with your schoolwork but also cared about your life issues. They knew how to fix where my heart hurt and taught me how to find hope again. I had finally found my place and somewhere to find myself. However, I had one thing that I couldn't shake—the drugs. I was a walking corpse with only the glimmer of hope to graduate. I still needed the drugs to numb the pain and guilt of the things I had done to others and myself.

Through Centennial and my parents, I ended up at Harmony Drug and Alcohol Rehabilitation Center in the mountains west of Estes Park, Colorado. I reluctantly went, but without much of a fight because I simply did not know what else to do. I knew I had to let someone else help me because I couldn't help myself.

With full support from everyone, I spent the hardest, weirdest, most surprising thirty-eight days of my life in rehab. I realized I had hurt my body, my family, my relationships, my financial status (not to mention my family's financial status), and understood the damage path created by the tornado of drug use. It was finally making sense to me. Maybe it was eating three meals a day for the first time in two years or the uninterrupted sleep, but things were very clear. I didn't just feel lucky to be alive; I felt my soul come back into me. I felt hope come back to me. I felt my options open up . . . for the first time . . . I felt!

Once I returned home, I started a job and became close friends with those I had previously met at Centennial. It made me miss school. Then I realized I actually wanted to return to Centennial. I knew I was ready to go back and move on with my life. It was an amazing feeling. I came back to Centennial as a twenty-year-old with a full year of work to complete before graduation. In the first term, I earned a 3.8 G.P.A., and in the second, a 3.9. I had never earned grades like that.

Today, I am working at a job I love and enjoying my parents, who are involved in all of my accomplishments. I also feel a sense of pride in myself, and the work I have done to repair my life. I enjoy a sense of family with my school, the entire school, and now I have been invited to talk to you. I wish you all could know how good it feels to be standing here. I will graduate at the end of this year with some of the same people I enrolled with in my first Centennial class. I have a love for writing that will hopefully turn into a career. I consider myself lucky to have had a chance to get everything out of school that I can, lucky to have a school like Centennial.

Now, I am on a road that actually goes somewhere and doesn't just pass everything by. Maybe I could have done it without Centennial, but I know I would never have believed I could without them. Thank you for inviting me to speak to you today.

When she completed her speech, there wasn't a dry eye in the room. More than one hundred Rotarians gave her a standing ovation. She embraced her mother, presented her with a bouquet of flowers, and thanked her for believing in her throughout the entire ordeal. In May of that year, she received a $2,000 academic scholarship from the Fort Collins Noon Rotary Club.

STRATEGY #6: A CLINIC, JUST FOR THE HEALTH OF IT*

In the early part of the 1990s, most of Centennial's student population lived on their own and worked forty hours a week to support themselves. The staff conducted an analysis of the school's yearly dropout rate, coupled with exit interviews with students who left the program. The findings fostered a need to create another public-private partnership designed to keep kids healthy and in school. When students became ill, they chose to stay in bed all day and cut school rather than miss work in the evenings. The more unexcused absences they accumulated, the farther behind they slipped in school and the less motivated they became to remain enrolled. Consequently, dropping out of school became an easily acquired, practiced pattern in their lives.

None of these students ever admitted they were dropouts. They believed the choice to depart was a temporary leave of absence from education. However, what these students failed to recognize was that each self-declared sabbatical distanced them from the goal of graduation for another semester. This pattern tended to continue until students reached the age of eighteen, viewed themselves as too old for high school, and dropped out to get a full-time job or pursued a GED.

In an attempt to address this problem, the staff went to the community for help. At a public health forum, the assembly was asked for assistance in establishing an in-school health clinic at Centennial High School to serve the needs of its high-risk population. A nurse practitioner in Fort Collins responded to the request and met with the staff to discuss possibilities.

The nurse practitioner and the staff formed an immediate personal/professional partnership that lasted for the remainder of the decade. In the absence of school board policy, a public-private health care partnership established an in-school health clinic at Centennial. The nurse practitioner rented a room in the school's basement for $1 per year. Physicians throughout the city were donated equipment, medicines, and other amenities to begin her practice. The clinic was supervised by one of the physicians at the city's Children's Clinic.

Interested parents initiated fund-raising campaigns and built an operating budget for the program so that taxpayer funds were not used to support a private clinic. By January 1994, Centennial opened its health clinic and served more than one hundred students during the spring semester. Students were charged a minimum of $5 per visit, and the nurse practitioner drew her salary and fees, as a part-time employee, from the donations secured from many private businesses and local service clubs.

Clear evidence suggests the nurse practitioner charged the account for less than half of the time she spent at Centennial. She called Centennial a "civic project," and her generous efforts paid off for students. The dropout rate fell dramatically that year. It dropped from a high of 20 percent at midyear to 9 percent by year's end. Daily attendance rose, and, due to her counseling, the baby boom, which is a typical pattern among high-risk adolescent females, dramatically declined. No birth control devices were dispensed from the clinic, but the presence of a medically oriented adult whom students trusted dropped the number of pregnancies from nine the previous year to only one in the year the clinic opened.

Today, the clinic is affiliated with Colorado Youth Naturally, a state health organization, and has enjoyed a working budget of up to $30,000 per year. Several medical associates have successfully applied for and received financial grants from diverse community sources including, but not limited to, the Belgium Brewing Company, the Stryker-Short

Foundation (now the Bohemian Foundation), Golden K Kiwanis Club, and the Poudre Valley Hospital Foundation. Currently, Centennial employs a full-time physician's assistant and a part-time psychologist. A health clinic advisory board, composed of students and community members, oversees the program's operation and continues to seek grants and private donations to stay operational. The facility serves more than 250 students annually.

STRATEGY #7: SMOKE 'EM IF YOU GOT 'EM*

Ninety-five percent of high school dropouts smoke cigarettes. That's a startling statistic but an understandable one. Cigarettes, if you believe the advertisements, provide a source of stress relief. From the beginning of its inception as an alternative school, Centennial provided a smoking area for students. Bending to the pressure of high-risk youth, Centennial's daily schedule called for ten-minute "smoke breaks" between classes. If you didn't smoke before coming to Centennial, you soon learned how to socialize with tobacco after you arrived. The staff recognized it needed to eventually address this issue, but they opted to first make major program changes before tackling student's personal choices.

However, the Fort Collins City Council forced the school to address the smoking issue, with imposed legislation. In February 1997, the city council passed an ordinance banning the use of tobacco products by any juvenile under the age of eighteen. The school board followed suit by banning all use of tobacco products on school property. The school's administrator testified before a city council hearing and was asked if he wanted a smoking ban waiver for Centennial High School. The principal responded with a definitive "no," indicating that Centennial applauded the council's courage and wanted to participate in creating a healthy environment for youth.

The school had a month to prepare students before the ordinance took effect in March. The first day of the new ordinance's implementation coincided with the first day of the new academic hexter. For a month prior to the deadline, counselors alerted students to the upcoming change and the new law. They instituted reduce-smoking events, passed out candy to use as a substitute, and provided incentives for students who wanted to quit or reduce tobacco use.

This effort was to no avail. On the first day of the new term, the school's smoking area was closed, and smoking on campus was banned. In protest, thirty-seven students walked off the campus and quit school. An education reporter for the Fort Collins *Coloradoan* called and asked what impact the new law had on Centennial's students. After the story was published in the local paper, *USA Today* picked up the information and included it in its "News from Every State" section. Interviews with all the Denver television stations followed, and a representative from the *Montel Williams Show* called to ask if it could produce a show featuring the smoker dropouts.

The staff closed ranks and informed all concerned they were not interested in such publicity. Centennial was a school and not a television studio. The school learned a valuable lesson in public relations. The media thrives on negative stories, and once a piece of information is released, it becomes public domain, to be used in ways that meet their interests and not those of the school or its students.

Centennial's staff spent the remainder of the year recapturing most of its wayward students and educating them. Instructors relied on their positive relationship with students to effectively address this challenge. It was one thing to teach students a new set of interactive, communication behaviors but another to intervene in students' self-selected choices to use nicotine as a stress reducer and a perceived rite of passage into adulthood. The personal efforts of Centennial staff members brought all but three of these students back into school before the end of the year. Of course, this information was never published or noted by the media.

As the staff developed a more sophisticated approach to the smoking issue, Centennial's health instructor volunteered to teach a smoking-cessation program. She received a grant from the Colorado Smoking Cessation Council and added a stop-smoking class to the curriculum. She helped students track their cigarette use and assisted them in a variety of ways to either stop smoking or to reduce their habit. She introduced various relaxation techniques, worked with the nurse practitioner to secure the patch and nicotine gum, and collaborated with counselors to provide students with chewing gum, candy, and personal support. If a student stopped smoking for a six-week period, Centennial presented the student with a $50 check in an all-school assembly. The smoking-cessation class was inviting and optional for students who wanted to look at the issue of smoking.

The school administrator was empowered by the city police to cite students who were smoking on campus and to have the school resource officer issue smoking tickets. Each violation cost the student $100. After issuing these citations, each student was approached and offered an opportunity to reduce the amount of the ticket. If the student agreed to enroll in the smoking-cessation class, a Centennial staff member volunteered to write a letter to the judge asking for a reduction in the fine from $100 to $50. If the student agreed to stop smoking for six weeks, the health teacher paid students the additional $50 from the smoking-cessation fund. This negotiation worked, and more and more students enrolled in the smoking-cessation classes.

A group of students who trusted the school's staff initiated a proposal that demonstrated their commitment to enhancing the learning culture. Speaking for a majority of smokers, these students presented a proposal for a new daily schedule at one of the weekly staff meetings. They claimed that the closure of the smoking area gave students too much time between classes to "think about" smoking. Therefore, they proposed the school cut the passing time between classes from ten to five minutes and reduce the lunch period from forty-five to thirty minutes. This proposal shortened the school day by forty-five minutes. Students believed they could delay their nicotine gratification if they kept busy and got out of school earlier. The staff endorsed the idea, and the students felt they had a voice in coping with the challenge of not smoking on campus.

The health teacher invited members of the Fort Collins community and student members from her smoking-cessation class to become part of a smoking advisory group for Centennial High School. The advisory group collaborated with the staff by finding additional grant money, instructional materials, and by volunteering to be guest speakers for the school. The teacher and the advisory group generated over $30,000 in smoking-cessation grant monies to implement new ideas and programs to help students quit smoking. Within the next four years, Centennial boasted a 13 percent smoking-cessation rate, compared to the national average of 5 percent. This success rate created a demand for Centennial staff members to speak at various state and national conferences. Centennial was also able to release the smoking-cessation instructor to model her program at a sister school within the school district for a six-week period so the program could spread to another campus.

This intervention strategy, based on fostering an effective relationship with students, not only proved to be a positive intervention strategy for Centennial students but established a collaborative rather than a punitive approach to dealing with tobacco use. Students appreciated school officials' showing a genuine concern for their health instead of trying to catch them breaking the law. Some students continued to smoke on campus and eventually got caught, but their attitude about accepting the consequences reflected an understanding of the staff's responsibilities under the law and school policy.

STRATEGY #8: PEACE IN THE VALLEY*

In 1992, Centennial experienced an ugly racial incident that led to several suspensions and two students' being dropped from the program. The student unrest that followed could have destroyed much of the cultural change being implemented in the program. As a result, a Centennial counselor proposed the creation of a peer mediation program and located student-training materials produced at the University of Illinois, Champaign-Urbana campus. The program, *Peer Mediation: Conflict Resolution in Schools* (Schrumpf, Crawford, and Bodine 1997), outlined ways for students to become trained mediators to help peers resolve conflicts before violence erupted. In time, another counselor created a quality-school mediation program that reinforced and expanded this initial concept. She helped students design and establish a peer mediation room, assisted the mediators in working through difficult mediations, used peers to train new groups of mediators, and acted as the staff liaison for the program.

All of the staff agreed to participate in the mediation process, an essential component to successfully incorporating the process into the school culture. Not only did students invite each other to settle disputes in mediation, but staff members and the principal also engaged in resolving conflicts through mediation. Even though confidentiality was the school norm, the word spread quickly when a student took the principal to the mediation table. The trained mediators were so proficient in applying their mediation skills that they were often viewed as unofficial assistant principals. The peer mediators conducted approximately forty mediations per year and kept the peace on campus.

Since the initial conflict-resolution skills were taught in the Discovery program, the student body knew peer mediation was a part of the Centennial culture. The process was confidential and was finalized by a written agreement of understanding between the two disputants. If a dispute occurred between two individuals, a form was available to request mediation. A trained mediator picked up the form placed in the mediation "staff mailbox," contacted each disputant, and arranged a time to meet in private. They followed a specific process throughout the mediation session, taking care to make sure each disputant listened to the concerns expressed.

Eventually, they reached an agreement that was signed and filed in the mediation room. If an agreement was broken, the disputants were required to return to the mediation table. If the agreement was violated a second time, the student who broke it was sent to the principal for a review of pledge card commitments. In over a decade, only four students were sent to the administrator for violating a mediation agreement or refusing to mediate. From 1992 until 2002, Centennial experienced only four acts of violence. Centennial established a reputation for being the safest school in the district. Following the violence at Columbine High School in Aurora, Colorado, many local parents actively requested admission for their children at Centennial.

Some of the young mediators were so skilled and effective, that they moved into mediation jobs after graduating from high school. They were also excellent trainers. In 1999, Centennial was invited to conduct a mediation workshop for faculty members from two different comprehensive schools. A Centennial counselor and two seventeen-year-old students arrived as the official trainers. Thirty adult, professional teachers expressed skepticism they could learn anything from high school students. In three days, their attitude completely changed. The young people demonstrated patience, insight, and integrity as they taught seasoned instructors how to implement a program that could change a school's culture. Participants left the workshop amazed at and pleased with the maturity and integrity displayed by these students.

Centennial's mediators not only knew they had an effective relationship with the administration and school faculty but felt a personal sense of satisfaction in realizing they could make a difference in the lives of their peers. They were empowered with the authority and skills to contribute to the program's culture. They proved to be the official peacekeepers in the valley. One Centennial mediator was nominated and selected as Colorado's Peer Mediator of the year for 1999 and maximized her skills as a mediator when she joined Serve America after graduation.

STRATEGY #9: DIVERSITY AS A CULTURAL NORM*

As Centennial's image changed in the community, students from various backgrounds began to seek admission to the school, because they felt the students and staff at Centennial had an accepting attitude. Centennial attracted students from the three comprehensive high schools in Fort Collins, neighboring cities and states, and from home and private school settings. Students who were loners, professed a different sexual orientation, had gang affiliations, wanted more individualized instruction, or wanted to be in a smaller, safer setting began to attend the school's orientations. This mix of such diverse needs could have created a social problem in the student culture. Such differences among students could have spawned social cliques and fomented tensions in a small setting, and overtaxed the skills of the peer mediators.

In response to this emerging mix of student needs, Centennial's counselors created an elective class that focused on diversity. The capstone experience of this class occurred when those enrolled chose to facilitate an all-school workshop on the most current diversity issues facing the school and the Fort Collins community. Diversity-class students created each workshop format, invited speakers and/or panel presenters, and organized the students into meaningful discussion groups. Various diversity workshops delved into issues surrounding racism, sexual orientation, gender differences, gang violence, and health topics. Students in the diversity class were trained in facilitation skills and handled every session in a professional manner. Centennial faculty members attended sessions, took attendance, and became participants in the workshops.

Every time a diversity workshop occurred, the student culture at Centennial improved. Students were more tolerant of individual and group differences. They expressed more courtesy to others and walked the halls with more pride. They felt honored to have time dedicated in a school setting to help them understand each other's differences. Such attention to current "hidden curriculum" agendas enhanced relationships and improved the student culture, which could now focus on learning rather than underlying social conflicts.

The counselors created such effective formats for student diversity workshops that they published their insights and success stories in an article, "A School Takes a Stand: Promotion of Sexual Orientation Workshops by Counselors," in the February 1998 issue of *Professional School Counseling* magazine. The article focused on ways to promote understanding and tolerance among students through empowerment and dialogue.

STRATEGY #10: SPANKY AND OUR GANG*

At one point in the mid-1990s, gang presence dominated Fort Collins and its many schools. The Centennial staff took time to meet with various gang members to discuss the meaning and purpose of Centennial High School. These students agreed Centennial High School was the only real second chance they had in the community. Subsequently, they agreed to make Centennial a neutral zone, where no intimidation or gang activity would occur. A group of students proposed a policy that required students to refrain from wearing gang colors, engaging in intimidating behavior, or flashing gang signs in classes. The policy was accepted by the staff and appreciated by the student body. Such an action demonstrated the continuous empowerment of students to impact the school culture and a growing sense of pride in their school.

The policy operated without incident for several months, until a group of students reported a problem during a lunch break. Five male Centennial students, all dressed in Chicago Bulls uniforms, had established a formidable presence on the school grounds. Other students complained that the group was intimidating since these colors belonged to a specific gang in the city.

All five Bulls boys were invited to the principal's office for a chat after lunch. The conversation began by asking, "What do five of us in this room have in common that the sixth person does not?" They looked at each other and smiled as one student said, "The way we're dressed?" This accurate observation prompted the administrator to suggest their choice of clothes had intimidated several students on campus. They protested, "We're just good Chicago Bulls fans!" The group was asked to name the starting five players on the team and promptly failed the test.

The administrator reviewed the student-initiated gang policy and presented them with several choices: 1) they could call each other to make sure they all didn't wear Bulls-imprinted clothes to school on the same day or, if they did, 2) the group could identify which ones wanted to model the new Centennial sweatshirts and hats for the day, or 3) if they didn't have enough money to purchase clothing other than red and black, a staff member would gladly take them shopping and purchase appropriate clothing from a special fund established by an interested citizen. Basically, the message asked the students to work inside of the culture. Centennial had a reputation as a safe school, and everyone deserved to feel safe, even members of gangs. They agreed, and the Chicago Bulls mascots disappeared from the campus.

During those years of social chaos in Fort Collins, Centennial High School experienced three incidents of tagging (spray-painted gang signs on the building), perpetrated by junior high school "wannabes" who had no knowledge of the school's culture. Gang members from throughout the city not only attended Centennial but also effectively worked together in classes to learn. For a few hours during each day, positive school relationships replaced social hostility.

STRATEGY #11: COURTING THE V.F.W.

Successfully implementing the new program required winning the trust and hearts of veteran students who had survived the old system and were now forced to change. The staff chose to implement the bulk of student culture changes over the course of the year and not require veteran students to attend the Discovery class. Therefore, the Discovery program was reserved for only newly enrolled students, who learned the new skills emerged from Discovery in groups of twenty-five. The logic was simple: the trained Discovery students would eventually outnumber the old-system veterans.

The staff implemented and enforced new behavioral expectations and policies without having a way to train the veteran students. Change was very difficult for these returning students, who had to live with a new system and resented the creation of the Discovery program. They felt anger toward those enrolled in Discovery and believed the staff was creating a privileged class by babying the new kids, who didn't have to learn the ropes the hard way like they had.

The administration and counselors frequently met with the veterans, explained the need for a change, and reminded them of their involvement and their approval of suggestions made throughout the previous year. These veterans mostly resented the closed-campus policy and often left campus at noon break to challenge the system. Discipline issues mostly emerged with veteran students who tested the new campus rules and behavioral expectations listed on the pledge card. Some students were suspended or given absences for walking off campus at noon, while others challenged the boundaries of policy enforcement that seemed contrary to a commitment to relationship rather than punishment. These violations were addressed with patience, consistency, and clarity as the culture of the school slowly changed.

By March 1992, veteran students were outnumbered by those trained in the Discovery program, and student behavior showed a remarkable positive change. By the following fall, only a handful of non–Discovery trained students remained. Graduation and attrition had changed the face of the school, and the new student culture was firmly entrenched.

A NEW CENTENNIAL CULTURE

By May 1992, three events demonstrated that students had not only embraced the new Centennial culture but also revealed a sense of pride and ownership in their school. First, a group of students who participated in the Principal's Advisory Board requested a meeting with the administration and counselors. They expressed the need to change Centennial's image with students who attended the comprehensive high schools in the city. They wanted to let others know Centennial was a good school that could meet the specific learning needs of certain types of students. They wanted to design and print for distribution a brochure that marketed the merits of the school.

Within a few days the students' work was complete. In a trifold brochure they had created a picture of Centennial; its mission and vision statements; a short history of the school's purpose; and a few paragraphs about the Discovery program, conflict mediation, and the pledge-card expectations. Student testimonials filled the back page. Brandy, one of the students who were quoted, wrote, "The theme of Centennial High School, Catch the Vision, has taught me to catch my dreams . . . to catch life and get motivated again. This statement has taught me to love learning again. It has brought me to a point where I am a successful student who can count on a diploma and a future."

The front cover captured the reader's attention. In bold letters underneath Centennial High School was the phrase "Catch the Vision," followed by an unattributed quote: "A vision without a task is but a dream. A task without a vision is drudgery. But a vision and a task together are the hope of the world." The students understood the new vision's concept and wanted to teach it to others. They saw Centennial as a safe haven and a place to turn lives around. They were ready to spread the word to their peers.

The second event literally offered a more dramatic presentation of the students' commitment. In late April, the school board scheduled a series of hearings to determine what programs needed to be cut in order to balance the district budget. Immediately, students, staff, and some parents formed the "Save Centennial High School" committee and created a fact sheet outlining the need to maintain the program and the benefits derived from the restructuring process.

More than one hundred Centennial students, staff, parents, and community members testified at meetings scheduled on May 1, 4, and 6, 1992. When the meetings ended, one school board member exclaimed how impressed he was with Centennial students and their passion for the school. He confessed he still didn't know what to cut but, based on the testimonies he heard, he was clearly convinced what he would *not* recommend to be cut.

XOX XOX XOX XOX XOX XOX XOX XOX XOX XOX XOX XOX

Don't Close Centennial

I do not officially speak for the Golden K [Kiwanis Club], but I know I reflect the sentiment of the majority of our members when I say we would deplore the closing of Centennial. It would be a great shame to deprive kids of a chance to succeed despite having made a mistake, to succeed despite having fallen upon dire circumstances not of their own making. We greatly approve of this unique effort to give direct, immediate and important support to where it is needed.

—Excerpt from letter to superintendent
Dr. Davis Hendrix from Don Wilkerson, May 7, 1992

XOX XOX XOX XOX XOX XOX XOX XOX XOX XOX XOX XOX

The program's districtwide supervisor, charged with the responsibility of creating the official "cut list," expressed the belief that Centennial's restructuring effort added value to the school system and successfully addressed the needs of high-risk youth in the community. Therefore, he continually placed Centennial lower and lower on the priority list every time the school board asked for current recommended program cuts. Centennial had survived another budget crunch and would never appear on any cut list again.

The final event that solidified student pride in the school was the addition of outstanding student achievement awards, worn with great pride at the graduation ceremony. The student culture had changed from a place to "hang out" to a place where one could take pride in demonstrating skills and abilities. Each staff member selected an outstanding graduating senior in a specific content area, and the entire school selected the male and female winners of the Catch the Vision Leadership Award.

Winners' names were engraved on metal disks, which hung from black and gold ribbons around students' necks as they marched across the stage to receive their diplomas. Twenty graduating seniors were honored in this way, and all wore their medals with pride. This format set a precedent for honoring students for the next decade. No longer was Centennial a school for losers. Centennial had established itself as a school where students earned a second chance, enjoyed a valued relationship with adults, and had clear guidelines and expectations to guide their progress.

5

HAND-CRAFTED

Results of the CBAM survey showed that staff supported the new program, but experience provided a major lesson about change. People will sing the virtues of a new vision, but bumps in the road often turn into potholes of resistance. The challenge facing the Centennial staff was to help its dedicated professionals move through the implementation phase, smooth out bumps as they appeared, fill in the potholes, and guide program modifications. This process would allow staff to celebrate successes at the end of each school year and reach the goals established for the five-year vision.

The strategies listed below were followed over a five-year period, from 1991 to 1995. Given what the staff knew about its students, their learning preferences, and personal and emotional needs, they acknowledged that changes and modifications would take time to fully implement. It was also acknowledged that veteran staff members required time, training, and patience to accept the logic and value of changing their content and instructional styles in order to meet the specific needs of the new program. For the most part, the Centennial staff followed the goals outlined in its five-year plan. In some cases, however, serendipity and/or unexpected opportunities allowed the school to move faster than expected. Dates accompanying the implementation of each strategy will assist readers to follow the changes as they occurred.

STRATEGY #1: BRICKS AND MORTAR

An effective leader often resembles a mason constructing a house. Starting with a strong foundation, the leader must work with well-blended mortar to set the bricks in place. As the mason prepares to lay the first row of bricks, he places a generous amount of mortar on the foundation to provide a substantial base for each brick and uses the handle of the trowel to gently tap each brick into place. The professional bricklayer knows how much mortar to use and how much pressure to exert on each brick. The remarkable thing about this work is that a row of bricks does not resemble the finished house by itself. However, the bricklayer sees the big picture and visualizes the beauty of the final product. Laying each brick requires skill and patience, and is often repetitive and tedious work. Every brick in the Centennial wall required each staff member to believe in his or her personal importance and contribution to the task that stretched ahead.

Program Implementation Dip

One of the most consistent findings and understandings about the change process is that all successful schools experience "implementation dips" as they move forward. The implementation dip is literally a dip in performance and confidence as one encounters an innovation that requires new skills and new understandings. All innovations worth their salt call upon people to question and in some respects change their behaviors and beliefs—even in cases where innovations are pursued voluntarily.

—Michael Fullan, *Leading in a Culture of Change* (2001), 40

In such a situation, the responsibility of the principal is to become the guardian and keeper of the school's long-range vision, share it with others, and begin the process of constructing a new future. The Centennial staff had established a strong foundation upon which to build. The communication process and consensus decision-making model empowered the staff and provided opportunities to have all voices heard. Surveys, data, and research provided the mortar to keep the plan in place. Finally, the principal, as the school's curriculum and instructional leader, used his authority to "gently tap" and help set each teacher (brick) in an appropriate place in the wall and to help each understand his or her importance in constructing the entire plan.

Pouring Mortar and Placing Bricks

The longer, seventy-minute blocks of class time called for staff development workshops to assist individuals in adjusting lesson plans to complement the new schedule. As each teacher wrestled with student issues that arose from structure and policy changes, leadership and collaborative intervention was required to coach teachers in developing appropriate instructional strategies to meet changing needs.

The task was simplified because one-third of the instructors were participating in the required three-year evaluation cycle, and the presence of an administrator in their classrooms was anticipated and often welcomed. These staff members were asked to gather data and explain the goals and objectives of curriculum choices and instructional strategies used in their classes and to report significant findings or challenges facing them. For the other two-thirds of the staff, not on an evaluation cycle, the principal announced his intentions to "wander around," observe learners at work, and gather data to monitor the impact of the program changes on the building culture and student performance.

Since the Discovery program was such an essential component of the new vision, the principal chose to spend a great deal of time with the Discovery teacher as he initiated the new social skills curriculum. The principal participated in the quality circle discussions and various lessons for almost twelve weeks, until he had a firm grasp on what was being taught and what student expectations were required. This knowledge helped the administrator work with other staff members to shape student behavior policies and suggest classroom procedures and protocols that were applicable throughout the school.

During this process, the principal continuously asked the instructional staff such questions as, "How does this content/skill support the new vision?" "Is there a way the staff can do this better?" "What should a senior at an alternative school know and be able to do after graduation?" In this way, emphasis was placed on fostering a continuous dialogue about the school, the progress being made, and specific benchmarks related to achieving the vision.

Inspection of the weekly purple feedback sheets provided signs of any emerging frustration or concern as the new program was being implemented. As soon as a problem emerged, an appointment with the concerned staff member was scheduled, a classroom visitation occurred, or the principal simply listened to the instructor vent. Genuine attempts were made to gently assist instructors become more comfortable with the place they fit in the Centennial wall, by "shaping the mortar" around them. This was accomplished by either providing data responding to their perceptions or with encouraging words to lift their sagging spirits. Continuous efforts were made to reduce stress levels caused by change so that "each brick" in the wall felt encouragement and hope in constructing the new program future.

First-Quarter Assessment

With the exception of some problems with veteran students, September and October 1991 ran smoothly. The Discovery program graduated its first twenty-five students, and a huge "trowel" of research data was added to the wall by examining student performance areas from the first two months of school. Statistics from the first two months of the 1990–1991 school year were compared with the first two months of the new program implementation year. The results bolstered staff confidence and supported a realistic belief that they were moving in the right direction. See table 5.1 for the results.

In a questionnaire completed by students, 92 percent endorsed the new six-week program over the quarter-length academic term. The reasons given included better grades, more time in seventy-minute classes to complete projects, and the ability to use the Friday zero period to make up work. In a similar survey, staff members indicated that 65 percent of their students had a better attitude about learning in the new structure, while 75 percent said students performed better in seventy-minute classes.

Table 5.1. First-Year Comparison

Data Item	1990–1991 (Sept.–Oct.)	1991–1992 (Sept.–Oct.)
Daily attendance	93.0%	95.5%
Dropout rate	40.0%	20.0%
Failing grades	70.0%	30.0%
"A" grades	5.0%	50.0%

Supporting these student beliefs, 71 percent of the staff felt the Friday zero periods provided an excellent way for students to stay on task, improve grades, and enhance their performance. In addition, the staff survey showed 88 percent were satisfied with student performance since restructuring. Not a single staff member suggested that student attitude was worse than the previous year. Given this show of approval, the staff continued with its implementation plans. The frequent assessment of the pace and success of the change provided staff with updates that used survey results or other hard data to guide midcourse adjustments.

Staff perceptions of their level of stress as of November 1991 proved to be another factor that encouraged continuous change. Six percent said they were "cool as a cucumber," while on the other extreme, another 6 percent complained they were "overwhelmed" or "out of control." However, a vast 88 percent indicated their stress level was about what they had expected it to be as they implemented the new program. The staff development committee devised additional strategies to reduce stress created by change as the wall of the new program continued to take shape.

The agendas at business staff meetings focused on developing or clarifying school policies to correlate all the program changes. None of these meetings resembled a gripe session, in which staff members publicly complained about the school's new vision, program changes, or their inability to adjust to the new order of business. As professionals, they handled one item at a time and moved ahead with implementation plans. For example, they discussed a depth of philosophical questions about the nature of the program. What is the purpose of an alternative school? What is the definition of alternative education? Was Centennial a transition school or a school of choice?

The staff also handled issues related to such mundane, but absolutely essential, topics as redefining the school's attendance and tardiness policies, which were changed frequently until a successful system was implemented. One of the Centennial staff, the philosophically conservative math teacher, said it best for all: "When it comes to policy change, I can live with anything for six weeks. If it doesn't work, we'll change it." This pervasive attitude of flexibility became the hallmark of staff cooperation as one program change after another was introduced throughout the year.

Midyear Evaluation

In trying to keep abreast of program changes, staff members completed a survey that assessed their perceptions of the new program after the first semester. In January 1992, three classes of Discovery students were now functioning in the school, and veteran students were feeling the pressure from new peers who seemed more mature and capable of handling the stresses of school life. The staff examined the performance and behavior of former Discovery students to see if this new program structure had made a difference in student achievement and attitude. The Centennial staff complimented Discovery graduates for using effective participation skills, leadership, and communication techniques. The Discovery program had had a major impact on the student culture.

The staff survey also revealed that 72 percent of the teachers endorsed the six-week, hexter schedule, while 20 percent of the staff preferred to return to the quarter system. Eighty-nine percent of staff members endorsed the seventy-minute class period but strongly requested help in developing more effective instructional strategies for that length of time. The counselors expressed concern over increased paperwork, and a few others were impatient with policy implementation or procedural logistics. These items would be addressed throughout the remainder of the year.

Tinkering with Instruction

The midyear program evaluation encouraged the principal to use his trowel in assisting "individual bricks" to settle into the new system. In many cases, the instructional leader took a more assertive role as the school's instructional leader and worked with individuals to suggest changes in the way they prepared and delivered lessons. The story of one particular staff member demonstrates his dramatic shift in thinking and performance as a teacher and speaks volumes about his commitment to Centennial, the vision, and the students.

One of Centennial's social studies teachers taught geography, U.S. history, and psychology. Originally trained in other subject areas, he had moved into the social studies position by necessity. For years, the teacher took comfort in lecturing students from a podium four days a week and on Fridays required responses to essay questions using a university-type blue book. Students accumulated a great deal of information through listening and note taking but were rarely actively engaged as learners in the classroom.

As information related to the learning styles of students enrolled at Centennial began to accumulate, it was discovered that 90 percent of Centennial students were abstract-random/concrete-random learners. In layman's terms, such learning preferences suggest these students require more group work and the need to develop a high relationship with their peers, teachers, and the content being studied. In addition, they performed best through hands-on tasks, thus tapping into their creativity in order to most effectively demonstrate what they learned.

Thinking Styles Lead to Achievement

Both students and teachers tend to exploit their preferred styles, which may or may not match. It is natural for people to seek activities that match their preferred thinking styles. People will be more motivated to perform such activities and often will be better at them. Therefore, it is important for teachers to be aware of their students' preferred styles so that they can capitalize on opportunities for student learning. The same activity that engages one student may bore another—not necessarily because the latter student is uninterested in the content, but because the style of the activity does not match the student's preference.

—Robert Sternberg, "Thinking Styles:
Keys to Understanding Student Performance," *Phi Delta Kappan*, 368

This huge "glob of research mortar" concerned the social studies teacher, who wanted to do the best job possible in the classroom and realized he was working harder than his students in the teaching-learning process. Through collaborated effort, the principal and teacher explored different instructional strategies and models that actively engaged students in the learning process. The teacher experimented with cooperative learning groups, then inquiry strategies, and finally simulation games.

After exploring the Australian concept of "walkabout learning," the instructor discovered the constructivist instructional model. Simply put, constructivism begins with a question or a concept. The teacher assists students to postulate a problem for investigation and then encourages them to explore a variety of intellectual avenues and resources to seek answers. Information is shared in class through frequent discussions, so a composite picture of the concepts or questions being investigated is enhanced by the collective work shared by individual student scholars.

The instructor embraced this approach with enthusiasm. He established protocols for students to plan individualized study formats, create final projects or products, and design formal class presentations. This approach permitted the teacher to restructure his instructional approach so he no longer played the "sage on the stage" but became an effective "guide on the side."

If you walked into his classroom today, you would witness students engaged in a beehive of individual activities, some watching a film, a few writing or consulting reference books, and others surfing the Internet for information. In a corner, huddled close together, you'll find the instructor and a student reviewing a paragraph or joking about some unrelated topic. There is a hum of focused, active work as students go about the task of constructing individualized understanding of the concepts under investigation.

The teacher's transition to a constructivist instructor was a remarkable celebration, because he explored a variety of instructional options until he found the right match for his teaching style. This exploration evolved as a shared journey between principal and teacher in a spirit of collaboration. It was a transition by choice rather than coercion by power. This staff member wanted to be a solid instructor; he was committed to addressing his students' learning needs. In his exploration to find an instructional style to match his comfort level and the needs of his students, the teacher relied on data and current research. Today, this instructor is one of the most effective constructivist teachers in the district.

Final Atonement

In preparation for the second year of program development and implementation, the staff met in late April 1992 for a program evaluation. For many reasons, April is a terrible time of year to meet and talk about the success of program implementation. First, it is spring, and adolescent hormones are running wild, adding stress to teachers, who must deal with human nature. Second, educators, like students, are tired and looking forward to the summer break. Third, frustrations and stresses, handled for months, often reach the breaking point as the school year comes to a close. Finally, even after all of its hard work, the Centennial staff realized the school was still on the school board's agenda as a program that could be cut. Worried about their individual and collective futures, they were not in the best place to examine the year with emotional neutrality.

However, there comes a time when the mason must put down his trowel, step back, look at his work, and accept criticism of the completed project. For eight months, the implementation process had unfolded and multiple interventions employed to reduce stress as change occurred. Collected data had supported the plan, giving the mortar a thick consistency and adding to an already solid foundation. The results of attitude surveys, administered and tabulated throughout the year, encouraged the staff to continue its work. Now it was time to invite the critics to speak up and take another step closer toward the center of the program's circle. This April meeting became the "watershed workshop of the year." The staff would either move forward as a team or move backward and let others control their destiny.

Most of the complaints that came from various sources had been anticipated. Concerns focused on the lack of student academic performance, territoriality and positioning among colleagues for power and influence, communication issues, and policy implementation. When all the venting had been heard, the staff gave a collective sigh and waited for the next step, which was easy to make.

The staff realized, with the implementation of a radical shift in program structure, that they had been through the toughest time and survived together. Data analysis indicated that the restructured program was working and making a significant difference for students. Centennial had become a better educational program than it had been the previous year. The staff development committee promised to examine and improve policies and procedures over the summer months, and return to school in the fall ready to suggest improvements and propose the next set of goals in Centennial's five-year vision.

The final meeting was a calculated risk, because people had to have an opportunity to vent feelings of frustrations about the change process. However, data-driven program analysis and continuous collaboration with instructional staff, students, and parents provided the school with the confidence and an intuitive sense that Centennial had turned the corner and was going to survive.

The house was going to be built with strong bricks, held together with solid mortar. With the school board's decision not to cut the program, the staff celebrated its success and launched into the 1992–1993 school year with a renewed sense of energy and commitment. The school board had removed Centennial from the cut list because the passion and community support for the program made it politically challenging to close the school.

STRATEGY #2: LEARNING BY DOING

Information about the learning styles of Centennial students made a significant difference to the instructional staff's approach to teaching. The knowledge that 90 percent of its students preferred hands-on learning reinforced the innovative methods used by many of the instructors to engage alternative learners. Actively engaging students in the learning process through hands-on projects, peer teaching, and experiential approaches kept students involved and motivated.

As staff members pondered the implications of their student's preferred learning styles, many began to expand learning into community settings. For example, Centennial's humanities teacher was awarded a grant to engage students in the production of a poetry program for a lo-

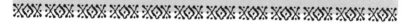

Authentic Student Achievement

The idea of authentic achievement requires students to engage in disciplined inquiry to produce knowledge that has value in their lives beyond simply providing their competence in school. Mastery of this sort is unlikely to be demonstrated in familiar testing and grading exercises. Instead, such mastery is more often expressed in the completion of long-term projects that result in the creation of discourse, things, and performances of interest to students, their peers and the public at large.

—Fred Newmann, "Linking Restructuring to Authentic Student Achievement," *Phi Delta Kappan*, 460

cal television station. As the poetry unit was taught in class, her students were required to write and refine their poems and essays, which they gladly did, in order to make them presentable for the television program. She collaborated with the owner of a local restaurant and videotaped her shows there to create a realistic "coffeehouse" setting.

Soon, these students were inviting peers from comprehensive high schools to join this class activity, and the televised poetry program became a community event for many district high school students. Through a similar grant, the teacher worked with another colleague to bring a poetry and reading program to sixth graders at a nearby elementary school. The elementary students appreciated their older mentors, thus creating feelings of pride and satisfaction for Centennial's students.

During the next few years, as new teachers were hired, members of Centennial's hiring committees specifically looked for instructors whose philosophy engaged students in active learning. A good example was the selection of an experienced junior high science teacher who joined the staff in 1995. He restructured the science curriculum to reflect hands-on, application learning. In both his physical and biological science classes, the instructor incorporated daily hands-on lab activities. Students learned science concepts in a variety of ways and then immediately applied what they had discovered to numerous experiments designed to reinforce learning.

In another case, a former junior high school English teacher taught students how to write with depth and passion. She connected hands-on learning to writing by having students artistically illustrate their written ideas. She eventually composed a writing manual for Centennial High School that established a standard format for staff members to use as they incorporated more written requirements into their programs. She also collaborated with the school's technology guru and taught students how to use computers to create a formal school newspaper. The creation of another hands-on learning product was filled with student articles and features, which were read by appreciative peers and the larger community.

An English teacher brought his passion for reading to Centennial students and invited them to explore the fascinating realm of the printed word. His reading workshops captured the interest of former nonreaders and engaged them in dialogues about books that matched their life experiences and interests. This instructor had a gentle touch with students. Even the most reluctant readers made every attempt to connect with his classes so they could read "neat stuff and talk about it with him," as one such student put it.

This instructor's passion to engage all students in hands-on learning impacted the curriculum. He engaged a shy, self-doubting student by tapping into her growing interest in philosophy. Using this insight as a way to make reading become more relevant for the student, the teacher requested financial support to purchase a set of introductory philosophy texts. He proposed that he and his student teach a philosophy class together. The PITS committee approved the request, and the teacher and his student co-facilitated the course. As the student-led discussions about meaningful life issues unfolded, the young lady's self-confidence soared. Her connection with the instructor kept her enrolled in school and helped her explore her passion and aptitude for philosophy, initiated by this reading seminar.

Such hands-on approaches to teaching promoted a myriad of curriculum ideas and ways to package learning. Centennial's social studies teacher, business teacher, and humanities teacher created an integrated curriculum that permitted students to complete required course work in an integrated time block. The three instructors each agreed to teach a specific content theme during each six-week academic term. Students could complete a part of required course work in humanities, geography, and American economic history by enrolling in classes taught by the three teachers for a six-week period.

For example, in this curriculum strand, the social studies teacher taught all of the geography standards related to Asia in his first-period class. Students who enrolled in this class could also participate in the business instructor's second-period international business class and master the content standards related to U.S. business and economic connections with Asian nations. The same students could move to humanities during their third-period class to study the art, music, history, and culture of Asian peoples. A different topic unified the program every six-week term. This kind of integrated approach not only assisted students in earning required credits but encouraged them to discover connections between the content areas being taught.

As years passed, Centennial changed its academic courses to correlate with district requirements and thus improved academic expectations to meet required content standards. The course titles and content resembled those being taught in other schools, but the delivery system remained unique and always focused on the students as active learners. Centennial staff continually employed instructional strategies that engaged student's heads, hearts, and bodies in the teaching/learning process. The main difference between the alternative school's approach to teaching and the comprehensive approach was to focus more on student involvement, inquiry, and discovery, and less on direct instruction by teachers.

STRATEGY #3: MOVIN' AND GROOVIN'

When the math teacher presented the staff with his proposal for six-week academic terms, the plan changed the traditional elective-week program from five days to three days per hexter. In the previous system, all elective courses were taught in the ninth week of the quarter's academic terms. Under the new plan, elective credits were earned in the last three days of each hexter. This shift required staff members to alter the ways they delivered elective credits.

At the end of each academic term, staff members created high-interest elective courses and marketed their offerings to students in an all-school assembly. Students enrolled in the courses of their choice, met with the instructors for specific instructions, and reported to the teachers at the beginning of the elective week (Wednesday). The purpose of the elective week concept was twofold. First, it provided students who worked hard throughout the academic term a special reward at the end of the term for continuous attendance and personal effort. The elective-week classes involved students in hands-on activities and provided an opportunity to explore interests and talents not included in most academic offerings.

Second, students and teachers had an opportunity to nurture their personal relationships. Elective classes were less structured, more casual, and quite often the teacher was a learner along with the students. In such informal settings, students gained insights into the talents, interests, and personalities of the adults who taught them structured content throughout the academic term. Adults learned more about students and engaged in a mini-form of advisory program as they pursued each elective topic.

The schedule called for elective week classes to run from 8 A.M. until noon, Wednesday through Friday, of the sixth week of each hexter. This schedule permitted staff to have time each afternoon to complete grades reports, plan lessons for forthcoming academic classes, collaborate with colleagues, or engage in staff development activities. This format provided staff members a precious commodity—time. They had scheduled time to be reflective about their instruction and the students they served, while the elective week awarded students variable elective credit commensurate with the number of contact hours each elective class met. The elective week granted the instructional staff time to be reflective about their teaching and to review and prepare for the next academic term.

In the first year of the new elective week format, staff members offered mostly academic classes, like "Colorado History," "Fort Collins History," and "Physical Education through Bike Riding and Hiking." However, the creativity and imagination of staff members quickly changed the format. A social studies teacher introduced the concept of "out-of-town overnight" elective-week trips. He owned an RV that accommodated twelve students. He offered long-distance trips that began on Wednesday morning of elective week and returned either Thursday night or Friday morning. These out-of-town adventures ranged from fishing and hiking trips in Colorado to long-distance trips to the Black Hills and Badlands of South Dakota or ski trips to Colorado/Wyoming slopes.

Beyond the Building's Walls

Recommendation: "The academic program will extend beyond the high school campus to take advantage of learning opportunities outside the four walls of the building."

—*Breaking Ranks* (1996), 45

Once this teacher opened the possibility of configuring instructional time in a different way, the "what if" thinking of staff members ran wild. Although some classes—"A Comedy Film Festival," "Strategy Games," "Ethnic Cooking," and "Planting Flowers for the Centennial Beautification Project"—kept students on campus, other far-reaching adventures emerged for students. A special education teacher invited students to participate in snow-cave camping and hiking trips to the top of St. Mary's Glacier in Rocky Mountain National Park. This became an annual winter trek, and each year students placed a Centennial flag on the glacier for the next group to reach during another challenging hike to that area. Students also spent time in the national park watching elk and listening to them bugle during the rutting season, and traveled to Denver or throughout the state to experience other learning activities.

Centennial's English teachers took students to plays and art exhibits in Denver and explored other cultures and lifestyles. The humanities teacher sponsored all-women campouts and instructed young women in mountain survival skills by showing them how to live off the land for two days. Counselors engaged students in self-discovery classes, trained peer mediators, or teamed with vocational instructors to explore small colleges, job sites, or training schools throughout Colorado.

The elective-week program provided an excellent interlude between academic terms, expanded the boundaries of instruction, and motivated students to remain enrolled in the program. The week was anticipated and relished by both staff and students, and it enhanced individual relationships between peers and adults. The elective-week format also set the precedent for a future "Roads Scholar" Program that emerged a few years later. (See strategy #8.)

STRATEGY #4: BEAM ME UP, SCOTTY

In 1992, Centennial hired a technology specialist who outlined a vision of excellence for the school that captured the hiring committee's attention and became a reality by the end of the decade. When the specialist joined the staff, Centennial owned five floppy-disc Mac computers for student use, two computers specifically designated for vocational use, and an outdated set of computers in a basement classroom designed to permit students to learn concepts in a rote-memory format.

The technology specialist's plan dramatically altered that reality. For more than a decade she demonstrated a phenomenal ability to work with staff members, some of whom did not consider themselves computer-literate souls. She had the uncanny ability to listen to and sense the needs of staff and students as they worked with confusing concepts of computer hardware and software programs. Through patience and persistence, she dragged the staff into the twenty-first century and changed the face of instructional strategies in the building.

Centennial's technology plan was simple and direct. Since the school did not have a library facility on site, instructional staff marched students six blocks to the public library or four blocks to the main library at Colorado State University to access resources, mass media, and print materials. Without the burden of allocating funds to build and maintain a library collection, the technology specialist proposed creating two to three computer labs in the building where students could access information online, use computers for word processing, learn computer technology in a structured class, and use various aspects of hardware technology in class or during their free time.

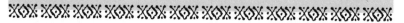

Technology as Learning Tool

Technology, in effect, extends the curriculum, enabling students to pursue in-depth study more readily and giving them access to information that they could formerly obtain only with an expenditure of considerable time and effort.

—Breaking Ranks (1996), 39

In the first five-year technology plan, all staff members were trained in effective computer use in the classroom. To accomplish this goal, money was allocated to staff through grants, building funds, and from district budget sources to provide a computer for every staff member. Meanwhile, each of the computer labs embedded as a core of the technology plan began to take shape. Centennial sold all of its electric typewriters and modified a vocational classroom to create two computer lab areas.

The first area was designated a computer-training lab, where all students had to demonstrate mastery of both keyboard skills and knowledge of software programs available in the building. Students who graduated from Discovery were assigned to this program as one of their first academic classes. Teaching students to be computer literate permitted them to use computers to access information and produce hard copies of assignments instead of handwritten work.

The second computer lab consisted of thirty computers connected to the Internet and school file server, supported by additional software programs that permitted students to conduct individual searches for information and resources. This room was an "open lab" for individual and classroom use. Every student had a personalized disc, kept in the lab storage files, that stored all his or her printed work and projects created for instructors. Several software programs were purchased to assist numerous instructors in implementing classroom projects, including formatting the school newspaper, yearbook, and literary magazines.

Eventually, the staff's effort earned Centennial a complete computer network system that connected all the buildings on campus and permitted every staff member to access district programs and the Internet from every room on campus. The technology specialist's passion moved district officials to provide top-notch computer equipment and software to learners who were often considered "throwaway" students by adults in other settings. Within a three-year period, the school moved from a paper-and-pencil culture into the technology age in a way that rivaled other district schools in its ability to use technology as an authentic learning tool.

One of the finest contributions to the program was the specialist's work with the computer learning lab in Centennial's basement. She immediately focused her attention on replacing all of the outdated computers and software programs. A skilled grant writer, she completed grant applications that produced more than $50,000 in technology funding over the decade, purchased computers out of newspaper want ads, and asked the community for donations of old computers.

As the face of technology education at Centennial changed, the computer specialist's rapport with the program's unique students emerged as another one of her assets. Even through she was not a certified instructor, the technology specialist effectively assisted students in earning credits as they worked through prescribed computerized curriculum packets that correlated with district course objectives. However, she quickly realized that computer programs could not maintain consistent student attention and often didn't match their reading skills or interests.

Consequently, she collaborated with the principal, a former curriculum specialist, to create over fifty individualized, self-paced learning packets that addressed academic standards and required skill acquisition. She turned the basement computer lab into a learning center for students who wanted the freedom to move through the learning packets at their own pace and to achieve success by completing interesting, and often bizarre, assignments created specifically for their unique learning styles. This approach worked effectively for many students in the program.

Rachel is probably the best example of a student who used this hands-on approach and moved through curriculum requirements at her own accelerated pace. Rachel came to Centennial in her sophomore year. As a comprehensive high school student, she had mixed with the wrong crowd, got into trouble, and lost interest in school. Her mother, a Centennial staff member, invited her to attend the alternative school. After graduating from the Discovery program, Rachel finally caught the vision of her success. In a career development class, a speaker from Front Range Community College motivated her to become a dental hygienist. Filled with a passion and a sense of urgency, Rachel admitted she had "screwed up" and wanted to know how she could reverse directions, get back on track, and graduate. She knew what she wanted to be and now had the motivation to realize her dream.

The counselor reviewed her graduation requirements and suggested she begin working on individualized learning packets by enrolling in the computer lab to work at her own pace throughout the remainder of the year. Working with the technology specialist and other staff, Rachel voraciously attacked assignments. She appeared in the office every day, turning in work and asking for more learning packets. She forfeited social life and sleep to complete assignments. Frequently, she came to school at 6:30 A.M. to turn in work or to complete another learning packet.

During one six-week academic term, Rachel earned credits in the five classes in her daily schedule and also completed enough credits through individualized learning packets to equal a semester's work at any comprehensive high school. By year's end, she had condensed two years of work into one year and graduated early. She completed the required course work at Front Range Community College and earned an associate degree as a dental hygienist. Once she was motivated to succeed, Rachel took full advantage of Centennial's effort to create a hands-on curriculum that permitted her to move ahead at her own pace.

Over the years, several noncertified staff members functioned as learning coaches in the basement computer lab, and each brought unique qualities to that position. But it was Centennial's technology specialist's inspiration and commitment to students that established the precedent of the computer learning lab concept. Each hexter, she worked with approximately sixty students who enrolled in the lab for individualized help. In addition, she handled the influx of students who had attendance problems and needed to be with a learning coach instead of dropping out of the program.

For these students, Centennial created an AP program that had nothing to do with advanced-placement course work. The AP program simply stood for "afternoon program." Students "dropped in" school from noon until 3:45 P.M. in order to receive tutorial help. The technology guru and another staff member, a remarkable writing coach, worked with these students to help them earn credit, recapture their vision of attending school, and prepare for re-admission to Centennial at the beginning of the next academic term. These two staff members worked effectively with students who often expressed the desire to stay in the AP program in order to work at their own pace instead of returning to the daily schedule of the academic term.

From the beginning of her tenure at Centennial, the computer specialist embraced a vision of technological excellence and used her authority, skills, and marvelous personality to produce a quality program for the entire building. Within a decade, the face of technology at Centennial had changed and the program boasted a 1:7 ratio of computers to students, one of the best in the school district. The new building plans, slated for completion in 2005, include another computer lab, a computerized resource lab, and a multimedia production lab.

In *Good to Great*, Jim Collins asserts that technology does not define the organization's vision. Technology is a vision accelerator. Technology provides the tools to accelerate the momentum of an organization on its way to achieve its goals.

STRATEGY #5: THE WALLS COME TUMBLING DOWN

In the early 1990s, the concept of service learning was practically nonexistent. A Centennial employee, working closely with the vocational department, penned a grant proposal that brought service learning to Centennial High School. As an unexpected bonus to the first year's restructuring effort, Action, the federal agency for student community service programs, informed Centennial it had been awarded a $20,000 grant to establish a service-learning program. A service-learning project coordinator accepted a partial position and became a passionate spokesperson for the service-learning concept, as well as an action-oriented, hands-on force within the staff.

The service-learning coordinator came to Centennial fresh from the private sector and demonstrated an assertive, businesslike approach to implementing the program. First, she proved to be an aggressive fund-raiser. Over the next five years, she turned her computer into a grant-writing machine. Using a database that accurately captured the learning needs and profile of high-risk students, the coordinator approached grant opportunities as if they were all earmarked for Centennial. She either wrote or coauthored applications that earned Centennial more than $50,000 in service-learning funds during the decade.

Centennial's service-learning program expanded to all aspects of the academic curriculum and moved education far beyond the school walls. The program created an extensive volunteer student network within the community, infiltrated the thinking of numerous academic teachers, promoted vocational placements, and enhanced the before/after-school programs. As a result, the community began seeing Centennial students in a multitude of settings. Students, in collaboration with the Colorado State University 4-H extension office, made several "Buckle Bear" presentations to preschool children, promoting seatbelt use. Other Centennial students planted a number of trees with elderly residents in the Red Feather Lakes mountain community to enhance a natural habitat for wild animals. Some students collaborated with other community agencies as they constructed a state-of-the-art playground at one of the elementary schools.

Using English and science class concepts, several of Centennial's students volunteered their services in Rocky Mountain National Park, under the direction of the Volunteers in the Park Program. As part of another English class project, students interviewed elderly persons in a number of nursing homes to gain insights about their life experiences. The students then constructed written and visual biographies of the residents.

Students who participated in these service-learning projects developed a renewed sense of self-esteem and connection with the adult world in the local community. At last, they felt a sense of respect for the well-being of others. The service-learning program at Centennial provided an effective vehicle to help students make the transition from childhood to adulthood. It provided students—even those with colored hair, numerous tattoos, and body piercing—a sense of personal empowerment. The students realized they could make a difference for

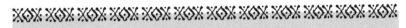

Risk Taking for Students

In summary, risk-taking opportunities for students should be:

- Plentiful
- Readily available
- Accompanied by explicit information
- Accompanied by immediate feedback that communicates competency and error information
- Associated with payoffs that vary with task difficulty
- Relatively free from externally imposed evaluation
- Presented in a relaxing and non-threatening environment.

—Margaret Clifford, "Students Need Challenge, Not Easy Success," *Educational Leadership*, 24

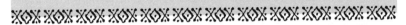

others and began to feel good about their ability to make such contributions.

STRATEGY #6: BEAUTIFUL DREAMING

The centerpiece of the service-learning program emerged in Centennial's own backyard. The school occupies a two-acre plot of land in an older residential neighborhood in Fort Collins. Constructed in 1906, the building originally served the community as a neighborhood elementary school, which many neighbors had attended. In the 1990s, four buildings occupied the grounds. The original building, located on the east side of campus, had ten classrooms to which a gym/cafeteria was added in the 1950s. A modular classroom, also situated on the east side of campus, was added in the 1990s to accommodate increased student enrollment. An annex on the far west side of campus that originally had housed the school's kindergarten program was shifted to a teen mothers' program in the 1980s and, in 1989, was replaced by the district's severe-needs special education program.

A large open space, which the neighbors called Centennial Park, occupied the area between the annex on the west side of the campus and the other structures. A high chain-link fence enclosed the entire area, presenting the neighborhood with a formidable obstacle to its use. It also created the illusion that Centennial was isolated and unwelcoming to its neighbors. The service-learning coordinator, collaborating with the school's science, math, vocational, and special education teachers, looked at the area and began to dream of possible ways to change Centennial's public image. Using the funds from the service-learning grants, they created the Campus Beautification Project, a vision that took five years to complete.

In 1992, a vocational teacher and self-admitted "green thumb," offered students an elective-week class to create an outdoor student garden, filled with flowers, benches, trees, and a flagstone walk. In three days, a dozen students created a beautiful area in the trees on the east edge of the park. Amazed at and pleased with their work, students wanted to do more.

A campus beautification team was formed, and a local landscape architect was hired to create a five-year project vision for the campus. The project became an all-school endeavor. The student body was divided into five work crews led by student crew leaders who were trained by the Fort Collins Nursery and guaranteed summer jobs as an outcome of the project. The science and math teachers incorporated the landscape project into their academic lesson plans. The science instructor taught lessons on Colorado flora, and the math teacher had students calculate problems like how much mulch would it take to cover a thirty-square-yard area to the depth of three inches. In the meantime, the special education instructor taught his students the merits of xeriscaping in Colorado's arid climate and designed a plan to change the appearance of the west side of the campus.

Students embraced the concept with delight, enjoyed being outdoors and engaged in hands-on learning, and viewed the landscape project as another opportunity to show the community they could make a difference. Students demolished the chain-link fence, built stone walkways that led into garden areas, and planted bushes and trees. The entire student body participated in the "planting" of huge moss rocks at the entrance to the school and placed "Centennial" roses and tulips around a split-rail fence. This added the final touches to an appealing, aesthetic invitation to the campus. The setting offered visitors a warm welcome, and the barrier between the neighborhood and the school vanished.

Every year thereafter, staff and students added more plants and flowers to enhance the beauty of the campus during elective-week classes or through projects embedded in course content. The campus beautification team continued to write requests for additional dollars, and organizations such as the Colorado Wildlife Agency endorsed and funded efforts to turn Centennial Park into an urban wildlife sanctuary.

The Campus Beautification Project was clearly noticed by neighbors. One resident of an apartment complex next to the school wrote, "What a beautiful job you've done landscaping your school ground. I have watched your progress with great admiration. It's like having a park right next door. Congratulations to you, the faculty and, most of all, the students."

Another neighbor composed the following letter:

> We appreciate the efforts of the staff and students of Centennial High School for the excellent job of landscaping the grounds surrounding the school. Removing the chain link fence, by itself, was a very positive gesture. Opening Centennial's land, constructing flowerbeds, adding benches, and cleaning up the recreational area created a new neighborhood park which is a definite plus for property values. Seeing the students outside physically doing all the work made us realize the valuable types of programs that are available through your school. Our neighborhood will soon be using the park for a neighborhood get-together. A place like this has not been available to us before the improvements were made. Living directly across the street from the school, we have observed a noticeable improvement in the esteem of the students and the school. The students and the school have become a real asset to the neighborhood as an educational and community resource. We would like to thank the staff and students for a job well done.

A leader of a public institution cannot purchase the kind of public relations Centennial's students and staff created. In two short years, Centennial had established itself as a positive presence in the neighborhood. More importantly, Centennial's neighbors saw its students as assets to the community, instead of the typical, negative image generally projected of adolescents.

In 1994, the city of Fort Collins honored the school by bestowing its annual City Environmental Award on Centennial for the Campus Beautification Project. The school's service-learning coordinator, nominated for the city's human relations award, was later selected as one of seventeen people to become a DeWitt Wallace Reader's Digest Fellow, reviewing service-learning proposals from schools throughout the nation. Eventually the Campus Beautification Project, evaluated by Brandies University, was listed in the National Directory of Student Community Service Learning Projects. The staff's passion for the service-learning concept motivated students and added another dimension to the school's hands-on-learning approach to education.

STRATEGY #7: A CHAMPION ON A WHITE HORSE

As the service-learning coordinator earned her teaching credentials and became more focused on vocational education and media production, the torch of service learning passed to another staff member. As a special education teacher, this instructor embraced service learning with an even greater passion. He taught students with special education needs in an adjacent program on the Centennial campus. This program was specifically designed to work with high school students who had severe emotional learning disabilities. This instructor recognized the power of hands-on learning as a vehicle to engage his students in activities that would help them acquire appropriate social skills, prepare them for future jobs, and help them develop strategies to compensate for their learning disabilities.

In addition to teaching all required courses in the special education program, he created a service-learning project called "the Centennial Eco-Warriors." The Eco-Warriors provided a recycling service for interested neighbors within a mile's radius of the school. He taught students how to write and distribute a neighborhood recycling newsletter, how to appropriately approach people in person or by telephone, and how to handle complaints with tact and patience. He organized students into recycling crews, collected waste products, and disposed of them at appropriate locations. Additionally, the teacher deftly integrated science, history, English, and economics into this project. Students organized a recycling business and paid student workers from the realized profits. These students created official Eco-Warrior T-shirts and wore them with pride.

Centennial's new service-learning coordinator believed this kind of hands-on application of learning would benefit students who had low self-esteem. He collaborated with officials at Colorado State University's Nature Center and engaged students in challenging work requiring intense physical labor. Students who lacked academic skills in the classroom achieved immense self-esteem and admiration from supervising adults and coworkers as they engaged in various physically challenging hands-on projects. They frequently exhibited a strong work ethic not noticed in their ordinary classroom work. The instructor used every opportunity to connect each hands-on project with lessons taught in the classroom. His service-learning reflection sessions, followed by individual writing assignments, evoked exceptional analysis and understanding from students who had often been academically discredited in the past.

In 1995, this instructor submitted a proposal that astounded the staff. His commitment to the service-learning instructional approach became so intense that he requested a radical change in assignment. He wanted to move from a full-time instructor to a half-time position for a one-year-only placement. He expressed the desire to model service learning for and with all of his colleagues, teaching them how to incorporate the concept into their content areas. He also proposed giving up half of his yearly salary so he could write grants and work with colleagues when appropriate.

The staff, amazed by his proposal, endorsed the plan, and hands-on learning became a permanent fixture in the school's culture. Throughout the next year, he team-taught with other staff members and incorporated service-learning concepts throughout the curriculum, organized all-school service-learning projects, and became Centennial's designated service-learning champion. Students flocked to his classes, due to his passion for social action and hands-on projects that took them into the community. His energy and commitment captured students' imagination and enthusiasm.

The capstone for this instructor's commitment to service learning occurred when he was invited to present the Centennial service-learning model, in partnership with Colorado State University, at the first international service-learning conference, held in London, England, in December 1997. Centennial sent the teacher and two students involved in the program to present at the conference. The director of England's Lighthouse Schools attended Centennial's presentation at the conference and listened with great interest.

Impressed with what he heard, the director insisted on visiting Centennial and arrived in April 1998 to witness a group of twenty students make a presentation in the school district's board room. They had just returned from a ten-day service-learning expedition in the village of San Lucas-Toliman, Guatemala. As the presentation progressed, students discussed politics and economics of the Third World, insights related to the recent civil war in Guatemala, and recounted projects that had placed them side by side with the locals in the village. They talked about working in the health clinic, constructing part of a house by making cement by hand, picking coffee beans by hand on the finca plantation, and grinding the coffee beans to sell for profit. Students evoked tears from audience members as they talked about the trip from a personal point of view and how their visit had proved to be a life-changing experience.

The Lighthouse director, moved by the presentation, vowed to return to Centennial with a group of students from his five schools. In the fall of 1998, he arrived with eighty students, ranging in age from ten to eighteen years. In order to accommodate such a span of ages and number of students, Centennial invited an elementary school and a junior high school to assist with the project. During the visit, British students were paired and lived with the families of local students. For ten days, Centennial High School, Lincoln Junior High School, and Juan-Fullana Elementary School, in collaboration with Colorado State University's Service Learning Program, engaged students in a multitude of volunteer projects, teaching the British guests how to create, implement, and assess a service-learning program in schools.

As a compliment to Centennial and its service-learning coordinator, the Lighthouse director informed the staff that Tony Blair, the British prime minister, had charged him with infusing a service-learning component into the British civic education program. The Lighthouse school visit taught British students and staff valuable lessons related to implementing such a program in Great Britain. To some extent, Centennial may have contributed its philosophy and service-learning program structure to the British civic education curriculum.

Every organization needs its "champion on a white charger" to motivate others. The Centennial champion was an exceptional, inspirational staff member. Sacrificing a half-year's salary made him almost a saint among his colleagues. His presence set the standard for passionate belief in the philosophy of hands-on learning and the positive impact it had on students. He exuded an energy that excited students and energized staff into approaching learning in more active, experiential ways. He challenged staff members to become better educators and to focus on greater possibilities, because he believed in the potential of every student. As a champion, this teacher gave Centennial a legacy of ideas and "what if" possibilities. His presence and passion evoked many dialogues among staff members and provided the catalyst for continuous change and improvement. One such improvement was the creation of the "Roads Scholars" program.

STRATEGY #8: POSTCARDS FROM THE ROAD

Establishing the Roads Scholars in early 1996 was spontaneous, almost an act of serendipity. At the time, the service-learning coordinator and a school counselor were team-teaching a course called "Current Issues." The curriculum invited students to study a group of people in the city for four days and on the fifth day serve them in some way. On one of those service days, students were loading a semitrailer truck with food and clothing items scheduled for shipment to the Navajo Nation in northern Arizona. During lunch break, one of the students asked, "Where are these things going, anyway?" Teacher and counselor responded to the "teachable moment" and discussed life on the reservation, the economic needs of the people, and the rich culture and historical legacy found among the Navajo. The students listened with interest, then one made the offhand comment, "Wouldn't it be neat if we could ride in the truck, go to the reservation, and help distribute the items we're loading?"

At that moment, the Roads Scholar program was born. When the two instructors returned to campus, their enthusiasm spilled into the school.

Their excitement attracted a group of staff members, who were drawn into conversation by their remarkable energy. The two staff members started speculating on the "what ifs" of learning. Could we send a group of students to work and learn on the reservation? What could we teach students before they left, while they were there, and when they returned? How could we raise the money to get students there?

As they were publicly pondering these ideas, Centennial's science teacher walked by and suggested he could teach some "roadside geology" on the way to Arizona; the journey could take students through the national parks in southern Utah. A social studies teacher added that he could teach a geography and history unit on the Southwest. The health instructor offered to teach a unit of study tied to food preparation, water consumption, and other topics. The school's art teacher joined the group and turned dreaming into reality. She had contacts on the Navajo reservation and offered to arrange with tribal officials to have students participate in Navajo ceremonies and camp on private land.

Within thirty minutes of exuberant discussion, a new program was created that altered the master schedule for the remainder of the year. The staff met regularly to plan, add detail, and resolve logistical issues. Students were invited to enroll in specific classes that taught content related to the trip, and fund-raising efforts began immediately. For two six-week academic terms, instructors adjusted course content to meet academic standards and to include information about the Southwest and the Navajo Nation.

In May, when most students begin losing interest in learning, forty students and five staff members climbed into district vans and personal vehicles to make an eleven-day trek into another culture. Earlier that year (February 15, 1996), a reporter for the Fort Collins *Coloradoan* had written an exceptional story titled, "Hands-on Learning." She declared the upcoming trip would not only provide hands-on learning for students but also "addressed the need to teach social and cultural understanding along with honesty, integrity and personal responsibility." The community responded by donating gifts for distribution and cash to defray student expenses. This approach to learning captured the attention and support of local residents.

During the trip to the reservation, students examined petroglyphs and rock formations in Utah, slept in an alternative high school's gym in

Cortez, Colorado, and worked with the Navajo tribe in Ship Rock, New Mexico, and Window Rock, Arizona. One of the high points of the expedition involved camping on a sheep ranch in Klagetoh, Arizona. Here students engaged in a traditional sheep-blessing ceremony and experienced several Navajo traditions. On their return to Fort Collins, the Roads Scholars stopped in Taos, New Mexico, where they donated time and energy to complete a service-learning project with the natives of the pueblo.

One of the trip's most unusual coincidences occurred when students had a chance to unload and distribute the clothing items they had earlier packed on the semitrailer in Fort Collins. Ironically, a student who had been involved in the original service-learning project found the pair of shoes she had donated the day she worked on the truck in Fort Collins. Her "wouldn't it be neat" statement had become a reality.

The staff learned a great deal about creating lessons on the road during those eleven days. The trip became a "shakedown cruise" for future Roads Scholar adventures. The staff created a policy and logistics handbook so others could pursue trips at different times. They established ways to engage students in class requirements, developed criteria for awarding credits, and created formats to gather the necessary funds and ideas to promote positive learning experiences.

Other Roads Scholar trips soon followed. One staff member used the guidelines to organize a Roads Scholar trip to Montana and the Wanuskewin Heritage Park in Saskatoon, Saskatchewan. Over the next five years, three Roads Scholar trips visited the town of San Lucas-Toliman in Guatemala. One trip sent students to experience daily life and culture in New York City, and several trips to the national parks of Utah became a regular part of a science/social studies curriculum. Each trip was filled with unique content and skill acquisition, and all trips included some kind of service-learning project designed to serve the people visited by the Roads Scholar team.

This ongoing program offered students another hands-on approach to learn and apply classroom concepts to the real world. The program's impact on staff and students has been immense. One student crafted an individualized program and completed her senior studies by volunteering to return to the Navajo reservation as an active participant in tribal life. Other students returned to Guatemala soon after graduation to continue their experience with the people of San Lucas. In fact, one of Centennial's former nurse practitioners was so moved by her experience that she and her husband quit their jobs and moved to Guatemala to participate in a two-year work-study program in San Lucas-Toliman.

STRATEGY #9: KEEPING THE VISION-EMBERS BURNING

As the Centennial staff began applying more and more experiential learning activities to their respective instructional repertoire, Centennial's leadership team continued to encourage change and, more importantly, collaboratively plan strategies to accomplish each of the yearly goals outlined in its five-year plan. Through observation and evaluation, the principal encouraged staff members to make the necessary adjustments to improve content and skill instruction in the classroom, develop assessment instruments to measure student achievement, and provide consistent implementation of school policies and management systems.

However, the most essential part of a principal's job is to ensure that staff, parents, and students keep their focus on the school's vision. A popular poster reads, "If you don't know where you're going, you'll wind up someplace else." To a principal, this statement must mean that employees and students should always know the organization's purpose, mission, and long-term vision, and be able to personalize actions that demonstrate their contributions to those ends. Every opportunity must be taken to define and redefine the circle of the culture.

From 1992 on, several strategies were used to keep the Centennial vision in the minds of all staff members. First, each school year began with a clarification of the vision and what it meant in terms of goals for the year. Collaboratively, the staff identified strategies to improve attendance, graduation rate, and academic performance in the classroom. In addition, staff members created professional goals derived from district and building goals and/or suggestions from formal conferences and evaluations conducted during the previous year.

Second, the staff development committee made a concerted effort to keep the culture of the program healthy and vital. Distribution of educational articles that emphasized quality achievement, promising instructional practices, or strategies that worked effectively with high-risk students became an ongoing occurrence. The staff collaborated with colleagues at Colorado State University to offer reading seminars, with college credit, specifically designed for Centennial staff.

The administration continuously monitored the purple feedback sheets, allocating more time to individuals who expressed concerns with implementing school policies. Each of the school's committees was encouraged to focus on long- and short-term goals that led to achieving the school's five-year vision. Staff development sessions always included topics that addressed both heart and head agendas. Some of these workshops addressed personal and professional challenges, while other workshops fostered a greater understanding of the school's unique culture, the changing student profile, and the immense possibilities of alternative education.

Third, the staff used surveys, distributed to both students and staff, to assess the effectiveness of school policies, learning-climate issues, and classroom activities. Results were shared with staff and students in order to foster a continuous dialogue about the program. Based on the school's philosophy, the staff wanted to guarantee that all voices would be heard. The staff held meetings specifically designed to model and role-play policy issues so all would know how procedures were handled. The Centennial staff continually talked about the impact that policy changes had on students, programs, and other policies in the building. They were keenly aware that a slight shift in policy often had a ripple effect on other aspects of the program and made a concerted effort to monitor changes as they occurred.

Fourth, all district testing and survey results were shared with staff and students in order to monitor academic progress and areas of needed improvement. The staff examined the responses of student attitude surveys related to alcohol and drug use, academic achievement, attendance, the dropout rate, and student profiles.

For example, in January 1994 the staff compared the profile of a typical Centennial student who enrolled in the program in 1990 with the profile of a typical student enrolled four years later. Staff members were amazed at the shift in student population and needs.

In 1994, the typical student was 16.2 years of age, lived with both parents, did not have a part-time job, and planned to attend college at some point. In the short span of four years, Centennial's students had become younger but exhibited more emotional deficiencies than the students of the previous generation. The staff used this information to adjust their instructional strategies and interactions to meet the newly identified needs. The process of change was continuous and required constant monitoring.

Ironically, in a high school setting the student population changes every three to four years. Program implementation, driven by long-term goals, must keep pace with the changing needs of each generation of students who walk through its halls. Collecting and analyzing data is an essential part of establishing midcourse corrections as people move toward achieving their vision. By constantly examining the changing needs of the students being served, the Centennial staff was able to adjust its programs and keep the school culture vibrant.

THE LAST PHASE OF THE FIRST STAGE

In the spring of 1995, the staff turned its attention to completing the last phase of its five-year plan. The Centennial staff and students prepared for a North Central Association accreditation visit in April. The staff completed a self-evaluation of the effectiveness of the elective-week program, instructional strategies, the counseling program, integrated curriculum ideas, and, most importantly, the relationship between the special-education program on the west side of campus and the general-education program on the east side. They surveyed students, parents, and staff members, summarized findings, and prepared for an inspection by the five-member visitation team of educators.

These findings, insights, and recommendations would be used to determine if the five-year vision had been achieved. From North Central recommendations, a new five-year vision would emerge and shape the next direction of the Centennial program. Had the hands-on approach to teaching and learning addressed students' needs? Did the brick wall, built over a five-year period, produce an aesthetically appealing, functional house with a program to match? The staff looked forward to the visitation team and its outsiders' view of program changes.

6

RECYCLING TO CREATE
A NEW VISION

From April 3 to April 7, 1995, a five-person team representing the North Central Association conducted an on-site review of Centennial's self-study. The North Central Association accredits private and public schools and endorses programs throughout the United States. During the visit, the evaluation team wandered the building; talked with students, staff, parents; and interviewed central office administrators. The Centennial staff asked the group to examine their effort to integrate curriculum and to review instructional strategies used to meet state and district standards and assessments. In addition, the Centennial staff requested that the team look at the special education and counseling programs. Centennial planned to make changes in these areas and wanted the perspective of this outside group of professionals.

Prior to the North Central team's visit, an article about Centennial's program was published in the November 1994 issue of *Educational Leadership* magazine. The article, "Empowering At-Risk Students to Succeed," initiated a flood of inquiries and promoted frequent visits by professional educators from around the country. For the next seven years, Centennial was graced by the presence of more than seventy visitors per year, which helped spread its program ideas throughout the country and promoted collegial relationships between Centennial and other institutions. Such attention increased staff confidence, because it showed the school had created a unique, successful program.

The Centennial staff anticipated a positive report from the North Central team that would validate the completion of its five-year vision. They were already basking in the accolades frequently expressed by visitors who came to see firsthand how the Centennial program empowered students to succeed. The school frequently received notes from visiting teachers who praised the program and its impact on students. A typical note read, "I appreciate the time you spent with us to show us your impressive school and the approach you use to lead students toward success who don't often experience success in traditional schools. I think of you and your program often as I search for ways to help my own students at MLK Junior High."

For five years, the Centennial staff, individually and collectively, had labored to create a shared vision for the school. They had changed and added programs, modified instructional strategies, redesigned the school's governance structure, created an exceptional learning climate for students, and fostered a positive image in the community. The burning question in September 1995 was: What does Centennial need to accomplish to rise to the next level of excellence?

The Centennial staff believed the North Central summary would provide the necessary insights and guidance to help create the next five-year vision. In his book *Change Forces*, Michael Fullan states, "Vision emerges from, more than precedes, action. Even then it is always provisional. Shared vision, which is essential for success, must evolve through the dynamic interactions of organizational members and leaders. This takes time and will not succeed unless the vision-building process is somewhat open-ended" (1993). Centennial had a group of seasoned change agents who had worked through five years of vision building and shared a belief in their ability to provide a successful program for high-risk students. The staff was ready to use current research on educational change, combined with personal experiences, to begin the "visioning" process for the second time.

This chapter outlines the strategies used to develop a second five-year vision for Centennial, and it can be adapted for any setting. Unlike during the first five-year plan, Centennial was no longer under pressure to produce or perish. The tension and accompanying anxiety about program survival was no longer a motivational factor for staff members. In fact, by 1996 two-thirds of the Centennial staff were new and had only a vague understanding of the motivation and challenging work that had consumed the staff as it created the first vision.

The process of identifying a second five-year vision evolved in a different way. First, the staff felt it had the luxury of time and a climate of flexibility to try new ideas at a leisurely pace. Second, members of the Centennial staff took the year to dialogue, debate, and modify shared beliefs about students, learning, governance, and school norms so all could step into the circle of a shared culture together.

There are advantages and disadvantages to this approach to change. An attitude of satisfaction, expressed by a majority of staff members, fosters complacency and presents the organization's leader with a dilemma. The principal must be compelled to keep motivating the team to create a new vision. As Jim Collins states in the opening line of his book *Good to Great*, "Good is the enemy of great" (2001). Satisfaction with progress achieved creates a barrier to becoming a great organization. Accepting a modicum of progress made as "good enough" is like the analogy of the frog that sits on the bottom of a bucket and can leap half the distance to the top. In every ensuing jump, the frog can cut the remaining distance in half. The question asked in this riddle is: How many jumps will the frog have to make to escape the bucket and meet its goal? Like all clever logic problems, the answer is that the frog will never jump out.

From a leader's point of view, the changes that took place during the first five-year vision were dramatic and awe inspiring, because Centennial's "frog" made huge leaps and visibly cut the distance in half with each jump. During the next five-year vision, each jump was less dramatic, and progress was more difficult to measure. At times, the frequent change in staff members was like adding water to the bottom of the bucket and cooking it over a slow fire. The frog became comfortable in its "bath water" and more hesitant to jump to the next level. Absent an urgent need, becoming comfortable strangles efforts to make dramatic improvements or changes in programs. The principal's role is to irritate the frog and create the need for it to jump. A leader must continuously coax the frog to jump by asking challenging questions in public and private, conducting surveys about school issues, and presenting thought-provoking topics for discussion at staff meetings.

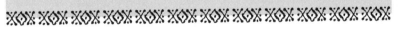

Four Principles of a "Living System" or Organization

1. Equilibrium is the precursor to death. When a living system is in a state of equilibrium, it is less responsive to changes occurring around it. This places it at maximum risk.
2. In the face of threat, or when galvanized by a compelling opportunity, living things move toward the edge of chaos. This condition evokes higher levels of mutation and experimentation, and fresh new solutions are more likely to be found.
3. When this excitation takes place, the components of living systems self-organize and new forms and repertoires emerge from the turmoil.
4. Living systems cannot be directed along a linear path. Unforeseen consequences are inevitable. The challenge is to disturb them in a manner that approximates the desired outcome.

—Robert Pascale et al., *Surfing the Edge of Chaos* (2000), 6

The first section of this chapter outlines the strategies used to create the next vision for Centennial High School during the 1995–1996 school year. The vision emerged from an analysis of the North Central report, reading seminars, and many staff development meetings during which the staff talked and talked and talked until they created a new, but simple, vision and a detailed action plan to achieve it. Strategies that follow identify programs and actions that moved Centennial toward this vision in the next five years. Many of the programs and ideas accelerated the process as new staff members were hired and their skills supported the next vision.

STRATEGY #1: MAKING SENSE OF THE REPORT

In essence, the North Central team's final report congratulated the Centennial staff for successfully turning the school around. One commendation stated, "The school is to be applauded for the continuous improvement and change over the past five years. The initial plan that was established four and a half years ago is almost complete and the school has positioned itself well for the next phase of planning and to accommodate change" (North Central Report, May 1995).

In September 1995, the Centennial staff formed a committee to examine the entire report and organize its commendations and recommendations into a potential plan of action. The strategy of categorizing evaluation findings attempted to make sense of the snapshot view of Centennial the five visiting individuals had experienced during their four-day visit. An organized approach to the evaluation document also permitted the staff to reflect on the implications of each proposed idea. The report included more than one hundred observations, commendations, and recommendations and responded to the request to challenge existing paradigms under which the school operated. After reviewing the report's findings, the Centennial committee placed them in the following categories of ideas that:

- Have been implemented already
- Could be implemented this year (1995–1996)
- Can be implemented within the next three years
- May be implemented within the next five years
- Missed the boat, did not match our philosophy.

The Centennial review committee presented these categorized ideas to the staff in September. Time was allocated at each ensuing staff meeting to discuss items, program implications, staffing use, impact on students, and how each suggestion might lead to the creation of a new vision. This process consumed a great deal of time, but by the beginning of second semester, the staff had a clear picture of what was needed to move the program to the next level and was ready to start working on creating a new vision.

STRATEGY #2: THE LEADER'S CHALLENGE

It is essential for the leader, as a key member of the organization, to personally analyze and synthesize such an evaluation report, interpret it for public consumption, and lay out his or her perceptions for the next challenge. All members of the organization need to know what the leader believes and how these beliefs will guide his or her actions. If the leader intends to be a key player in moving an organization to the next level, he or she cannot enjoy the luxury of keeping ideas and beliefs close to the vest. At this point in the process, it is important to model motivational beliefs and passions for all employees. These passions and beliefs, in turn, must reflect or be close to the passions and beliefs of the employees. If there is a mismatch, the leader must reassess his or her ability to lead the organization to the next level and consider moving on.

After examining the list of recommendations from the North Central report and listening to staff discussions, the principal asked the staff to focus on higher levels of student achievement by raising academic standards and increasing student expectations as independent learners. Teachers and counselors were asked to create a list of skills, knowledge, and competencies expected of graduates from an alternative high school and to develop a common format and assessment rubrics for all student written work. In addition, the staff was asked to explore instructional strategies that would accelerate learning.

In order to move in this direction, Centennial began collaborating with the Education Department at Colorado State University and conducting reading seminars in brain-based learning, multiple intelligences, and authentic assessment strategies. As a result of these discussions, the need to enhance the vocational component of Centennial's program was identified. Efforts to improve this aspect of the program emerged into a program that would create meaningful, real-life transitional experiences to position students for post–high school life.

The North Central report underscored the need to create a more appropriate balance in program emphasis. The team noted that the Centennial staff spent a great deal of time and effort promoting personal growth at the expense of academic and career growth. It also requested the staff to seek approaches to create more independent, self-actualized, academic learners by eradicating the subtle belief that some of the students were "damaged goods" because they had personal issues. The North Central team wanted staff to determine if Centennial was an authentic alternative school or a transition program designed to "fix up kids" and return them to the comprehensive school setting.

As a staff moves through the analysis process (a period of transition between thoughtful analysis and purposeful action planning), the organization's leader needs to model vision and verbalize expectations in order to motivate and support continuous improvement. The Centennial principal took a position on these issues in early September and expressed the desire for Centennial to become a school of excellence, with a program committed to graduating students with skills, knowledge, and competencies that would rival those of any high school graduate in the city. Given the clarity of the principal's position, the staff knew how he planned to allocate staffing units, distribute funds, seek district support, and utilize other resources. Until the staff had time to collaboratively design a new five-year vision, the principal used his leadership position to guide the program through a year of transition and analysis. Such clarity fostered understanding of the principal's role and promoted confidence in him as a trustee of a program in transition.

STRATEGY #3: EXAMINING THE BIG PICTURE

In preparing to create the next five-year vision, the staff initiated a reading seminar, with attached continuing education credit, through Colorado State University. One of the readings included Tom Sergiovanni's book *Moral Leadership* (1990). As the staff members read chapter 7, "Collegiality as a Professional Virtue," and chapter 8, "The Virtuous School," they recognized that Centennial had a larger mission to develop a program that provided students with skills, attitudes, and aptitudes for a lifetime of success and learning. Sergiovanni's chapters reinforced the notion that Centennial's cultural "glue" was tied to its shared values and beliefs about the nature and potential of students. Teachers were motivated by Sergiovanni's criteria of a virtuous school, finding correlations between Centennial's program and his list.

The Centennial staff endorsed beliefs that a virtuous school:

- Makes a commitment to develop a spirit of curiosity, inquiry, and reflection that touches adults and students alike.
- Believes that every student can learn and does everything in its power to see that every student does learn.

- Has an ethic of caring and views caring as a key to academic success.
- Honors respect—respects teachers for their professional commitment and knowledge of their craft, and respects students for their commitment to learning.
- Acknowledges parents, teachers, and community members as school partners (Sergiovanni 1990).

Armed with this information and the desire to improve its virtues as an effective school, the staff launched a series of staff development workshops aimed at reinforcing the cultural norms that bound the program together as a learning community. This reinforcement provided the driving force to create a new five-year plan and vision.

Scheduled topics of discussion included:

February 21:	Celebrate Success!! What is working and producing the results wanted?
February 27:	What is Centennial's belief system in 1996?
March 6:	Compare 1996 beliefs with 1991 beliefs—any changes?
March 19:	Define the characteristics of the current student enrolled at Centennial.
March 27:	Do current Centennial beliefs match student needs?
April 2:	Do current practices, procedures, and policies match belief system?
April 17:	How does the school adjust its program to meet needs that have changed? Part one.
April 23:	How does the school adjust its program to meet needs that have changed? Part two.

Like the first vision, the second vision took more than four months to construct. However, based on the belief that an organization must go slow in order to go fast, the recycling process was worth the amount of time spent in lengthy discussions. Extensive time was necessary because the Centennial team was working with a new cast of characters in the vision play.

Through retirements and transfers, only one-third of the staff members who had participated in the first vision process in 1991 were still employed at Centennial five years later. Even though the school's culture and vision had held the staff together over the years, it became uncomfortably obvious that the addition of each new staff member slightly changed perceptions of the vision, its goals, the cultural norms, and the implementation of procedures. Assumptions related to "this is how we do things around here" were challenged by new staff members who seemed to "know better." They often modified or gave a different interpretation to school policies and procedures. The new staff members did not fully understand the logic and consequences of the policies or procedures based on the school's history and student needs. Veteran teachers resented the subtle, sometimes frontal, attack on a system that promoted student success.

Assigning teacher-mentors to new staff members and staff orientation meetings did not help acclimate new teachers into the program or help them make decisions based on established protocols. Therefore, the total staff needed to take time to fully understand how the Centennial program had emerged and the reasons for establishing practices and procedures to match practiced beliefs. Centennial's staff development committee scheduled time to examine the parameters and scope of the program and redefine the circle that held the culture together.

This strategy is imperative for every organization to consider whenever it adds new employees. The principal could help one or two new people become comfortable with the system through the interview process or through personal coaching during the year, but massive changes in personnel can create havoc with cultural norms. Challenges or modifications in policy implementation foster distress for veteran employees and cause unrest and divisions in previously successful working relationships. As the staff became more aware of this phenomenon, more discussion items related to school norms appeared on the business agendas at staff meetings and staff development days. For, as suggested by Sergiovanni, shared vision and common beliefs become the essential glue that holds an organization together.

STRATEGY #4: CREATING AN ACTION PLAN AND A NEW VISION

By May, the Centennial staff was ready to create an action plan in order to translate the new vision into words. The staff's thinking was supported by the publication of *Breaking Ranks* (An Executive Report on High Schools by the National Association of Secondary School Principals, 1996). Thus encouraged, the staff identified five core belief statements, outlined an action plan for implementation, and penned Vision 2001.

Belief statements included:

1. People at Centennial are treated with courtesy, respect, and dignity.
2. The six Ps (Prepared, Prompt, Polite, Participate, Positive mental attitude, and Produce) establish the ground rules for appropriate student and adult behaviors and expectations.
3. All students can succeed, given the appropriate time, personal commitment, and a flexible learning environment.
4. A successful learning environment is free of alcohol and other drugs.
5. Centennial is a safe, nonviolent school in which conflict between people can be resolved through personal negotiation or mediation.

The essence of the new vision statement, oddly enough, was embedded in the parent section of the North Central report. A suggestion offered by the parent group said it wanted Centennial to prepare students for jobs after high school. Centennial's staff looked at that statement and modified it to read, "All students who graduate from Centennial will position themselves for success after high school." The new vision was born! To staff, this meant they needed to help students understand there were many visions in the future. As one of the school's counselors said, "To catch the vision of earning a high school diploma is only the first vision, with many more to come." Centennial needed to build a program and engage students in learning activities and experiences that helped position them for college scholarships, improved academic and technology skills, and prepared them for jobs that brought upward mobility and increased responsibility.

Staff members committed themselves to a list of seven goals that needed to be developed and measured during the next five years. These were:

1. Teach students to demonstrate basic academic skills in reading, writing, math, science, social studies, and technology.

2. Increase career-training opportunities for students and emphasize the attainment of advanced training or technical proficiency.
3. Develop an individual educational plan and a portfolio by which all students could measure individual progress.
4. Teach students how to develop and use resiliency skills to independently plan and seek alternative options, without Centennial's help.
5. Provide a learning program that delivers skills and content in a variety of formats, including, but not limited to: self-contained classes, independent study packets, self-paced learning programs, service learning, experiential activities, thematic content units, or other innovative delivery systems that match student learning styles.
6. Develop alternative methods of assessing academic and skill proficiency.
7. Develop more partnerships with the Fort Collins community, the parents, and various educational/business institutions to assist the staff in achieving the vision.

This exercise unified the veteran and newer staff members, provided a common vision and purpose for the next five years, encouraged creativity, and provided a set of seven measurable goals for program improvement.

STRATEGY #5: EQUALITY THROUGH INCLUSION

During one of Centennial's reading seminars, participants examined John Goodlad's belief that public schools had a moral responsibility to provide a structure to acculturate the young into political democracy and to develop persons with an understanding of truth, beauty, and justice (*Phi Delta Kappan* 1992). Most staff members believed this statement applied to *all* of their students, even those with labels created by special education experts to guarantee the delivery of special educational services for specific learners.

The special education program at Centennial High School had an inauspicious beginning. In the fall of 1988, much to the chagrin and dismay of the Centennial staff, the district's severe emotionally disturbed program was placed in the school's gym. It was an ill-planned move from the outset. Soft-sided removable walls created temporary classroom space. Every day, the walls had to be disassembled at 11:30 A.M. so the room could be used for lunch and reconstructed for classroom use at 12:30 P.M. Neither the Centennial staff nor the special education professionals were happy with the situation. In fact, animosity openly flowed between the two adult groups.

A year later, in another poorly planned move, the special education program was moved to the building on the west side of campus, replacing the much-loved teen mothers program that had occupied the old kindergarten space for several years. The displacement of the teen mothers added to the disdain for the special education program and its staff, and created a virtually self-contained program that was separated from the Centennial program by more than the two-hundred-yard park between the two buildings. When the new principal arrived in 1990, the special education program was barely acknowledged or tolerated by the Centennial staff. The new principal was not required to supervise this program, and it remained a remote site on the west side of campus during Centennial's year of program restructuring.

As the analysis of student profiles began in 1990, it was discovered that more than thirty students had previously been served by special education before they enrolled in Centennial. The school's structure did not officially serve students with special learning needs. Therefore, these students had voluntarily withdrawn from the special education program at their home high schools in order to be eligible to enroll at Centennial. Consequently, the instructional staff at Centennial struggled to find appropriate teaching strategies for these students. Placing them in classes with educators who were untrained in the instructional skills required to address special-need students frustrated both instructors and learners. The system had inadvertently created an environment in which some students were denied the additional help they needed to succeed.

As the 1990–1991 school year came to a close, Centennial requested and received district approval to provide a half-time special education staff member, trained to work with students who had learning disabilities. The instructor was asked to reexamine the needs of each former special education student and create individual education plans (IEPs) if they still qualified for special education support services. Parents of these students were asked if they wanted to reenroll their children in a special education program on the Centennial campus. Most of them accepted the invitation as a way to help their children succeed.

By the end of the year, Centennial's half-time special education teacher was serving twenty-seven students, which far exceeded Colorado's guidelines for a special education teacher-student ratio. Using this knowledge as a bargaining chip, Centennial's principal asked the director of special education to provide a full-time staffing unit in special education for the upcoming year or move most of these special-needs students to other sites, where they could receive appropriate services to meet their learning needs. The director of special education agreed to support Centennial's program with additional staff, on the condition that the principal begin supervising the ED (emotionally disturbed) special education program and its staff on the west side of campus. Through these negotiations, Centennial's program expanded—but so did the responsibility of all, including the staff and students in the ED program. This action set the stage for a full inclusion program.

The special education program on the west side of campus was officially called the Mathews Street Center, named for the street it faced. It consisted of a social worker, three teachers, two paraprofessionals, and twenty to thirty students who were all diagnosed with severe emotional disabilities. The student enrollment changed frequently, as some dropped out, some were incarcerated, or new faces were added as programs in other district schools transferred students with high needs into the Mathews Street facility. The program's behavioral system was a modification of the Boys Town model, in which students were given points for appropriate behaviors and lost points for inappropriate behaviors. The accumulation of points moved students to higher levels of trust, responsibility, and consequently, more privileges.

In general, this behavior-modification model established an external focus and control system for students. Such a system often works best with elementary school–age children, not high school students. The latter easily spot the artificially controlled overtones in the model, see little to respect in earning or losing 10,000 points within a few minutes, and proceed to create ways to sabotage its impact.

The Mathews Street Center was often in crisis. The adults, who gave more than a 100 percent effort to make a difficult situation work, were frustrated by the number of students who dropped out or were dumped into the program by the district. Frequent acts of violence or defiance resulted in daily police calls and some arrests. The staff used to measure their degree of frustration by the number of large bags of pretzels consumed. At times, pretzel consumption exceeded three bags per week.

The behavior protocol used by the Mathews Street program was philosophically opposed to William Glasser's philosophy of student self-empowerment that the Centennial program followed. As a result, consistency of behavioral management was frequently challenged by the needs of staff and students in both buildings. This was especially problematic at lunch or other times when students from both programs interacted. Discipline issues were handled differently, and consequences for behaviors confused both adults and students. The situation became an administrative nightmare and often created feelings of schizophrenia among supervising adults.

By 1993, however, the culture on the west side of campus was beginning to change. Staff changes at the Mathews Street program, the positive image created by the formation of the Eco-Warrior recycling program, and participation in the aforementioned Campus Beautification Project increased collegiality among professionals in both buildings. The level of trust between staff members in both programs began to grow. Even the Mathews Street Center students realigned their allegiance to the larger Centennial campus.

In an unprecedented move, students at the Mathews Street Center drafted a petition to the district's director of special education and requested a name change for the program. They wanted to rename their facility Centennial West High School. Students articulately explained the reasons for the change by stating:

1. We would like the name of our school to show that we are part of the Centennial campus and are major contributors to all school projects such as the landscaping project.

2. We would like our name to show that we work hard in class and do academic work and earn credit like our peers in other high schools.
3. We would like our name to send a positive message to the community about who we are. When we collect the neighborhood's recyclables, we call ourselves "Centennial's Eco Warriors." The media, though, on occasion have identified us as students in legal trouble attending Mathews Street Center.
4. Our teachers, school staff, and the principal at Centennial support us in this request.

The Mathews Street Center was officially renamed Centennial West.

In the next two years, the process of integrating both programs unfolded. Centennial's art teacher was assigned to offer an art class to the Centennial West students, permitting the Centennial West staff to have a common planning time. The team's social worker received training in the Discovery program and, along with other program components, created a social-skills training class for Centennial West students, modifying the Boys Town model.

Due to increased enrollment, a modular classroom was moved onto the Centennial campus, and a Centennial West teacher was assigned to one of its two classrooms. Her program became known as the "island." When students reached "merit level" in the Boys Town model, they transferred into this class and used it as a staging ground to earn placement in Centennial's Discovery program or other mainstream classes.

Although this approach provided more flexibility for students, it did not qualify as complete educational equity for all students. Special-learning-needs students labored under educational labels that separated them from their peers and the professionals that served them. Labels remained artificial barriers that created a social distancing phenomenon between peers and adults. These labels lowered the academic bar and minimized social/behavioral expectations among teachers who served these students. The myths that swirled around the aura of special education confused and limited teacher and student potential.

In February 1996, a bold move was proposed that shook up the entire Centennial campus. The complete integration of the Centennial West staff and its students into Centennial's program was planned and implemented in the fall in order to attain a total-inclusion model for the campus. The Centennial West building now housed the campus art facility and science lab, and teachers who formerly only served students with severe emotional needs moved into Centennial's main building, taught mainstream content classes, and served a combination of both regular ed and special ed students. If a self-contained program was to exist at all, it would be of short duration, with the intent of mainstreaming as many students with special needs as possible. With the anticipation of adding more staff, Centennial planned to hire individuals with special education training and, more specifically, experience in developing an all-school inclusion model.

The proposal evoked a mixed reaction from both staffs. After expressing some initial concerns, both staffs cautiously accepted the change. For the remainder of the year, the Centennial West staff joined Centennial's faculty meetings and shared insights about their professional needs and the social/academic needs of their students. Such discussions began the process of developing greater collegiality among the professionals from both programs.

In the fall of 1996, Centennial had another opportunity to hire a special education teacher who had an expertise in implementing an inclusion model. The instructor impressed the hiring committee with her passion, commitment, and desire to provide equity for all students. In addition, she brought to the program strategies and program ideas that had been successfully implemented in another setting.

The teacher's first approach was to demystify the language and aura of special education. She distributed a survey to the Centennial staff asking them to identify their needs, fears, and beliefs about special education. From this feedback, she crafted a series of workshops to dispel myths and teach the instructional staff how to understand and deal with students who had emotional and perceptual/communicative disabilities.

Traditionally, regular education professionals do not have the necessary training or experience to work with students who have special education needs. Typically, they view special education teachers with distrust and feel "dumped on" when asked to include a student with special learning needs in their classes. However, in a school like Centennial, most of the staff had already successfully dealt with the unique learning needs of high-risk students by creating positive relationships with them and providing many hands-on learning projects. Therefore, the staff welcomed the information provided and effectively eliminated lingering communication barriers.

For the first months of school after the inclusion model was implemented, the special education staff took twenty to thirty minutes of each staff meeting to teach Centennial instructors how to identify and accommodate students' special needs. This process included modeling instructional strategies, providing instructional modification techniques, and offering methods to handle students' emotional crises. They shared information about specific disorders and their treatment, including Asperger's syndrome, ADHD (attention deficit and hyperactivity disorder), depressive conditions including bipolar disorder, severe anxiety or panic disorder, and traumatic brain injury disorder. With more detailed information and understanding, the staff's confidence and acceptance increased.

By implementing several behavioral management plans, the Centennial staff began to observe a reduction in students' emotional outbursts and an increase in self-esteem and academic production. These changes became apparent immediately. By including students with special needs with peers in a supportive, respectful, and kind environment, these formerly self-contained students began to think differently about themselves and others and rise to higher academic and behavioral expectations. At all times, Centennial maintained a full spectrum of services available to these students when needed. The school's goal, however, was to continuously prepare students for a full-inclusion learning environment.

Logistically, Centennial created a "mini-Discovery" class for one special education instructor to teach all new students with special learning needs who were assigned to the program. This program was called "Home Base." The students affectionately called it "home basement," due to its location in the building. Home Base was a one-period, six-week social-skills program in which special-needs students learned the culture and expectations of Centennial. The primary goal of the class was to move these students into regular education classes and/or into the Discovery program as soon as possible.

Each special education teacher, who formerly had worked in a self-contained classroom, now taught regular education classes. These teachers' schedules often included reverse mainstream classes (those including both regular ed and special ed students), such as U.S. history, British literature, U.S. literature, and prealgebra. In addition to teaching, these special education instructors maintained their case-management load of individuals assigned to them.

Another teacher with special education certification became the case manager for all of Centennial's students with learning disabilities (LD). She prepared lists of accommodations for each student and distributed them to staff members in the building. She also reviewed the files of all new students and assisted the Discovery teacher in working with students with identified special learning needs.

This instructor effectively exchanged her training and experience in the Boys Town model for the behavioral approach used by Centennial. She implemented the Centennial model with great clarity and consistency, much to the chagrin of some students who attempted to negotiate variances in the system rather than strictly adhere to the established protocols.

In addition, she demonstrated amazing flexibility as an instructor. Due to her generalist educational background, the instructor agreed to teach a variety of subjects that ranged from math to English and reading to physical education and speech. Her classes included a balance between regular education students and students with special needs. As the special-education team members expanded their instructional repertoire, the lines between students with special education labels and regular education students blurred and the inclusion model became a way of life in the school, providing equity for all learners.

Whenever the district placed a student with special needs at Centennial, the principal took the time to have "the conversation" with him or her. It sounded like this: "John, your file indicates you have a special learning need. Is that true?" Sheepishly, John responded, "Yes, I am ED" (emotionally disturbed). Continuing, the administer added, "You know John, there is no such thing as an ED adult; only school students have such labels. In this school, you will have three years to learn strategies to help you make the transition successfully from high school to adulthood without a label. If you don't mind, from this point, I'd like to think of you as just John and not John who is ED. Is that OK with you?" With some amazement in his voice, John replied, "Yeah, great with me."

The principal expanded on how the school planned to work with him, still providing the additional help and services he needed but without placing him in any self-contained special program. The student would still have a case manager, who planned to assist him as his guide and family liaison. The student was also assured that the staff would be patient with him as he learned new strategies for success. They knew he might take a couple of steps forward and occasionally slip backward. When that happened, the staff would talk about the event, plan a different strategy, and try again. John, like many others who had this talk, knew that Centennial would be different from the other schools he had previously attended, that students would be treated with respect and dignity and not as damaged pieces of merchandise.

Over the years, many students with special learning needs moved into the Centennial program and succeeded well beyond previous expectations. These students attended and excelled in academic classes, enrolled in college classes to earn dual high school and college credit, and graduated with honors. Of the many examples of student successes, the most remarkable story is that of Nate.

Jake, Nate's father, found Centennial High School on the Web. After talking with the special education department head by phone, the family moved to Fort Collins from Baltimore, Maryland, specifically to enroll Nate in Centennial. According to Jake, his son had been born with pervasive developmental disorder, a condition closely related to autism and Asperger's syndrome. Nate had normal intelligence but difficulty learning or handling many social interactions. Jake realized that Nate's continued isolation from society was also isolating him from a normal social setting with peers. Jake wanted his son to attend a school that accepted even students with unique learning challenges.

In the first weeks at Centennial, stress triggered body-rocking and attempts to hit his head against the wall. However, concerned students, staff, the school's culture, and the learning climate soon eliminated such behaviors. Nate found students and staff who cared about him and supported his growth as a person. With counseling and redirection, he began to relax and explore his interests as a learner. He enrolled in several classes where peers took him under their wing and helped him adapt to the program's social culture.

Two students, Ryan and Ali, were exceptional guides in Nate's development. Ryan taught Nate how to dribble a basketball, even when some students were frustrated by his feeble attempts to play the game. Ryan was so exceptional with Nate that it was suggested he consider going to college to become a certified special education teacher; the school district provided scholarship money to enroll in such programs. Ryan had other plans for his future but was honored by the offer. Ali taught Nate the subtle nuances of interacting with members of the opposite sex. She coached and guided him in distinguishing appropriate and inappropriate behaviors, and they became close friends. Nate earned the acceptance of his peers at Centennial and was recognized for his unique sense of humor, his intelligence, and his friendly interactions with others.

At one point, Nate earned a $25 award for perfect attendance. When students were presented checks at an all-school assembly, Nate stood to accept his check and told his assembled peers how much he appreciated them and the school. Students clapped, cheered, and gave him a standing ovation.

As Nate's confidence grew, his horizons expanded. In his senior year at Centennial, Nate created an interesting schedule for himself. First, Nate attended an advanced math class at Rocky Mountain High School, on the south side of town. Then, he loaded his bicycle on a local bus and traveled farther south to take a horticulture class at Front Range Community College. After that, Nate rode his bike to Centennial High School to attend three afternoon classes. At the end of the school day, he returned to Rocky Mountain High School to participate as a member of its track team. Nate was an exceptional long-distance runner and contributed to the team effort. Centennial's vocational program secured a job for him as a weekend sacker in a local grocery store. In addition, he continued his piano lessons and presented a concert for interested Centennial staff at the end of the year.

In two years, Nate, a student who had previously been limited to restrictive programs and treatment centers for students with learning disabilities, emerged as a very talented, respected student in Centennial's learning community. He was bright, articulate, humorous, and expressed remarkable passion that captured the hearts of Centennial staff and inspired many students. He applied for the Fort Collins Breakfast Rotary Club Scholarship and overwhelmed the members with his passion and dedication. After graduation, he enrolled in the horticulture program at Front Range Community College, received an associate degree, and planned to open his own business as a landscape architect.

Nate's story provides an excellent example of Centennial staff's commitment to help position all students for success after graduation. In spite of seemingly major obstacles, the belief that all students have the potential for success created an atmosphere of hope for every Centennial student. Centennial's commitment to help students with special learning and emotional needs motivated the staff to create an inclusion model that reduced the emphasis on labels and developed strategies and approaches so all could succeed.

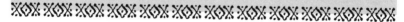

What Matters

The proof of school reform is to be found in the students. All ultimately turns on them and what kind of people they are after they graduate.

—Ted Sizer, *Horace's Hope* (1996), 76

STRATEGY #6: EVEN OUT THE THREE-LEGGED STOOL

From the beginning of the restructuring process, Centennial was like a three-legged stool with one leg shorter than the others. The school's mission statement claimed that Centennial provided a "nurturing, intimate environment in order to promote personal, academic and vocational (career) success." Based on staff analysis and the North Central visitation team's report, the Centennial program excelled in providing opportunities for personal growth and did an adequate job of creating academic challenges. However, the vocational program seemed to be the short leg on this three-legged stool.

The vocational program proved to be perplexing because it seemed to be in a constant state of transition and never enjoyed a clear purpose in the alternative school. The original program had prepared students for jobs in the community, with students attending school half-days and working the other half. Then in the 1980s, school policy required that all students enrolled in Centennial be sixteen years of age and be employed. If they lost their jobs, students were dropped from school. That policy soon ended as the staff addressed the changing needs of the school district and restructured the program. Given its small size, however, Centennial's vocational program could never completely match the requirements or scope of a program designed for larger comprehensive high schools.

In the early 1990s, the vocational program still seemed to function as a job-placement service. Students who enrolled in this program could earn up to 10 percent of the credits required for high school graduation. All they had to do was go to work and turn in time cards to vocational teachers. These teachers held periodic conversations with employers and granted appropriate credit to students.

This approach to career training frustrated many. In more than one meeting, staff members expressed the belief that this strategy for vocational exploration simply gave Centennial students minimal experiences and trained them to accept minimum wage as a lifestyle. Centennial struggled with the work-related program until the Vision 2001 statement was created. As the staff examined the new vision statement, they developed plans and strategies to revitalize Centennial's career program in order to help position students for success after graduation. The staff responded by creating ideas for a five-year action plan. These included:

1997:

1. Develop an advisor-advisee program to help graduating seniors plan for a successful post–high school transition.
2. Expand technology to permit students to develop computer and technological skills that will position them for post–high school careers.
3. Expand and emphasize community service-learning opportunities as a means to connect students with adults who may be potential employers.

1998:

1. Expand the computer-learning center to help students improve math and reading skills.
2. Develop means to initiate and monitor student apprentice placements in the community.
3. With the anticipated additional staffing allocation for the fall, hire a teacher to focus on career development.

1999:

1. Develop new career-related courses to add to the current master schedule.
2. Engage students in hands-on activities in all classes that relate to community and career opportunities.
3. Develop and implement a senior seminar program to permit individual students to explore research topics in the community as graduating seniors.

2000:

1. Secure the services of community mentors to assist students to make connections between academic success and career opportunities.
2. Create a student-run Centennial business in partnership and collaboration with a local business.

2001:

1. Assess successful strategies and reinforce or change approaches as needed to position students for success after graduation.

As with all enthusiastic planning activities, some of the ideas captured the imagination of the staff, while others received minimal support. As it turned out, the advisor-advisee program was the first plan to be implemented and the only one to fail. The intent of this program was to help graduating seniors make the transition from high school to post–high school life. Several staff members volunteered to work with seniors once a month to discuss topics related to their future. Students, divided into groups of five, met with these adults every other week for approximately forty-five minutes each session. The program lasted approximately twelve weeks and ended abruptly.

It failed for two major reasons. First, it only applied to graduating seniors who wanted to sleep in the mornings, did not like being singled out for special attention, and/or chose to work on completing graduation requirements rather than chatting with an adult about the future. Their life revolved around immediate gratification and not future plans. Second, staff members were somewhat ambivalent about talking with students about career topics. Many wanted to use the advisory time to engage students by discussing personal issues, while others felt uncomfortable talking with students in a structured setting. As a result, the first attempt at futures counseling ended without protest.

One counselor's approach for seniors proved more effective than the structured advisor-advisee program. He collaborated with members of the vocational department to position students to enter college. The counselor and the vocational staff helped students prepare college entrance forms, positioned students for scholarships, and personally escorted many on tours of small colleges throughout Colorado. His efforts created an atmosphere of future possibilities for many seniors, and he personally worked with every student who applied for a college scholarship. The counselor reviewed their essays and coached them on effective presentation skills so that every graduating senior who chose to apply for a scholarship earned one.

In order to meet another strategy listed above, Centennial's technology specialist collaborated with a career teacher to improve technology training at Centennial by teaching students post–high school skills. The career specialist explored video production and turned her classroom into a television studio. Within months, students who enrolled in her class were mastering the art and skill of television production, videotape editing, and sound production. Several graduating seniors enrolled in colleges and technical schools specifically geared to train professional sound and video technicians. A Centennial graduate, for example, informed her that he graduated from such an institution and started his career with a $40,000 salary.

In another career-related program, El Pomar, expanded community service learning activities helped turn students into philanthropists. The local paper reported that the El Pomar Foundation in Colorado Springs had invited students in Fort Collins's three comprehensive high schools to participate in its EPYCS program (El Pomar Youth in Community Service program). If students at each school could raise $500, the foundation would match the sum with $7,500. An EPYCS student committee at each school reviewed applications from needy organizations in the city and proceeded to grant them money. Some of the total funds could also be allocated to in-school organizations that applied for a small portion of the grant money.

The El Pomar Foundation was contacted to inform its personnel that there were four high schools in Fort Collins and that Centennial would like to participate in the program as well. They invited the school to participate the following year. Centennial's service-learning coordinator organized students and raised the needed $500 in a short period of time. He turned his current issues class into the El Pomar selection team. As organizations from around Fort Collins applied for some of the grant money allocated to Centennial, the instructor used the requests as an opportunity to send students to each applying agency and complete a volunteer service project on site. In this way, students not only learned about the social service organizations throughout the city but also experienced, firsthand, how these agencies operated and what social needs existed in the community. The opportunity to collaborate with the El Pomar Foundation greatly assisted in Centennial's goal of expanding students' experiences in the city.

STRATEGY #7: IF I HAD A HAMMER

The addition of a building trades teacher to the Centennial staff in fall 1998 accelerated the development of Centennial's career program and vision. This instructor had an intense passion for teaching students the skills required in the construction trades. After being hired, the teacher wrote a grant to purchase hand tools and wanted to know if he had approval to submit the grant. Since grant writing had become a way of life at Centennial, the principal endorsed all efforts to add supplemental resources to the program. Within a few weeks, the instructor proudly announced he had received a $5,000 grant to purchase hand tools. With little planning, Centennial added to its master schedule a construction program that taught students carpentry skills.

The building trades teacher used his ingenuity to expand program resources by approaching the management of Home Depot Building Center. He made a commitment to purchase his hand tools at the local Home Depot store if its employees could assist him in some way. With little publicity, the company doubled the amount of the Centennial grant, giving the school a total of $10,000 in hand tools, though no place to hold class. The first class met in an open space in Centennial's basement. The sound of lathes turning and sandpaper scratching may have been music to some ears, but the custodian and computer lab technicians began objecting to the dust and noise. Soon it was discovered that the construction program was in violation of several Colorado health laws and needed to be housed in an approved space in order to continue.

Fortunately, the district's assistant superintendent helped purchase a sea-land container for Centennial to use as its outside construction classroom. Placing the structure on the blacktop and running electrical cords from the modular classroom created a fine work site. The program grew and prospered as the teacher added more tools and more projects. Male and female students advanced from turning pens on lathes to building doghouses, sheds, and lawn furniture. Within the first year, in order to accommodate increased student enrollment, another sea-land container needed to be purchased, and a third was added a year later. The construction program paid for itself, as community residents purchased most of the student-crafted projects. The unplanned addition of a construction program had little financial impact on Centennial's building budget. The construction class, now called the building trades program, provided another way to position students for success after high school.

A Building Trades Advisory Board, composed of contractors from throughout the city, added credibility to Centennial's program. When possible, several contractors assisted the program by teaching demonstration lessons, arranged for discount purchases of lumber and tools, and provided jobs for building trades graduates. Centennial students were manufacturing quality products, and the program received local attention. Subsequently, Front Range Community College administrators approached Centennial and offered to develop a collaborative building trades program. They intended to close the college's building trades program and offered to provide Centennial with approximately $90,000 in equipment if the staff agreed to share the training facility with them. This was an intriguing offer and was eagerly endorsed by the district.

In 2000, Fort Collins voters approved a multimillion-dollar bond issue for building construction in the school district. Centennial was one of the buildings slated for remodeling. Centennial's construction plan included the addition of a building trades facility that could be shared with Front Range Community College, local carpenters and construction workers, and other students throughout the district. In the final proposal, the Centennial site was allocated $5,000,000 for overall improvements, and the building trades concept proved to be a key selling point. Along with the building trades facility, a redesigned art room, science lab, elevator, administrative office, and classroom spaces were included in the improvement package.

The presence and vision of the building trades teacher helped solidify Centennial's career emphasis and moved the school closer to developing a balanced three-legged stool. His vision and effort met several of the goals outlined in the 2001 vision statement and created a new sense of energy among Centennial's staff. Students learned a special set of skills, created their own manufacturing business, and expanded their presence in the community.

STRATEGY #8: ICING ON THE CAKE

As 2001 approached, most of the career program plans had been successfully implemented. Centennial's career department developed classes in marketing, management, and entrepreneurship. It collaborated with the Center for Community Participation at Colorado State University and used its personnel to teach an entrepreneurial class, culminating in the creation of a student business called The Grub Hut, which supplemented the school's lunch program. Centennial worked with another CSU organization, Bridges, the staff of which coached some of the students with special learning needs to help them find jobs and paths to permanent employment.

In addition to these efforts, Centennial's art teacher created another innovative career-oriented program. She owned a ranch and horse-boarding facility and proposed offering an equestrian class during the warmer academic terms throughout the year, using her ranch and boarding facility as a classroom. Students who enrolled in her class learned how to ride horses and also received insights into barn management, horse care, and breeding. This popular class provided students with another skill to take into post–high school life.

The art teacher also added a glass-fusing program to the art instructional repertoire, through Centennial's efforts to develop sister-school relationships with professionals who visited the program. When a team of teachers from La Entrada Alternative School, located in a suburb of Sacramento, California, attended a Discovery training seminar, one of the teachers shared that she was also a professional glass artist. Arrangements were made with La Entrada's principal to send the art professional to Centennial for a three-day elective week and to teach Centennial's art teacher and a group of interested students the skills of glass fusing. In exchange, a member of the Centennial staff offered to conduct a learning styles workshop for the La Entrada staff. With a three-day workshop, Centennial's art teacher was trained in the skills of glass fusing and enabled to add another component to the program.

A former special education teacher from Wyoming was hired to serve as Centennial's career transition coordinator in 2000. She created instructional seminars for graduating seniors and located shadow experiences, job placements, and apprenticeships opportunities for them. Many students felt comfortable and confident within the confines of Centennial but struggled in the world beyond its walls. Her personality engaged students and filled them with confidence as they ventured outside of Centennial's realm. When students expressed doubt, the teacher personally escorted them to interviews and appointments, gracing them with the accumulated wisdom of one who knew how to become employed. As Centennial's transition specialist, she provided students with opportunities to develop confidence and experience in the adult world. Her efforts filled a missing piece to help students make a successful transition into a post–high school experience.

Another teacher embraced opportunities to continually engage students in the community. One such opportunity came when the executive director of the Center for Community Justice Partnerships in Fort Collins approached Centennial with a marvelous idea to involve Centennial students. Having authored a grant to teach students restorative justice skills, and having an awareness of the school's reputation as a violence-free site, she selected Centennial to become a partner in the project.

Centennial used its government classes as the basis for exploring the causes of violence in America, the city, and its schools. The grant provided money for several students to become peer trainers in applying the skills and concepts of restorative justice. Students in the government class hosted an all-day workshop for local residents and students and played a key role in spreading the concept throughout the community. This opportunity further enhanced the status of Centennial students in Fort Collins and provided another avenue to transition students into post–high school life.

The Senior Project program offered students another connection with the larger business community. The concept was predicated on the belief that seniors could apply what they learned in high school to community issues. If students were to create an effective project from a personal interest in an issue of local concern, the outcome could benefit both the student and the community. Centennial teachers helped senior students define issues appropriate for inquiry and locate community mentors to guide and assist them in researching and preparing a final for a panel of interested people.

One of the first students to express interest in this program wanted to examine the causes of school violence and the impact programs like Centennial's Discovery and peer mediation could have on reducing school violence. Because this was an educational issue, she worked closely with school administrators. She prepared and distributed surveys to six junior high schools and interviewed school principals, students, and police resource officers. She carefully analyzed the data and compiled her report. She earned rave reviews at the formal presentation, marked by thorough data analysis and insightful conclusions. Her presentation substantiated the conclusions reached by national studies related to the importance of establishing strong relationships between adults and students in an educational setting.

STRATEGY #9: MEASURING STUDENT ACHIEVEMENT

Measuring student achievement was never easy at Centennial. High student achievement is another indicator of a quality school that requires increased yearly progress on standardized test scores. However, generating appropriate numbers in a consistent fashion was always challenging at Centennial, because the population was extremely mobile. With new students entering the program every six weeks, some having been out of school for more than a year, the staff had a difficult time assessing students or measuring the effectiveness of their instructional programs. Students often resembled Swiss cheese. They possessed "exceptionally flavorful" attitudes and "robust" enthusiasm, but often revealed large holes in their intellectual makeup from missing too much school. Therefore, it became Centennial's responsibility to blend its version of "ricotta cheese" created by the Centennial culture and fill in the empty spaces.

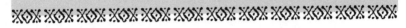

Motivating At-Risk Students

Teachers who are successful in reaching low-achieving students combine a high sense of their own efficacy with high, realistic expectations for student achievement. . . . [Teachers need to help students] set performance goals, develop learning strategies that work, enjoy successful learning experiences, and recognize that success come from within.

—M. Kay Alderman, "Motivation for At-Risk Students,"
Educational Leadership, 28–30

The assessment of student abilities began before they were admitted into the program. During orientation, all students were required to complete the TABE (Test of Adult Basic Education). This test is often used as an assessment tool to earn a GED. Test results indicated that 70 percent of Centennial's students were at or above grade level in reading and writing skills but had not produced quality work on academic assignments required in classes. The Discovery program, coupled with the staff's instructional approach, was designed to promote self-confidence, higher self-esteem, and practice in performing skills and demonstrating essential knowledge. The program worked for most students, but a substantial number were still two to four grade levels below acceptable high school reading skills. In addition, math skills, often taught in a sequential manner, proved frustrating to students whose attendance in school had been anything but sequential. Consequently, math test scores in every standardized test administered were always well below acceptable performance levels.

Centennial made a good-faith attempt to engage in the district's testing process. The staff wanted to have some measure to examine the strengths of its program and track student improvement. However, the district, looking for an appropriate way to communicate student achievement to the public, changed its measurement instruments three times during the ensuing decade. In the early part of the 1990s, the district used the Iowa Test of Basic Skills to identify district student achievement. Then the high schools shifted to the California Achievement Test in the mid-1990s. Finally, in 2001, the state of Colorado mandated that all high school sophomores take the CSAP tests (Colorado Student Assessment Program) in reading, math, and writing, and that all juniors take the ACT (American College Test).

As Centennial continued to earn credibility over the decade, the district also required students to participate in the district's own version of teacher-made, standardized tests. As Centennial participated in nationally normed tests and district tests, the staff attempted to level the playing field by limiting participation to those students who had been enrolled in the Centennial program for a minimum of one semester. If these tests were designed to measure the effectiveness of a school's program, it was only fair to test students who were actually veteran participants in the school. The district officials accepted the request, and only a selected group of students was included in the testing pool. However, this process changed with state-mandated testing for all sophomores and juniors.

Test results were analyzed and reported in annual accountability reports to the community. The analysis yielded several conclusions. First, tests results did not provide a clear picture of the strengths and weaknesses of the instructional program. The students tested, year to year, were never identical. Even if follow-up testing occurred, with assessments administered the next year, the student pool was drastically reduced due to Centennial's high mobility rate, making analysis difficult. Therefore, Centennial could not measure or track statistically significant differences in student achievement caused by program changes or instructional improvements.

Second, impressive gains in reading and writing skills were consistently tied to the quality, passion, and length of service of the English or reading instructors who worked with students prior to testing. Harold Hodgkinson's (1991) research on school improvement suggests long-term student contact with excellent instructors is the key to academic improvement. If high student achievement is an important mark of a program of excellence, it is absolutely essential that the school employ passionate, knowledgeable, and skilled instructors who teach students reading and writing skills and the proper test-prep techniques to employ when taking standardized assessments. However, the other half of the equation requires students to be present in their classrooms in order to have a long-term relationship with these teachers. With new students enrolling every six weeks, it was virtually impossible for teacher and student to develop a solid relationship in such a short period of time.

Students also have a tendency to reflect the passions and beliefs of their teachers. In the early stages of state-mandated testing, the political arena required that a teacher's personal feelings related to the law be left outside the classroom door. Many teachers felt imposed upon and resented the state requirements. In such cases, some teachers often expressed doubt about the purpose and legitimacy of mandated testing. In reaction, some students subtly or overtly sabotaged their performance in an effort to please their teacher or demonstrate disdain for the new requirement. If, however, a teacher encouraged his or her students to "show their stuff," students would follow the teacher's lead and engage in the testing process as if it were an intellectual challenge.

One of Centennial's English instructors is a perfect example of the latter approach. He had a passion for teaching at-risk students and wanted to teach them how to express their ideas in writing and to expose them to literature that would bring out their passions and interests. Using Centennial's Sophomore Academy to improve student achievement, this English teacher created a focused reading/composition program.

First, he convinced a school board member to become an anonymous donor for Centennial. Using the board member's funds, the instructor provided copies of the local newspaper to all staff members and, more importantly, dozens of bagels and cream cheese, breakfast for students who arrived at school without nourishment.

Second, like the Discovery class, he started each day with a sharing circle, to get students grounded. However, his approach was somewhat different. He passed out copies of the local daily newspaper and asked students to introduce themselves and then report on a specific article. In this way, he checked on their emotional readiness for learning and had them practice the skills of reading, summarizing, and analyzing the written word. Third, the teacher invited students to read high-interest books, provoking debate and controversy among his students. Using writing formats designed specifically to match the state assessment, he challenged his students with numerous writing prompts to practice their skills with topics related to the books used in class.

This approach proved to be successful for sophomore students. The English team was able to help students raise standardized test scores from an abysmally low school rating, 22 percent at the proficient level in 2000, to double that level in 2001. The scores were still well below average when compared to the district but represented a significant improvement from the previous year. Centennial still had a long way to go to close the achievement gap. However, the instructor's passion with students and teamwork with colleagues provided continuous improvement for the program.

Prior to the state-mandated testing, Centennial's students compared favorably with their peers at the comprehensive schools on district and nationally normed tests. Although Centennial's test results rarely surpassed district high school averages, it was clear that its students had academic potential. Over the decade of the 1990s, Centennial students' average ACT scores were 20+, which qualified them for admission to most state colleges in Colorado.

Reading percentiles were higher than national averages but lower than the district's. When the Centennial staff began emphasizing reading skills, its teachers successfully helped students raise reading percentiles on the Iowa Test of Basic Skills from the 38th percentile in 1992 to the 78th percentile in 1998. In district written-expression tests, scored locally, students moved from a 5.0 average score (on a 0–9 point scale) to a 6.5 average score. Centennial's students also scored approximately the same as students from other schools on district standardized tests in reading and language.

Centennial students demonstrated academic excellence in several ways during the decade. Jason, one of its former students, for example, took the ACT and earned a cumulative score of 34. He wanted to a perfect 36 and expressed the desire to take the test over to prove how intelligent he was. The staff convinced him that it wasn't necessary to be perfect on such a test to be admitted to college. When Jason graduated, he received Colorado State University's Presidential Award, which entitled him to receive tuition waivers and a new computer.

As the staff began looking for a positive indicator to measure the 2001 vision, an interesting statistical pattern emerged. Every May, the district administered a "graduate plans for next year" survey to seniors. The survey asked graduating seniors to indicate their intended plans for the ensuing year. Choices included working full time, entering military service, seeking vocational training, attending a two- or four-year college, or undecided.

The Centennial staff members were frequently frustrated after the completion of the graduation ceremony. Students who had just received their diplomas were often asked, "Now that you have earned your diploma, what are your plans for the future? What's your next vision?" Most would shrug their shoulders and say, "I don't know!"

Such a response became a professional irritation for the adults who had worked so hard to help students succeed. How could the staff labor to help students see the "vision" of earning a diploma, only to watch them shrug and admit they had not formulated any future plans? The high numbers of "undecided" survey responses troubled dedicated professionals. This undecided category became an appropriate indicator to measure progress toward achieving the 2001 vision of positioning students for success after high school. The undecided student responses became a testament to the school's inability to reach its vision. Therefore, staff began tracking the results of the district survey and challenged key personnel, specifically counselors and career teachers, to reduce the number of students who fell into the undecided category.

Using the 1999 survey as baseline data, analysis revealed that 50+ percent of Centennial's students, like other high school graduates, planned to enter a two- or four-year college. However, 30 percent of graduating seniors indicated "undecided" on the exit survey, and none of the graduates chose to seek technical or vocational training. Centennial needed to help all students create the next vision in their lives. The staff believed that the fewer number of kids who graduated as "undecided," the closer Centennial was to achieving its 2001 vision. The next year, the Centennial staff placed more emphasis on helping students plan alternative futures.

In 2000, survey results indicated the number of college-bound students remained constant, and the "undecided" group dropped to 26 percent, still an unacceptable number. Choices to seek technical/vocational training increased from 0 to 3 percent. With the added emphasis on helping students develop their own plans for the future, the 2000–2001 school year provided an atmosphere where staff members talked about futures with students. As a result, when the 2001 graduates filled out the survey, the number of college-bound graduates remained the same, but the number in the undecided category dropped to 13 percent. A larger percentage of students (27 percent) chose to seek full-time employment, an increase from the previous year's total of 11 percent.

After Centennial hired a career transition specialist, she was assigned to work with all seniors to help them develop a post–high school action plan. Collaborating with the counseling department, the building trades teacher, and other staff members, potential graduates began to visualize many options. On the 2002 survey, two- and four-year college options remained at 50 percent. However, the number of students considering military service increased from 3 percent the previous year to 12 percent. Undecided students hovered at 12 percent, and those choosing to pursue additional technical/vocational training increased from 0 percent to 7 percent. This data provided staff with a guide to measure success.

Cautiously, standardized assessment data was used to measure program and student success, even though the data provided a limited tool to measure organizational goals. Testing is one source of measuring success, but other data helped Centennial realize it had successfully awakened the imaginative potential in students. Daily attendance always hovered around 95 percent, a remarkable accomplishment for students who had barely attended class 50 percent of the time in their previous academic settings. In September, of the students identified to graduate by the end of the year, Centennial graduated between 90 and 95 percent. Over a twelve-year period, Centennial experienced only three fights, and no student was expelled from the school system. Attitude surveys, conducted by the school district, indicated that 98 percent of the students felt safe in Centennial, enjoyed a positive relationship with instructional staff and administration, and believed they could succeed.

These indicators are remarkable considering that many students previously had had toxic relationships with the educational system and, at best, expressed ambivalence about possible futures. As a leader, it is imperative to look at every aspect of the organization to measure and assess its effectiveness. These nonstandardized indicators played an important role in measuring the success of the Centennial program.

In summary, Centennial's "ricotta cheese blend" never produced National Merit Scholars. However, its academic program repaired some major deficits in students' knowledge and skills. The school's career program created greater awareness of options never dreamed of when students first enrolled at Centennial. Finally, emphasis on empowering students with prosocial skills created young adults who were self-confident, assertive, and willing to take risks to succeed in the adult world.

VISION 2001 RESULTS

In 1990, an immense vision for a restructured Centennial High School was outlined in a position paper to central office administrators. The document envisioned a school where alternative approaches to teaching and learning could be explored. It pictured a Centennial program that could work as a learning laboratory for in-district staff training and instructional experimentation. The document proposed that Centennial become the center for the district's summer school for students and teacher training and postulated that the alternative school would become a place visited by educators throughout the nation, observing effective and promising instructional practices.

Centennial achieved this status immediately after the completion of its first vision in 1995. The school hosted an average of seventy visitors from national and several international schools every year. They examined the Discovery program, service-learning program, the vocational program, and the Roads Scholars concept, replicating one or more in their own settings.

Dave Turner, from Widefield, Colorado, and several of his staff members visited Centennial on two occasions in 1998. They attended a Discovery training seminar conducted by Centennial's Discovery teacher and began an alternative program in the Widefield School District. Dave asked permission to call the new alternative school "Discovery High School," in reference to the program used to empower students. With great appreciation and humility, the staff expressed gratitude and honor to have a school named after one of its programs.

Other visitors were effusive in their praise for Centennial High School. Laura Theimer, a community member, wrote,

I was often touched to tears as I witnessed the interactions between you and the students. I knew the minute I walked through the door there was something very different and very special about the people who came together each day. I felt community, I felt freedom, I felt respect, I felt a multitude of things, but what I most felt was love. The building and all in it were truly alive. I am glad your program is being replicated little by little in other places.

The principal of Fremont School in Florence, Colorado, wrote,

We are very interested in "stealing" from you some of those things that you have developed into your culture. My teachers were impressed with the "feeling" of your school and spent the three-hour ride home talking about the Discovery program, the single vision of your students and the willingness of your staff to share their wisdom with us. The concern for student success and the dedication of your teachers and staff were very evident.

Mike Daniels and Bryce Anderson from a Centennial High School located in Peoria, Arizona, wrote, "Your collective vision and dedication to meeting the needs of all students is inspiring and humbling when reflecting on how schools conduct business. From the moment we approached the front step and saw the phrase 'catch the vision,' it was amazing to see that reoccurring theme in every facet of how the school functioned."

After such accolades, the district's assistant superintendent was approached with a simple question. "Isn't it interesting that Centennial hosts many visitors each year and several take away program ideas, yet the Discovery program and other ideas are not known or embraced by any schools or staff members within the Fort Collins School District?" He agreed and proposed a plan to move Centennial's successful program into other schools in the system.

He assigned a staff member from the district's alternative junior high school to collaborate with the Centennial staff. The new teacher worked with Centennial's Discovery teacher and developed an appropriate Discovery instructional model for the district's junior high schools. District support was appreciated, because it was believed that this intervention could reduce potential dropouts if the Discovery skills were taught to students at an earlier age. This type of instruction would empower younger students with the skills needed to succeed later on.

The two Discovery teachers proved to be effective planning partners and quickly designed a modified Discovery program for the junior high school level. District staff development money was dedicated to provide training seminars for interested staff members who wanted to learn these new instructional strategies or to teach the Discovery program at their schools. More than 150 staff members from the Fort Collins School District participated in these training seminars. The Discovery program is currently being used in five of the district's eight junior high schools. These training seminars were offered in addition to the workshops conducted annually by the Sopris West Educational Services Company, which purchased the training rights and now offers Discovery workshops throughout the United States.

By the spring of 2002, Centennial had successfully achieved the goals of both of its two visions. Ninety-five percent of the staff organized professional presentations of their ideas and instructional strategies to colleagues at local, regional, or national conferences. Several published their action research projects through Colorado State University. The program had empowered most of its students to succeed and to create visions for productive futures. The Centennial program and staff had significantly impacted public and private education and had offered its ideas to others with pride, honor, and humility. For over a decade, the collaborative energy of professional colleagues struggled, planned, created, and experienced as a team, dedicated to helping students become the best they could within the program.

Centennial flexed, moved, and changed as each new generation of learners passed through its doors. The program did not change in isolation, for it was never isolated. The staff was responsible and accountable to a larger community of stakeholders who observed and supported its efforts to become a quality program. These stakeholders included students, parents, neighborhood residents, the School of Education at Colorado State University, the school district administration, and the school board. Each group, along with other significant individuals, assisted in the school's transformation. Collaboration and cooperation with these stakeholders became an essential part in transitioning the program from the cutting block to an exemplary program.

7

SPREADING THE TENT
FOR THE STAKEHOLDERS

To paraphrase William Shakespeare, all the world's a stage and we are mere actors upon it. As the lead actor in the school play, the principal must exercise exceptional stage presence. It doesn't matter if you are the principal of a large or small school, in a rural or urban setting; you represent the school no matter where you are or what you are doing. You have no specific lines to memorize but need only to project your voice to capture attention, interest, and admiration from the community audience.

If you aspire to be a school principal, you must learn to accept the fact of being on stage all the time and an observed public figure. You represent the school in every setting in which you find yourself. People watch and judge your school by what they see you do in the shopping mall, the restaurant, the park, or driving down the street. The principalship requires you to become a diplomat, emissary, cheerleader, fund-raiser, counselor, and sage—all dramatic parts for which no formal training exists.

The mantle of success or failure falls on the school's symbolic leader, the principal. The image and role of principal carries a public mystique that can be used as an effective public relations tool. The principal has the capacity to mobilize public sympathy and financial support for ideas and programs. The leadership role provides the ability to motivate others to volunteer countless hours to help students succeed. The school leader has the public forum to convey his or her vision to others and to create an image of quality and excellence in the community.

Of course, the principal must have more substance than the Hollywood version of a Henry Higgins when trying to change the image of a school or program. The role of principal also brings an incredible amount of responsibility to deliver promises made and to demonstrate significant progress. Such commitment drives the integrity of the person who accepts the position and role. If one does not walk the talk, community observers will be the first to call the game and withdraw their support.

The previous chapters documented the exceptional effort and many hours professional educators dedicated to planning and implementing ideas in order to develop a quality program for Centennial High School. They came to work every day, engaged students in lessons, dealt with discipline issues, and handled paperwork responsibilities. Then, after the school day ended, they committed time and energy to debating, creating, and planning new ideas and strategies in order to improve the program for the benefit of the students served. Their dedication was remarkable.

However, another group of individuals, often on the fringes of the school arena, emerged and sought opportunities to contribute to the success of the program. These people were not professionally trained educators, only interested parties who wanted to contribute time, talent, and financial support to Centennial's continuous commitment to improve.

One of the principal's public roles requires him or her to become a catalyst to organize community volunteers and the resources they offer. The opportunity to work with community members and groups necessitate the creation of appropriate public relations strategies that will be discussed in this chapter.

STRATEGY #1: NURTURING PARENT INVOLVEMENT

One of the indicators of a school's success is the presence of a vibrant, active parent group. The number of participating adults whose children are under one's care provides the principal with a barometer to test the vitality of the school's vision. Parents will mobilize like a hostile mob if they feel the school is creating programs or permitting instructional activities that will harm their children. It is often more challenging to motivate parents to engage in school-related committees if they accept the quality of the status quo or feel disenfranchised by the system.

Sometimes parents emerge and offer their time and energy if they feel they can contribute to the improvement of the educational program. More often, however, when students reach high school age, parent participation in the school dwindles to a trickle. After all, these parents contributed many hours to their children's schooling during the early years, when they were elementary age. High school students, especially those who enroll in an alternative school, do not need or want their parents present in the school building.

In an alternative setting like Centennial High School, this attitude seemed most prevalent during the early years of the change process. Curiosity alone should have drawn parents to the back-to-school night in September 1990, but the staff outnumbered the handful of adults who attended, two to one. Some parents and community members served on Centennial's Vocational Advisory Board during the 1980s, but no PTA/PTO organization or site accountability/improvement team existed. Using a proven mode of communication, notices were sent home informing families of the scheduled Parent Advisory Board meetings. Throughout the fall the principal sat alone, waiting for interested parents to arrive. No one came. Since Colorado requires every school to have an organized Parent Advisory Board or accountability committee, the pursuit of adults to participate on the program's Parent Advisory Board site team continued in earnest.

In December, one parent responded to the invitation. He had been drinking heavily and came to complain about the school system. His daughter had recently enrolled in Centennial after being dropped from two other high schools. His concerns were respectfully noted, a different future was promised for his daughter, and he was invited to return.

During the holiday break, the administration resorted to personally calling all the parents. Personal contact or phone messages were left with almost one hundred families. At the January Parent Advisory Board meeting, ten parents appeared. The first official Parent Advisory Board was formed and charged with the responsibility of monitoring the progress of students and programs, examining educational opportunities, analyzing accountability data, and suggesting areas for program improvement. The discussion was lively, but many present expressed a sense of hopelessness about improving students' attitudes and potential for success. Parents learned about the restructuring process taking place and were invited to collaborate with staff members to improve the program.

By March, one of the parents presented the Parent Advisory Board with a list of questions for discussion that revealed the healthy concern these adults had for their children. Some of the questions she asked to discuss were:

1. How is Centennial equipped to work with students from dysfunctional families?
2. What types of professional training does the staff have in the areas of alcohol, drug abuse, and teen pregnancy?
3. Do you feel students who attend Centennial learn how to make their own decisions and experience the natural consequences of their actions, or does the school rescue them, like some parents do?
4. What is the definition of an at-risk student, and how is Centennial different from other schools in the way they handle them?
5. Is Centennial too late for most students? Should the school district provide earlier intervention programs?
6. What are some of the unique educational needs of students at Centennial, and how are teachers addressing them?
7. Is progress monitored in any other way than through grade-point average?
8. How important is the relationship between attendance and academics?

These questions provided a perfect platform for a thorough discussion about the need to restructure the school's educational program. Parents were also aware that Centennial had become a place for students to hang out rather than a challenging educational program to prepare students for adult life. For the next two meetings, these questions were discussed and recommendations made to the staff for program improvements. Then the weather turned pleasant and spring arrived; the parent meeting scheduled in May attracted no participants.

At Centennial, advisory board parents disappeared as their students chose to withdraw from school or lost interest in participating in the re-structuring process. The limited parent participation taught the staff several lessons. The parents were deeply committed to their children's success but felt powerless to intervene with adolescents who were phys-ically as big as they were and who constantly challenged adult authority, especially theirs. In addition,

- The adults believed they lacked adequate parenting skills to suc-cessfully deal with adolescents who challenged everything.
- Many were intimidated by the school system, didn't trust school of-ficials, and felt betrayed when their children were dropped from other schools for nonattendance.
- Parents did not feel as if they were in a partnership with professional educators. They felt the system had let them down, due to lack of communication and a lack of perceived concern for their child.
- They expressed intense passion about the educational system, re-membering with nostalgic fondness their own experiences as stu-dents. They longed for guidance from professional educators in a system that had once provided them with many of life's answers.
- In addition, they lacked consistency and time to follow through with the required actions to make change happen. As a result, the frequent turnover in participants at Parent Advisory Board meet-ings immobilized the group, and they languished into frustrated discussion sessions.

In order to ensure that parents functioned as significant participants in the program, the program needed to find consistent leadership to an-chor the goals and direction of the parent organization. In time, Cen-tennial was blessed with seven parent leaders who guided the Centen-nial advisory board, asked hard questions of the staff, stepped forward as the school's most staunch supporters, and became some of the most effective fund-raisers.

Tom and Judie emerged as parent leaders with the arrival of their son, Greg, at Centennial in September 1991. The couple organized various committees to support the school's new vision and mobilized many par-ents to begin participating in school functions and contributing funds to support new program ideas. Tom and Judie provided the missing leadership catalyst needed to ignite and hold the interest of adults.

Greg, blessed with wonderful artistic talent, designed the school logo but lacked motivation and vision in academics, and he worried his parents throughout his enrollment at Centennial. He enrolled and withdrew from the program five times, but Tom and Judie continued to support the Parent Advisory Board throughout Greg's academic wanderings. As a result, they cochaired the Parent Advisory Board from 1991–1994 and provided the leadership consistency Centennial needed to establish a solid parent voice in school affairs. They made a commitment to assist the school and to stay in touch with all the professionals in the building, especially Greg's teachers, and to assist where and whenever needed. Judie wrote letters of inquiry and support to district officials, the local newspaper, and community members whenever she believed the voice of a Centennial parent should be heard.

Judie viewed Centennial with a special interest. After Greg graduated, Judie wrote a letter of thanks to the Centennial staff. She recounted her experience as a teenager after dropping out of school and completing course work at night. Her former high school principal had rejected her request to receive a diploma from her original school and belittled her for making the request.

In the letter, Judie recounts,

That conversation with my former principal stayed buried for many years, causing hurt and a sense of not quite being good enough—not smart enough. But, Centennial staff, you have healed a lot for me by the caring and acceptance you show your students. Letting them know and feel you accept them and they are worth so much to their families, communities, but most of all to themselves. It has healed a lot of buried pain to see you help students reach goals and attain success when others have given up on them. You have helped me to realize that negative cycles can be broken. Thank you all for being strong in your beliefs that we are all someone special.

In 1994, parent leadership passed to two dynamic women, Cheryl and Karen. The two ladies saw leadership as a means to help Centennial become more financially self-sufficient. By 1994, the first five-year vision was becoming a reality and the parent support group witnessed results as their children began to blossom and succeed under the revised program structure. Grateful to Centennial for helping their kids turn themselves around, the ladies personally organized fund-raising activities and annual garage sales to provide additional funds to support elective week events and field trips and to purchase needed computers. They also became avid supporters of the school's health clinic and successfully represented Centennial's needs in the community.

In 1996, Doug became the president of Centennial's Parent Advisory Board and added a business approach to the organization. He supported the school's new vision to position graduates for success after high school and used his authority to challenge the staff to expand its horizons. He expressed a keen interest in the development of the building trades program and Centennial's connection to Front Range Community College. He also pressed the staff for answers related to academic preparation and helped secure more assistance in the career development program.

As the Centennial learning experience expanded to embrace a total inclusion model for students with special learning needs, the parent group began to reflect this emphasis. First, Jake, the parent who moved from Baltimore to enroll his son in Centennial's program, became the president of the advisory board in 1998. He continued to ask the staff to expand its role to ensure equitable educational opportunities for all students. He was impressed with the program and asked staff members to make presentations to the Parent Advisory Board by outlining the accommodations made to help each student succeed in the academic arena.

Jake's leadership was followed by Eileen. A former New Yorker, Eileen took pride in being assertive and getting the most for the school. As president, she regularly made her presence known in the school, dropping in to chat, monitor staff morale, and spread cheer and encouragement. Eileen volunteered as a classroom aide and collaborated with many staff members in order to discover how students were taught and how they learned. She spearheaded fund-raising events and became the program's community voice. Eileen adopted the school's vision and expressed a deep passion for the program, the staff, and the administration. She was extremely dedicated to the success of all students and pushed the professional staff to become better educators.

The key to effective parent support revolved around leaders who caught the vision of the school and supported its goals and operations. Like most organizations, the average Parent Advisory Board meeting ranged in attendance from five to twenty people on any given night, but the capacity to mobilize larger numbers to participate in various school activities became a simple task. As each new student enrolled at Centennial, parents completed an interest survey sheet. Parent involvement occurred in several areas. Some parents served on the Health Advisory Board for the in-school clinic, while others volunteered to participate on the smoking cessation committee. Still others chose to initiate a parent support group to discuss issues of raising teenagers, while others were more involved in various fund-raising events.

Parent Note

Dear Centennial Staff:
    You have shown us the hope that lies within our teens. The struggle for an education and to find out where they fit in has been an uphill climb for many. You seem to never give up. The accomplishments achieved this school year have been many. Your efforts to work as a team show real commitment to your students. Thank you,

—The Centennial Parent Support Group, May 1999
(This note was attached to a large box
of cookies left in the front office.)

By the late 1990s, parents at Centennial had become a visible presence. Each fall and spring, the Parent Advisory Board sponsored two all-school potluck dinners in which 100 to 150 staff, students, and parents shared supper and conversation. After dinner, staff, students, and parents were invited to step to the microphone and share dreams for the upcoming year or to celebrate the year's achievements. These meetings resembled an old-fashioned Fourth of July picnic in small-town America. The sharing was joyous, spontaneous, and heartwarming. Centennial had created a family atmosphere and established a unique feeling that the school was a special place to be.

Parents felt a sense of pride in the school and the environment created for their children. Even when some of their students did not succeed at Centennial, they still expressed gratitude to the school.

One parent wrote the following note:

> I just wanted to thank you for giving me the privilege of serving on the Parent Support Committee at Centennial. It has been a blessing to our family to learn about the school and the amazing things that are happening there for so many students. . . . Jenny received much from your school. Although she may never get a diploma, she has been truly blessed with support, understanding, appreciation, encouragement, and knowledge. I am sure it grieves you as much as it does us when you "lose" a student. Yet knowing how many kids you are helping and how many students will graduate from Centennial in the years to come is so encouraging to us and to the many people we are always telling about your school.
>
> We know that Centennial gave Jenny the best opportunity she could have ever had to get that diploma. For every "Jenny" that doesn't make it, there are so many who catch the vision and get that diploma because of your dedicated and caring staff. God bless you all for what you are doing for the students and community, many of whom would have no place to turn without Centennial.

In a later conversation, Jenny shared her post-Centennial life with staff members. After leaving Centennial in 1998, Jenny earned her GED and moved to California to travel and explore the world. Jenny said she needed additional time to discover her passion for learning and focus of life. In the next few years, Jenny developed an intense interest in environmental politics and music. She indicated that her participation on the Roads Scholar trip to Guatemala stirred her thinking about environmental issues.

Today, Jenny is enrolled at Front Range Community College in Fort Collins and plans to earn an associate's degree in environmental studies. In her spare time, Jenny sings, plays the guitar, and writes music. Jenny said she still uses the anger-management, planning, and effective communication skills mastered as a Centennial student.

STRATEGY #2: DISCO FOR PARENTS

After the restructuring of the Centennial program, both students and staff were trained in the skills taught in the Discovery program. The school culture had effectively improved its learning environment and provided consistency for students to succeed. However, something seemed to be missing in the program. Staff members soon realized they were leaving out an essential program component.

The Discovery program helped students learn how to deal with the school system, the work environment, and with authority figures, but in many instances, students were still operating in a crisis mode in their homes. Skills taught and used in school were not transferring to the family system, because old communication patterns were still operating as usual. One of the counselors recognized that parents felt inadequate to effectively deal with their students, because they did not have the skills to do so. When their students participated in Discovery program skills training, both they and their parents felt a sense of frustration. The parents were frustrated because they did not understand the language and cues related to their offspring's new behaviors, and students expressed dismay that nothing at home changed, because the new skills they learned didn't work in the family setting.

In response to this "cultural gap," a counselor volunteered to teach a Discovery training class to parents in the evenings. He was guaranteed a full house, because all parents were required to pay a $25 refundable check when their student was admitted to Centennial and the Discovery program. If the parent(s) attended all five two-hour sessions of the parent Discovery class, Centennial returned their uncashed checks. However, if they missed a session, their check was cashed and added to the school's general budget. At first, parents or a significant adult in the student's life attended sessions just to get their money back, but as the weeks unfolded, they came to class to learn new ways to deal with their student. In this manner, more than 90 percent of the parents attended these adult Discovery training sessions.

The counselor organized the class around topics that paralleled the Discovery curriculum being offered their students during the day.

Week One

Parents received information about Centennial's learning culture and definitions of attending skills, attendance policies, and the six Ps. At the end of the first evening, parents "circled up" into a conversation group, modeled after the sharing circle established for students in the Discovery program. During this activity, parents soon realized they had a lot in common with other adults in the room and were not experiencing the trials and frustrations of raising conflicted adolescents in isolation.

Week Two

The counselor engaged parents in exercises dealing with effective groups and anger management skills. Parents learned how Centennial emphasized collaboration rather than competition and how to use strategies to avoid angry confrontations with their children.

Week Three

Parents learned the transactional analysis communication skills, which defined the difference between the critical/nurturing parent, the angry/playful child, and the adult communication patterns taught to their students. They had an opportunity to role-play these skills using new strategies to present clear messages to their frequently "manipulative" children. The role-playing provided great entertainment for the adult audience and a way to practice improved communication skills to be used at home.

Week Four

Joel, the director of the Jacob Center, took parents on a "night of drinking" by showing them the kinds of games students play with alcohol. He also exhibited his collection of marijuana paraphernalia, providing parents with insights about how to identify a child who had chosen to become a substance abuser, and appropriate intervention strategies.

Week Five

The skills of conflict resolution and problem solving were outlined, and a mini-graduation ceremony was held by distributing certificates of completion and returning checks to those parents with perfect attendance. At the graduation ceremony, many parents openly expressed thanks to the school personnel for working with their child and helping the family renew its sense of hope in a positive future.

As the course was taught to parents, they were instructed to go home and ask their students to "teach" each skill to them. In this way, parents demonstrated interest in what their student was learning and provided another opportunity for the student to reinforce recently learned skills by directly teaching them to his or her parents. This assignment also provided an opportunity for parent and child to communicate in a non-combative mode and confirm for students that their parents cared about their success.

During the graduation ceremony, parents had a chance to express, verbally or in writing, their thoughts about the changes they saw in their children. Parents were thrilled with the changes they witnessed in their home life and in their student's attitude toward learning. A typical note stated, "Our family's use of the techniques taught in the Discovery program and parent Discovery class has proved to all of us, kids and parents alike, that we could interact with each other in a rational manner. We have emerged from the last five weeks with a renewed sense of hope for our son's future."

The counselor did not require additional compensation for teaching the night classes to parents. Every six weeks, he accrued an additional ten-plus hours of work time. In exchange for his teaching the parent class, the counselor was compensated by taking two "comp" days every six weeks, which met his needs more than financial remuneration. He liked to play golf, read, and hike. Having two days off every six weeks provided him with the incentive to continue his night class for the next several years.

STRATEGY #3: CREATING MORE FROM LESS

Most school administrators today complain they must live with budget cutbacks and do not have the staffing to create small classes or to expand curriculum offerings. Such complaints will always be cyclical and reflects the national and local economy as a whole. However, there are ways to do more with less if the principal is willing to think and act outside of the box and see restrictions as opportunities for creativity. The following job placements are examples of ways Centennial expanded its instructional staff with minimal cost to the school district or program.

As changes began to alter the school culture, enthusiastic conversations about the school dominated many public settings. At a restaurant one morning, a staff member was talking about the merits of the Centennial program and the impact it was having on students. During the conversation, the waitress, Judy, seemed to be hovering around the table and lingered more than expected for good service. Finally, unable to contain her curiosity, she broke into the conversation with an apology and asked what school was being discussed. Learning that the program being discussed was Centennial, she arranged to visit the school.

In August 1995, Judy appeared in Centennial's front office. After a brief tour of the building, the enthusiastic visitor explained she wanted to teach dance to students at Centennial. The principal thought it was a great idea, but Judie had a valid Colorado teacher's license; with no additional staffing funds, the administration was challenged to create a job using innovative funding sources.

Conducting a district search for additional funding to hire Judy, a rarely used pocket of money was discovered. Annually, the district sets aside several thousand dollars to pay stipends for assistant coaches. Noncertified community members were frequently hired to coach sports for the school system. Therefore, by stretching the definition of a modern dance class, Judy became a paid dance coach, and a one-period modern dance assignment was added to the master schedule. Centennial's new "coach" was placed under the supervision of a certified instructor.

Judy was an excellent addition to the staff. She motivated students with her enthusiasm, energy, and talent and ended the school year by taking a group of Centennial students to Colorado State University for a dance recital in May 1996. Centennial dance students also participated in the community homecoming parade that year, and the dance group helped the school win first place in its entry category. Due to this positive experience, Judy enrolled in the education program at Colorado

State University, earned her teacher's license, and is now an instructor working in Alaska.

John became a Centennial staff member in a similar fashion. He walked into Centennial to talk with one of counselors about the program. During the course of his conversation, John offered to teach karate to Centennial students. Centennial did not have additional budget funds to pay John for his services. However, as the discussion progressed, a mutual agreement that satisfied the needs of everyone was reached. John agreed to teach a one hour karate class to students as a physical education credit in exchange for permission to use Centennial's gym, free of charge for three days per week, so that John could have a place to begin his business as a karate teacher in the community. The counselor agreed to supervise John, who, like Judy, did not have a valid Colorado teacher's certification. John worked for Centennial for two years and offered students a skill that helped them develop mental and physical discipline.

Elizabeth was another community member who walked into Centennial High School and offered to teach students. Elizabeth, considering a career in music education, wanted to volunteer in schools to determine if she wanted to pursue a teaching certification. Elizabeth received a stipend from the building's instructional budget for twelve weeks. During that time, she created a music appreciation class and then an instrumental music class. She tapped into the creative curiosity of many Centennial students and motivated several to pursue their musical talent. Elizabeth completed requirements for a teacher's license at Colorado State University and is currently teaching in the elementary program in the Fort Collins School District. Elizabeth's presence at Centennial offered students an opportunity to explore avenues for personal growth.

Other sources of instruction emerged within the ranks of the Centennial staff. Many classified staff members are dedicated individuals with an exceptional work ethic. They complete routine and often mundane daily tasks, charged with addressing the business needs and details of running an organization. They work for an hourly wage that is far less than that paid to salaried staff or school administrators.

Each of these individuals has life experiences and talents that extend well beyond the limits of their job descriptions. For example, Sally, Centennial's registrar, participates in a local theater company, designing sets.

Her deep passion for theater prompted an offer to teach Centennial's drama class. She was hired as a drama coach and paid by the district's supplemental language arts funds. A certified instructor supervised Sally, and the drama class was added to the master schedule. Sally's class presented short plays to the student body every hexter, such as *A Christmas Carol* and *Ten Angry Men*. The drama class provided students with an outlet to explore their acting talents.

One of Centennial's receptionists was as a former magazine editor and writer. Marci requested to teach a journalism class to help students create a school newspaper. Marci, a credentialed instructor from New Jersey, had not applied for her Colorado teaching certification but had the experience and knowledge to guide students in the skills of creating a school newspaper. The program's instructional budget paid Marci an additional hourly wage, and interested students enrolled in the class. They created the school's newspaper, the *Centennial Times*, published once every academic term.

Susan, a Centennial parent, became the school's receptionist and stepped into the tradition of teaching classes for Centennial. She created a home economics class and sponsored a 4-H club. Susan exchanged one of her hours as the school's receptionist for the pleasure of teaching students. Her dedication to the program and student's success motivated her decision to do more than her job description required and expanded students' choices.

In September 2001, Al, the former owner of the local Harley-Davidson motorcycle shop and now a substitute teacher, had an opportunity to work in Centennial for several days. He was captivated by the school's learning culture and the positive attitude of the students he served. Al substituted at Centennial again, and within a few days, he offered the staff an inviting proposition. He had recently sold a few businesses and was in semiretirement. Since he had the additional time, Al offered to teach three classes at Centennial without compensation. As a result, Al taught two classes in business and one in English for a six-week hexter. He liked the assignment so much he volunteered to teach for a second academic term. Al was eventually compensated for his time and generosity with a token stipend for his contribution to the program.

In another opportunity to expand Centennial's staffing, the building-trades teacher collaborated with a local investment manager to team-teach a class in finance. Peter Villeneuve used the concepts from his book *Want to Be a Millionaire?* to teach Centennial students how businesses operate and how to invest in the stock market. He helped students form an investment club and track stocks purchased by the group. He also offered parents an investment seminar in order to help them plan secure financial futures for themselves and their children.

The strategy of creating additional staffing from community sources provided adjunct personnel and expanded Centennial's master schedule without begging for any additional staffing units from the school district. The school stretched the definition of "instructor" to include many interested community members who had talent, time, and skill to enhance the students' education. The staff carefully supervised and monitored their presence in the building to ensure that the safety and well-being of its students was never compromised. This approach enhanced the master schedule, reduced class size, and permitted the school to offer classes with content well beyond the expertise of the professionals on the staff roster.

STRATEGY #4: HIGHER ED CONNECTION

In the mid-1980s, in response to the *Nation at Risk* report, John Goodlad (1983) and the Holmes Group (1990) initiated a movement toward the creation of professional development schools. This concept called for teacher colleges and universities to collaborate with public schools in facilitating higher levels of learning for children, promoting better school environments in the preparation of teachers, creating opportunities for authentic inquiry and research in the public school arena, and fostering renewal for professionals in the field.

In 1993, the School of Education at Colorado State University collaborated with the Fort Collins public school system and initiated its first Professional Development School, at Rocky Mountain High School. In its infancy, a group of future teachers, taught by a university professor, met on the high school campus for six hours, two days a week. The students learned theoretical concepts and practical strategies of instruction, followed by hours of practicum experience in Rocky Mountain High School's classroom with mentor teachers.

In 1993, an education professor at Colorado State University's School of Education proposed making Centennial High School another PDS site. In her view, Centennial would provide teacher candidates with an excellent training opportunity. The school had a 20 percent minority population, the largest in the district, and more than 40 percent of its students were labeled with some sort of learning disability. The vast majority of the student population fit into the at-risk category and would present future teachers with many challenges. From Centennial's perspective, such a connection would expand the one-on-one adult relationships for its students. If an energetic, optimistic future teacher could connect with one of Centennial's at-risk youth, the student might find the encouragement to continue in school.

This relationship also presented the staff with an opportunity to work with potential teachers in a school setting. Professional educators have a responsibility to infuse future teachers with a passion and desire for educating all students who grace their classrooms. This PDS relationship would help potential teachers understand there are no "throwaway" kids. It is an essential part of their teacher preparation to develop a positive relationship with students and not be limited to the role of conveyors of content and skills.

Many students do not attend school to master subject matter. They must be coaxed, motivated, and challenged to learn. The most essential component in a teacher's tool bag is the ability to form a meaningful relationship with all of his or her students. An alternative learning environment stretches one's skills to develop such essential personal relationships.

A Professional Development School, housed at Centennial, created a forum for its staff to impact the future of education. The Centennial PDS would arm these future teachers with skills and insights to make them indispensable and in high demand for any educational setting in the United States. If an instructor can teach successfully at an alternative educational setting, he or she can teach successfully anywhere.

For the next two years, Centennial began to accept practicum students in its program. Subsequently, in spring 1996, a professor in Colorado State University's School of Education taught the first section of "Exceptionality, Diversity, and Human Relations" on the Centennial campus. Her students contributed more than forty practicum hours

Soul Searching

I would prefer to use the Professional Development School experience at Centennial High School to really help future teachers who are more directed to the kid than the content. . . . Ninety percent of the students who come and talk say . . . "I want to be a history teacher; I want to be an English teacher." Then there are about 10 percent that come in and say, "I really want to teach kids." Those are the one who should be at programs where they can do the most good with students. And sometimes the most good is being done at places like Centennial High School, because you save souls at Centennial.

—Interview with a Colorado State University education professor, included in Terry Deniston's doctoral dissertation notes

each of collaborative time with staff and students. This pilot program proved that a Professional Development School, within an alternative school setting, benefited both university students and the public school it served.

In the fall, Terry, a doctoral student at CSU's School of Education, replaced the former professor, creating a skyrocketing effect for Centennial's PDS. The professional chemistry between Terry and the staff was electric. She shared the same passion for students who were perceived as castoffs and endorsed a similar philosophy related to teacher preparation. Terry's personality and professional work ethic captured the imagination of the staff. She became an "insider" in heart, spirit, and dedication. Her high energy and compassion for high-risk students attracted staff members and opened opportunities for her to collaborate and team-teach with them.

Terry worked with a Centennial counselor and combined both high school and college students as collaborative learners in a diversity class that focused on college content and curriculum. The class served as a forum for interaction among college-age and high school students. Their shared learning experience was marvelous to observe.

Terry became so involved with the Centennial Professional Development School that she used Centennial's PDS program as the topic for her doctoral dissertation. Completed in 1997, Terry's dissertation, *Authentic Inquiry and Collaboration at a Non-traditional Professional Development High School*, used a qualitative approach to determine the value and quality of a Professional Development School housed in an alternative high school. As part of her research, she interviewed twenty-six university and high school educators. Her analysis demonstrated the important role Centennial played in the teacher-training program at Colorado State University.

Following her graduation, Dr. Terry collaborated with Centennial's administration to expand Centennial's role in CSU's teacher-training program by adding a methods class in 1998. For many years, the Centennial PDS was considered a "mini-program," because it did not have the necessary staffing to teach a pre–student teaching methods class on site. As a result, college students in CSU's education program attended the methods courses offered at comprehensive high schools and requested student-teaching placements at the sites, where they had a working relationship with classroom teachers.

In order to address this situation and encourage college students to choose Centennial as a place to complete their student teaching, the Centennial principal volunteered to be the on-site "teacher of record" for a methods class that was taught at the high school. Every Tuesday morning the administrator teamed with Terry and presented pre–student teachers various models of teaching, lesson-planning strategies, organizational skills, discipline techniques, and professional responsibilities. These college students were then assigned to work with mentor-teachers at Centennial in order to complete required practicum hours. On Thursday afternoons, the class met again to discuss the differences between the theoretical approaches presented on Tuesday mornings and the practical applications of the theories observed in the classrooms.

Professor and principal provided students with an excellent balance between head and heart. As the building principal taught theoretical foundations behind each concept as applied to an alternative school, Terry provided wonderful insights by combining personal teaching experience and research with her passionate reflections from the heart. In the second year of the Centennial program, the methods class was overwhelmed by requests from college students seeking admission. The section was limited to eighteen students, but requests far exceeded that number. In a four-year period, more than sixty pre–student teachers were trained at the Centennial Professional Development School.

Centennial received more than a dozen requests for student-teaching placements. This change added to the professional development needs of the staff by asking them to coach and share professional insights about instruction, classroom management, and teaching various types of learners. Every college student who successfully completed his or her student teaching at Centennial was employed at some location within the year. The Centennial staff was confident in its program and its ability to train exceptional teachers.

The connection with Colorado State University proved to be beneficial for Centennial staff members in several ways. First, each staff member could ask Terry to place a practicum student in his or her classroom. These students were often assigned to mentor Centennial students who had reading problems or needed more one-on-one attention. Second, Terry assisted the staff in creating and implementing self-directed reading seminars with attached college credit. Based on Centennial's PDS relationship with CSU, the staff members received a 40 percent tuition discount for college classes.

Third, staff members who had a successful relationship with a practicum student often requested that Terry place that student with him or her as a student teacher. Finally, the PDS program offered staff members an opportunity to conduct authentic research at Centennial, earn college credit, make presentations, and have their work published. During the 1998–1999 school year, Centennial's business teacher engaged in an action research project that studied the question, "How Do the Roads Scholar Trips Impact Centennial High School Students' Learning Styles?"

This study was followed by two additional research projects conducted by Centennial staff members. An English teacher published a pamphlet titled *Best Practices in Secondary Reading Instruction—Students Have Their Say*. This publication was followed by "Exploring the Possibilities of Social and Emotional Learning with At-Risk Students," a research project conducted in a collaborative effort by three Centennial staff members. These instructors presented their findings at local and regional conferences, adding to the credibility of the Centennial staffs professional commitment and the contributions being made by teachers in alternative settings.

The director of the Research and Development Center at Colorado State University expressed compliments to a Centennial instructor after she presented an action research project at a local conference sponsored by the University of Colorado at Denver and Metropolitan State College in April 1999. Her note read, "Her project titled 'Why Roads Scholars?' was exemplary teacher-as-researcher work. She was well-prepared, articulate, and contributed significant findings. Feedback from participants was very positive. The work was cited as an outstanding example of good questioning, excellent data collection and analysis process, and having action-oriented results."

For the college pre–student teacher candidates, the PDS provided many insights and practical understandings. Terry often asked her students to summarize their practicum experiences at Centennial. The responses speak volumes for the successful impact of the student's experience. Excerpts from several papers collected by Terry in spring 1997 offer the following insights:

> I think my practicum experience at Centennial was valuable for me personally. I wasn't sure what to expect from special education students in an alternative high school. I thought these students might be uncooperative and disruptive. I am happy to report this was not at all the case. I also thought these students would have problems comprehending the book. While some students read slower than others, they all could read with understanding. I probably learned more than the students. I learned that these students aren't "bad." They learn better and enjoy learning under different conditions than a traditional school. I also learned that if you treat students with respect, they will treat you with respect. (Vicki M)

> I have learned a lot about what it feels like to be in front of a high school class, instead of behind one of the desks. I have also experienced the difficulties and frustrations that can occur within the teaching profession and the huge challenge teachers are confronted with. Overall, I feel that I came away from my practicum with a greater understanding of the work teaching takes. I treasure the experiences I have had at Centennial for opening my eyes to the reality of how far I still have to go, and how hard I still have

to work before I am the teacher I want to be. I have the passion to teach. . . . What I still need are the skills, guidance, and, most importantly, more experiences like the one I have had at Centennial. (Ashley H)

What do you say about an experience that has changed your life? Words on paper don't seem to convey the excitement or emotion that Centennial has brought to me. I am so grateful for the experience. I am changed because of the students. I want so much to take the hand of every person who has ever uttered a negative comment about "at-risk" kids, and introduce them to the students I have been fortunate to work with. All it takes is getting to know them one-on-one. They are no different than any other student, in fact, some put my education to shame. . . . I have been able to hear about their good times and bad, their joys and fears, their anger and frustration. More importantly, they taught me that it was necessary for me to get in touch with those feelings in myself to become a better teacher. (Debbie L)

The Professional Development School added luster to Centennial's program. In any given week, the program permitted Centennial to add twenty-five to thirty caring adults to its staff in order to coach and motivate students. Colorado State University became a marvelous partner and valued stakeholder for Centennial.

The long-range impact of the program is still being measured, but an example, recorded in Terry's dissertation and observed by others, reveals the power of the connection. In 1997, the Arthur Vining Davis Foundation contributed funds for an evaluation of the Colorado PDS partnerships in Fort Collins. A group of educators visited sites and interviewed staff and students who participated in the program.

Nik, a Centennial student who had worked with a practicum tutor in the program, was invited to chat with the reviewers. Nik did not like school, often expressed a negative attitude, and used his multitude of invisible learning disabilities as an excuse to avoid completing work. He had given his tutor, Roberta, a difficult time throughout the semester. However, Nik was direct and honest in his interview. He expressed appreciation for Roberta's presence in his life, her patience with his behavior, and the assistance she had provided in helping him complete a history project.

The committee members, who had previously interviewed Roberta, remembered her telling them of her frustrations when working with Nik and pressed him with a question. "When Roberta leaves you at the end of the semester, how will you succeed after she's gone?" Without hesitation, Nik responded with an answer that brought tears to some eyes. "She will never leave me," Nik replied. "You see, Roberta is a little angel that will always sit on my shoulder . . . with a ruler . . . and will keep me on task."

Nik's impact on Roberta was powerful. Almost two years later she sent him the following letter:

> Dear Nik:
>
> I don't know why I'm doing this. I haven't spent any time with you in about a year and a half. I haven't kept in contact with you, and I haven't seen you except in passing. But maybe I need to tell you that working with you was one of the best experiences I have ever had. And now for some reasons I am cursed with this investment I have in you and in your success, particularly in your success in school. I know that school has been difficult for you, but I do not believe that school is impossible for you. I believe that your story is about perseverance, that your story is about tribulation and hard times, that your story is about success and victory over labels, victory over difficulties, victory over past failures. I believe your story is one about promise. These are the things I know about you—and I hardly know you. I have no idea where you've been, what your family is like, what you've done, or why you are wanted in twenty-five of the fifty states (okay, that was a joke)—but I do know that you can thrive if you put a little mind to it. You can be successful. You can do the work. You can beat the odds. You can show all those people who looked at you and expected you to fail. Maybe none of this is relevant to your life. If it isn't, then politely set this letter aside and go on your way but ultimately, Nik, the decision you make today will impact your life in the years to come and you, and only you, will have to deal with that. Where do you want to be in five years? What kind of job do you want to have? What kind of education do you want to have? Where do you want to be living? Perseverance, victory over hard times . . . success in the midst of failures. These could be the outcomes that await you. So, what will you choose?
>
> Someone who believes in you, Roberta

Nik left Centennial High School in December 1999 with less than a semester's credit to complete before earning his diploma. He completed his GED and enrolled in the Denver Institute for the Arts. He earned a certificate in culinary arts.

STRATEGY #5: PENNIES FROM HEAVEN

Based on its size, excluding staff salaries and building maintenance, Centennial had a yearly budget of approximately $30,000. A penchant to try the new and unexplored instructional strategies for the school's hands-on approach to learning, travels by the Roads Scholars, and creative electives exceeded its limited funds. Based on Centennial's positive image in the community and the district, stakeholders with deep pockets, huge hearts, and compassion for the school's needs, continuously stepped forward and provided financial assistance.

The district's assistant superintendent provided a compassionate ear and an open pocketbook for Centennial. He realized that the economy of scale limited the amount of money allocated annually to Centennial. At the beginning of each school year, Centennial's student population, on which district budget appropriations is based, was a great deal smaller than the total number of students it served throughout the year. Centennial worked with three times the number of students than the group that began each school year.

At high school principal meetings, Centennial's administrator frequently asked colleagues to transfer the activity fees of the students who had withdrawn or dropped out of their respective schools and enrolled at Centennial. They smiled and refused every time. In jest, requests were submitted for an allocation for Centennial's athletic program, which matched those of the comprehensive high schools. Since Centennial had no authentic athletic program to justify such an expense, these requests were politely discounted with a smile. However, the assistant superintendent did respond to Centennial's needs as a small site. He asked the staff to create a "wants and needs" list and submit it to him at the end of the first semester of each school year. If he had unspent dollars left in various accounts, he used some of that money to pay for items on this list.

Eventually, the district and building administrators created a formula to account for the increasing number of students who would swell Centennial's ranks during the course of the year. Centennial's enrollment figures were provided during the first week of school, along with a projected estimate, based on previous history, that accounted for the number of students Centennial planned to enroll over the course of the year. Using this number as a base figure, the district provided a supplement to Centennial's operating funds, which supported its instructional budget.

The school district's assistant superintendent became Centennial's strongest advocate. He supported the program through the initial years of restructuring and backed requests for policy changes and decisions made regarding student discipline and parent issues. In return, the school never hesitated to assist whenever he encountered a student problem that required a creative solution, student placement, or assistance with other district matters. Centennial became the district's safety valve to handle some of the most challenging students, and, in turn, the Centennial staff accepted these challenges and gladly worked with each placement made by district officials.

Community Image

Schools must compete for public funds with many other worthy recipients—agencies for health care, the aged, public safety, and transportation, for example. . . . We urge schools to seek goodwill and to keep their message in public view at all times so that it does not get obscured or forgotten.

—*Breaking Ranks* (1995), 92

In 1994, Centennial received an unexpected financial donation from the George and Louise Thornton Charitable Foundation, a family-managed foundation. The Thorntons chose to donate money to Centennial because they observed its commitment and progress in transforming Centennial into a quality school. During the previous years, the local newspaper had published stories about Centennial's changes and improvement in program and structure. In addition, the Campus Beautification Project received attention and the student's community service projects earned public praise. Due to this recognition, the foundation members believed the school could use a helping hand.

George and Louise asked to remain anonymous donors, because they did not want to be solicited by organizations looking for additional funds. For them, the choice to contribute foundation money to various causes was a private one. On a note attached to the first check sent to the school, they told the administration to use the money to motivate students to remain in school, and to send them a written summary of how the funds were used. Every year the school submitted a financial report to the foundation, and every fall the Thorntons sent a larger check. They chose to increase their yearly donations because Centennial never used any of the funds for administrative costs or as a supplement to an existing budget code. All of the money from the Thornton gift was used to serve unique student needs and to support "out-of-the-box" ideas created to motivate student performance.

The gift provided the flexibility to add value to many of the programs in the building. Each year, their contribution to Centennial grew, and the staff used creativity and flexibility to find unusual yet important uses for the funds. For example, since daily attendance was an important ingredient for success, the staff started rewarding students with perfect attendance by giving each eligible student a $25 check, one dollar for every day of the term. Money often provides a motivational incentive for teenagers, and every six weeks, ten to twenty students received checks for perfect attendance.

Some of the foundation money was used to support the operation of the school's health clinic and as a supplemental fund for Centennial's alcohol and drug intervention program. By the late 1990s, these funds were also used to purchase books and materials for students who could not afford them, for peer mediation training and partial scholarships for Roads Scholar trips, and to buy tools and tool belts for students who graduated from the school's building trades program.

In 1998, Rachel, a bright, articulate young woman, wanted to enroll at Front Range Community College but her family could not afford the tuition or the required books, uniforms, and supplies. In August, a distraught, frustrated Rachel visited Centennial to see if the staff could help her figure out how to find the additional money to attend college. Even though Rachel had already graduated from Centennial, the staff stretched its authority and gave her the additional $500 from the Thornton funds to start her on her way. Rachel was told the funds came from an anonymous donor. In a thank you note, Rachel said, "I was so happy to find you were able to contribute to my financial situation. I have received the money and with it have purchased scrubs, uniforms for dental assisting, books for class, and other school-related materials. I am very thankful for what you've done for me and words can't begin to express my appreciation. You are a wonderful person with a kind heart. Your money will not go to waste, and I hope that one day I can do for someone else what you have done for me."

Kathy, Rachel's mother, also sent a thank-you card, which read, "Recently you gave my daughter $500 to assist her with college expenses. With school rapidly approaching she/we found ourselves coming up short of funds. All I could tell her was God would provide. Within a week she was guided to you. You have enabled Rachael to continue on her path to success and I wanted to thank you. I know how important an education is and I deeply appreciate your contribution to her. She is a wonderful, intelligent young woman and I am sure with this opportunity she will achieve her goals."

Rachel graduated from Front Range Community College with an associate's degree in 1999 and has been a successful dental assistant ever since.

The most unusual use of the money provided by the Thornton funds was the purchase of an Angus calf. One of Centennial's students wanted to raise a calf for a 4-H project and "borrowed" $650 from the fund to pay for the steer. The student housed the steer at a staff member's ranch throughout the summer and displayed the calf at the Larimer County Fair in August. He sold the steer for $1,250. After paying expenses and the loan, he made a profit of $75. He didn't get rich, but as the Thorntons were told in the annual report to them, "Your funds provided him with the opportunity to try something that was far beyond his life experience. He worked at the ranch every day and learned a great deal of personal responsibility and the value of hard work."

As a financial stakeholder in Centennial, the Thornton Foundation added the little extra to make creative use of imagination become a reality. George and Louise granted the staff the flexibility and trust to use the funds to enhance and expand Centennial's program possibilities and to find ways to motivate students to stay in school.

Another financial stakeholder appeared on the steps of Centennial one day in the spring of 1998. Michael Moravan, a community patron, expressed a desire to assist Centennial in some way. He explained that he and his wife, Elaine, had no children in the school district but had closely followed the school's progress in the newspapers. They had attended some of Centennial's commencement exercises and were impressed with the school's alternative approach to education. He related that they had wisely invested in the stock market and wanted to contribute some of those earnings to the school. He concluded by asking if Centennial could use an additional $10,000.

The staff's new vision of positioning students for success after high school was described to Michael. Due to the characteristics of students who attend alternative high schools, however, they rarely proceed in life in a continuous, sequential approach. That is, some students often choose many directions and stop and start several times before they figure out what they want to do and what special interest captures their attention. Many of these students graduate from high school and explore the world for two to five years before deciding what course to pursue. They often return to Centennial looking for scholarships or grants, only to discover that none exist. Unfortunately, service organizations in Fort Collins, like other localities, take pride in interviewing and selecting scholarship winners from graduating seniors with lots of potential for immediate success. They rarely hold money in their coffers for years, waiting for students who will *eventually* design their life goals.

Therefore, it was suggested that Michael consider using his proposed financial contribution to establish the first "post–high school" scholarship fund. Under the scholarship guidelines, any graduate of Centennial High School could apply for a scholarship. In return, scholarship recipients promised to return 10 percent of the scholarship to the fund or contribute time to tutor and assist other students still enrolled in school. As tutors, they would serve as models of post–high school success for current students. Michael liked the plan, presented Centennial with a check for $10,000, and turned over the details of granting scholarships to Centennial's counseling department.

Slowly the word spread throughout the community that Centennial had established a special scholarship for graduates. In the first year, the school granted seventeen scholarships, ranging from $500 to $1,500. Michael and Elaine, pleased with the success of this program, renewed their contribution for another year. During the 2000–2001 school year, nine more scholarships were granted. The Moravans were community members who saw potential in students who were attracted to Centennial's alternative educational approach. They had the resources to provide the financial needs of post–high school students and created a unique program that still exists. Several community members continue to contribute to the scholarship fund established by this couple.

Many other financial stakeholders committed to Centennial's success surfaced over the years. At Rotary Club meetings, in grocery stores, at church gatherings, or in the mail, the school received checks from people who wanted to contribute to Centennial's program. No matter if the amount was $25 or over $100, each one of these community members generously endorsed the program with financial support. They believed in the school's vision. They recognized the need and wanted to contribute to the continuation of the program's success.

STRATEGY #6: POLISHING THE COMMUNITY IMAGE

The Centennial staff was constantly in awe at the kind of passion community members expressed when they visited the school and experienced the learning culture. Lewis Lachman, a retired educator, moved to Fort Collins and became a self-appointed educational observer. He visited all of the Fort Collins schools and also asked to spend a morning at Centennial. After the visit, he sent a letter that read, in part,

> Prior to my visit to your facility I believed that there were three high schools and Centennial. My mind has changed. There is Centennial and three other high schools. Without any doubt, your school is student oriented as opposed to curriculum run. If what I saw done for one student in seven days is the norm, there is little doubt that every student passing through the portals of Centennial will successfully graduate. Each room I visited reflected the individuality of the instructor with the singular purpose of providing each student with the tools necessary to make him or her a citizen of the school, community, state, nation, and world. The teachers I met made me feel that being in their class was the place to be.

Even Centennial's next-door neighbors complimented students for community spirit. In the early 1990s the administration used to receive negative telephone calls from senior citizens who lived in an apartment complex next door to the school. They complained about the noise, trash, and the presence of unusual-looking adolescents in their parking lot. In those early years, a leadership class was added to the program to help build a positive student culture. After another neighbor complained about the school, students enrolled in the leadership class were asked to find solutions to this problem.

After examining all aspects of this public relations problem, one of the students offered a simple solution. She contended that these people had once had homes and backyards and envied Centennial for its park. She proposed that the school could eliminate the complaints by sharing some of its land with the neighbors.

Implementing this solution, the students cut a hole in the fence that divided the apartments from the school, added a gate, and planted raised vegetable beds for the neighbors to use. Each May, Centennial students planted a vegetable garden during an elective-week activity, printed flyers inviting apartment residents to use the garden, and left for summer break. The garden was the seniors' to use and was effortlessly watered by the Centennial lawn sprinklers.

Dennis Tobin, Vickey Nastav, and Kathy Mass, residents of the next-door apartment complex, sent the following note to school: "All of us garden squatters would like to extend a warm appreciation for your offer of maintaining the garden plots at Centennial High School. It provided us with the means of community contact, as well as a reprieve from the hectic worries of modern existence." The school never heard complaints from neighbors again.

The public relations effort was expanded to the neighborhood by sending a letter to residents every fall. The staff hand-delivered the letters to all residents within a two-block radius of the school. The letter announced that school would be starting within the next two weeks and that many high school students planned to return and park in front of the neighbor's houses. The staff invited residents to call the school if they had any concerns about students making noise, parking in driveway areas, loitering before or after school hours, dumping trash, or smoking. The letter expressed the expectation that adults could collaborate to help young people develop the skills and attitudes necessary to become good citizens of the community.

In this manner, the staff developed a positive relationship with neighborhood residents, and calls received reflected a cooperative tone rather than one of complaint. These conversations were in the nature of information sharing, because the people knew the staff wanted to respond to their needs. One telephone call requested that students save a parking place in front of a house adjacent to the school. The resident was physically incapacitated and needed to make frequent trips to his physician. The neighbor's request was announced in a school assembly, and thereafter a free parking space was available, due to student awareness and a spirit of cooperation.

Centennial stakeholders emerged from various corners of the community. They contributed time, talent, and money to help the program succeed. The staff appreciated its stakeholders' financial gifts, donations of books and computers, participation in school events, and presence in the building. Centennial was the fortunate recipient of an outpouring of genuine community spirit, forged by the recognition that Centennial had changed, improved, and offered students a quality program.

STRATEGY #7: A ROSE BY ANY OTHER NAME

To a certain extent, Centennial's graduation ceremony represented the culmination of the staff's effort to help students succeed. However, the staff also viewed this ceremony as an event that united all the students and community stakeholders in an hour of personal triumph and celebration. Each year, Centennial graduated between fifty and seventy-five students.

The graduation ceremony drew six to eight hundred people into a community auditorium. Unlike the fast-paced program of the comprehensive high schools, which were forced to move three to five hundred graduates through the ceremony in less than an hour, Centennial's ceremony focused on recognizing the accomplishments of each individual graduate. The rose ceremony, an integral part of Centennial's graduation, became the hallmark event of the celebration. As school board members suggested, "It's a two-tissue event."

The rose ceremony was designed to give every graduate a personal opportunity to speak to the audience for two to three minutes. During that speech, each graduate, with two roses in hand, selected two people from the audience to thank for helping him or her graduate. Recipients of the roses were asked to come forward and accept the gift. The students' words, coupled with embraces that followed, were visible symbols of the healing and joy that took place between family members, former teachers, current instructors, and significant others in the auditorium. The emotions that poured forth became overwhelming at times, as hurts and struggles of the past were washed away with tears and hugs.

One particular rose ceremony event demonstrated the power of this ritual. During the ceremony a female graduate stepped to the microphone and held only one rose in her hand. She began by saying, "I have only one rose to give out tonight, but it goes to two people who don't like each other very much. I present this rose to my mother and father for their continuous love and support for me."

The victim of an unfortunate, unpleasant divorce, the young woman looked about the audience for her parents to step forward. From the far right corner of the auditorium a man made his way to the podium, while a woman, seated on the far left side, walked forward. They met in the center of the auditorium, and all three embraced to the thunderous applause of the packed arena. That moment may have consumed a microsecond in their lives, but the three of them celebrated the success of a young woman's accomplishment. The community participants recognized the power of the Centennial program to impact young people and celebrated every time the graduation ceremony transitioned another group of students into adulthood.

THE CENTENNIAL TENT

Centennial represented, and still represents, a tent that shelters high-risk students who need a positive relationship with adults, an alternative format for learning, and opportunities to demonstrate personal, academic, and career successes. Every tent is securely anchored to the ground by stakes supporting each corner. Centennial was supported by individuals in the community who planted their stakes firmly in the ground and had a place in the successful completion of the organization's goals.

Centennial was blessed by a diverse group of community members who not only cheered on the school but also backed it with time, talent, and financial support. By the end of the 1990s, Centennial had changed its image in the community. Centennial High School had become the city's golden child, for its educational success in Fort Collins. As Fort Collins mayor Ray Martinez stated in a letter to the school, "You are right that there is no such thing as a throwaway kid. By being a positive role model and caring about youth, you have improved our community."

For over a decade, the staff learned many lessons about creating visions, developing implementation plans, dealing with human differences, and practicing public relations. The last five-year vision may have been easier to implement than the first one, but it presented different kinds of challenges. Without the pressure to fix it up or shut it down faced by Centennial in the early 1990s, the biggest challenge Centennial faced was small by comparison. The continuous turnover in staff required its members to spend more time reviewing and renewing components of school culture, norms, and the new vision. The staff needed to collaborate and embrace a shared vision. With a 50 percent turnover in staff during the last five years of the 1990s, progress was often slowed by the need to re-articulate common practices and beliefs. Within the walls of Centennial, progress seemed to move at a snail's pace, but for the most part, the late 1990s earned the Centennial program continuous public support and praise for all of its innovations.

8

REFLECTIONS

People who choose to enter the educational profession need to decide where they can make the biggest impact on the future. Some choose to remain in the classroom and touch the lives of students every year, while others go into middle-level administration or write curricula to guide teachers or impact the school district. Some opt for the challenge of becoming a school principal, because they want to be on the front line, engaging students, parents, community members, and teachers in the ongoing process of educating the next generation.

Of all the positions in the field of education, it is amazing to observe the influence, power, and authority the principal commands, coupled with a huge dose of responsibility that challenges heavily one's integrity and character. Most principals are effective program managers and successfully maintain expectations of schools. They provide stability and guidance for their respective schools year after year by orchestrating the development of building goals, managing school budgets, assisting and evaluating teachers, negotiating parental concerns, and implementing district directives and school policies.

The current professional literature refers to another type of principal, the transformational leader, who approaches the position in a different way. This type of leader uses the power and authority of the position to expand the concept of leadership by embracing futuristic thinking and risk taking. He or she empowers and collaborates with others, creates reality from imagination, and experiments with ideas. This type of principal is willing to attempt the impossible and take responsibility for failure if and when it occurs. He or she believes that student programs can become more efficient, less expensive, more productive, and more enjoyable for staff, students, and parents. This principal uses evaluation data to measure progress or to create new ideas as a daily routine; creates big-picture thinking for the school, staff, and community; and develops action plans that are quickly implemented. (See, for example, M. Fullan or P. Senge books/articles for more detailed descriptions of this leadership style.)

The transformational principal nurtures collaboration by empowering staff, students, parents, and community members to believe in the school's vision and purpose in order to achieve lofty goals. The leader challenges others to become contributing members of the school team and leads with passion. He or she does not see the position as a job but as a cause to be embraced.

The transformational principal must learn how to master many people skills, create and implement visions and ideas, orchestrate the change process, anticipate future needs, communicate with a variety of audiences, and maintain a positive sense of self in order to remain healthy and viable under daily stresses. The current belief that power comes from "sitting in the principal's chair" has become a myth, because it is a rare occasion. The real job responsibilities occur in the halls and classrooms, on the school grounds, and in the community. Most of the time, one's ability to effectively operate as a principal evolves through on-the-job experience and not through prescribed actions embedded in administrative preparation classes. The following reflections address attitudes, ideas, and behaviors that should help make the job of the transformational principal much easier.

COURTING THE CENTRAL OFFICE

Reflection #1: Put on Their Moccasins for a Short Visit

If you are a new principal or, more importantly, new to the district, this approach may be essential in establishing a long-term, successful tenure in your position. There are several key people in the district with whom you must develop and nurture a professional relationships. These people will make your job much easier if they know you, trust you, and understand your goals. They include the following department heads and service personnel: grounds, maintenance, security, curriculum, staff development, personnel, records, transportation, and book acquisition. As diverse as these positions may seem, the combined responsibilities and activities of the people that fill them represent an infrastructure critical to the success of your building program.

Schedule time to visit, on their turf. Make appointments to talk with them about their communication needs, protocols to follow, how they prefer to handle crises, and how you can reach them in an emergency, and vice versa. Spend time getting to know them as individuals, not only as school district service providers. The amount of time you spend front-loading an exchange of ideas, needs, and personal preferences will pay huge dividends later when you need assistance from any one of them, or if they need your help in correcting situations created on your campus that impact their area of responsibility.

It is also important to be on a first-name basis with the district office receptionist, your supervisor's secretary, the superintendent's secretary, and the person who delivers the interschool mail. Take time to say thanks for a job well done or save a special joke or story to share without asking for anything related to business. Such additional acts of kindness let these people know they are more important than mere service providers. Such familiarity breaks down barriers created by loosely coupled organizational structures that are often too big to support personal relationships.

Centennial High School had a tradition of hosting a Thanksgiving meal the day before the holiday. The staff and students invited personnel from all departments who had supported or assisted the program during the previous year. At the meal, staff and students gave public thanks to specific individuals and made an effort to call each support provider by first name. When the principal and staff make a concerted effort to develop this kind of relationship with support personnel throughout the district, the school is never viewed by others as a "high-maintenance" building filled with difficult people. Support personnel will serve you out of courtesy and respect, not merely out of contractual obligation.

The institutional position of building principal earns the mantle of power and authority that sets him or her apart from peers. Depending on the principal's personality, the position can either foster a tacit tolerance for the role or create a marvelous support system based on honor and respect. Taking time to develop personal and professional relationships with key service providers, whether through a phone call or by individual contact, will quickly correct problems and earn continual cooperation.

Reflection #2: Talk a Little, Communicate a Lot

After you have been hired or appointed to your new job as principal, communication with others must be expanded. It is important for your immediate supervisors to know how you process information and what you believe about your role and responsibilities. Share your belief statements with your supervisor in writing first, then in person. Your supervisor will extend more trust and respect for your decision making if he or she knows how you think and process ideas before a crisis occurs—and crises will always occur.

Take time to nurture a working relationship with your supervisor's secretary. She or he is the first one to receive a call from an irate parent or a neighborhood resident's complaint about student issues. How the secretary responds to that call and how the situation is presented to your supervisor will dictate how effectively the problem is resolved. If your supervisor's secretary knows how you operate, how you cope with crises, and how you handle such situations, every event will already be positioned for a successful resolution.

It also helps if you give the secretary a "heads-up" when you know a call is going "up the chain of command." If you are unable to dissuade an angry parent from pursuing a complaint, it is necessary to let your supervisor know of the impending caller. Secretaries in the public school system do not make salaries that justify being the doormat for callers who want to vent. Professional courtesy dictates an appropriate level of communication to solidify your relationship with the central office staff. A brief call will save a thousand words of explanation and time on the computer.

Reflection #3: Do More Acting than Asking!

As a principal, you are given authority to run your site, follow school law, and implement district policy. You are paid a reasonable salary to live on the firing line and to handle situations as they arise. If school board policy does not exist, create a short-term policy for your school to expedite an unexpected situation until the school board or district lawyers can provide an official answer. On site, you need to handle the safety and welfare of your students and staff—and some situations cannot wait for an official ruling.

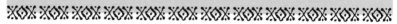

The Principal's Leadership

They must display the courage to lead even when no one else offers to don the mantle of school leadership. A principal who leads well keeps the objectives of change in everyone's sight through the most trying times, when clouds of despair block the view of the future and prospects for improvement appear bleakest. The principal helps people believe in the larger possibilities in order to sustain the hopes of those who want to create a better high school.

—*Breaking Ranks* (1996), 100

Don't ask permission to try new ideas or for an official district interpretation of current programs. If a situation calls for a risk, take it, as long as you are willing to be responsible for the consequences that follow. That is where integrity and responsibility converge. Whenever a leader requests official clarification of a policy or procedure, he or she will usually receive a more restrictive definition than wanted. If, however, one applies a professional interpretation to a policy in order to meet the school's specific needs, and it works, central office approval usually follows. As long as the school's practices do not jeopardize the health and safety of students or cause a massive protest from the parents or community, the system's stability will tolerate such behaviors from site leaders who desire to try new ideas or handle situations for which no policy statement or precedent exists.

This proposal is not advocating administrative anarchy, but the reality of the principalship is that you are empowered and charged with the authority to run a successful program at your site. As the Nike Company says . . . "Just Do It!" Such authority often calls for you to provide an immediate and/or creative response to events and situations that occur. As long as each decision is measured against your professional beliefs, appropriate data, and the vision/mission of the school, your leadership skills will generally be supported and endorsed by the district.

ESTABLISHING SITE-BASED LEADERSHIP

Reflection #1: Nurturing Credibility

Getting hired for the job of principal does not automatically ensure immediate credibility, trust, and integrity. You need to earn the respect and following of the employees at your site. In your initial months, all you say and do will be scrutinized, analyzed, and judged, even if only limited information is available. Here are some suggestions to formalize your credibility as a principal.

First, in order to earn your leadership stripes, it is essential for you to be extremely clear about your philosophy and beliefs related to leadership, students, public relations, employees' expectations, and decision making. You may need to send your staff written statements and post them for public consumption. Never miss an opportunity to continuously state and reinforce your beliefs when you attend various meetings.

Second, effective communication and relationships with employees and students are key components to establish credibility. Become familiar with the learning styles of each employee and discover how each responds best: to written notes, one-legged conversations, or longer sit-down talks. Use multiple formats to communicate information. Do not rely solely on e-mails, hard copy, or the public address system. Staff members need to hear and process the message in their preferred style, not just yours.

Third, in order to monitor the morale of the building, select specific employees to be your "cultural barometers." Select a couple of staff members, without their knowledge, and observe their reactions to events, policy implementations, and staff discussions. These staff members become your "mine canaries." Before the advent of sophisticated technology, miners used to take a canary into the mines with them to detect odorless toxic gases. As long as the canary sat in the cage singing, the miners knew they were safe. When the bird stopped chirping, they knew deadly gas was present, and they evacuated the mine.

Select "staff canaries" who reflect different learning styles. Each style will react to events in a unique way. For example, if one of your selected staff canaries is a concrete-sequential, he or she will thrive best when order, quiet, and structure prevail in the building and will have an adverse reaction when the culture seems to get too chaotic. Other staff members who are abstract-random learners exhibit a wonderful intuitive sense and make decisions from the heart and feel most comfortable when the daily interactions among people exude laughter and an easygoing manner. If you watch your staff canaries and are sensitive to their change in moods or reactions to building events, you can anticipate and analyze the situation and plan intervention strategies that need to be made.

Fourth, avoid creating the impression that the principal listens to an exclusive "inner circle of influence." There is nothing more demoralizing for a building than to inadvertently foster the image that a select group of people has more influence than other groups in the principal's decision-making process. In larger schools, access to the principal is often a key determiner in labeling members of an inner circle. For example, assistant principals or counselors are often accused of owning the principal's ear. In order to avoid this dilemma, hold forums or pizza lunches with an open invitation for all building constituents to attend.

Fifth, since we are all human and not always on the same page with each other, conflicts occur and are a normal part of a working relationship. Establish a protocol for a mediation process in order to quickly and honestly resolve conflicts between disputants. Many people go to great lengths to avoid conflict and often harbor resentments that interfere with effective job performance. With a conflict-resolution process in place, run by trained mediators, issues can be resolved to the mutual satisfaction of both parties, and job productivity and harmony reestablished.

One of the most time-consuming and energy-draining activities a principal encounters is to legally craft a letter of reprimand to a disgruntled employee or to become mired in the legalities of the district's grievance procedures. This process is not enjoyable for the principal or the employee involved and erodes the morale of the building. Even though such a formal process is confidential, the grapevine within the building creates rumors, fosters unfounded speculations, and often polarizes the staff. Avoid this headache by being proactive in establishing a mediation process. Such a process requires staff members to have the professional integrity and courage to trust that the system is designed to maintain and enhance a solid working relationship among peers.

Reflection #2: Out of Sight, Out of Mind

Once a vision has been created and goals identified, a tendency exists to check this exercise off the yearly to-do list and put it aside. However, an organization trying to pursue a long-term vision must keep each goal leading toward that vision in public view, at all times. If it is out of sight, it is out of mind.

For example, one of Centennial's early goals was to have students achieve 95 percent daily attendance. The staff created an attendance chart on a whiteboard and posted it in the school's lobby. One axis of the chart had numbers 100 percent to 88 percent and the other axis listed each month's date. The 95 percent level was marked in a bright color so all could see how close students were to the attendance goal each day. The daily student announcements started with "Yesterday's attendance was," followed by words of praise for achieving the prescribed goal or words of encouragement to try harder to get to school in the upcoming week.

The message was clear to students and the community: Centennial valued student attendance and set its goals of achieving or exceeding 95 percent every day. Once the goal was achieved on a regular basis and was no longer emphasized, and with a change in administration, the chart came down. The central office tracked attendance for the accountability report, but the goal of achieving 95 percent daily attendance no longer captured the attention of the students or staff.

In another example, a colleague interviewed for an administrative position in another school. At the end of the interview, when time is usually allocated for candidates to ask questions, she inquired, "What is the vision and purpose of this high school?" Search committee members were caught off balance, looked at their shoes, and one or two of them tried to express some vague notion of student success for productive citizenship. Clearly, the interview committee did not sufficiently understand the vision and mission of their program to convincingly convey these ideas to the prospective candidate. Consequently, the candidate was unimpressed with the commitment and focus of the interview committee and chose not to work in that building.

The vision of an organization must be the dominant theme of the program and the central understanding and passion of its employees. If all personnel have the same focus, they can achieve marvelous results. However, if creating a vision and yearly goals is reduced to an annual exercise and placed in the bottom of a desk drawer in September, then the organization is merely treading water for another year. Keep what is important visible!

Reflection #3: To Decide and Not to Decide

Decision making and building governance often present the principal with an uneasy balance between authoritative use of power embedded in the position and the empowerment of staff and students to have a voice in and ownership of how their school functions. The principal must clarify and be comfortable with his or her philosophy related to decision making and shared authority. Today's principal is often in the precarious position of finding the most effective balance between top-down decision making and collaboration. No correct formula exists. Every site and every combination of players presents a different picture.

In order to be most effective, the leader needs to establish several models and protocols to follow with the organization. First, the leader must clarify what aspects of the decision-making process are autonomous—that is, identifying what decisions are totally made by the organization's leader. For a building principal, these include, but are not limited to, decisions related to the health and safety of students, enforcing legal requirements dictated by the state and district, personnel decisions related to evaluations, and hiring and firing.

Next, the leader should establish the protocols for a communication process that invites advice and counsel from others on issues related to shared decisions. These may include soliciting input on policies, procedures and practices, program changes, master-schedule building, or other areas associated with the school culture. Finally, if the principal chooses to create a consensus decision-making process, with the staff having the power to vote for new programs, policy changes, and so forth, the leader must develop specific protocols and procedures to follow to handle the minority position when a vote is taken.

In similar fashion, students, parents, and community voices need to be included in the decision-making process in a meaningful and legitimate way. The National Association of Secondary School Principals believes the involvement of students, teachers, family members, and the community in the decision-making process is one of the cornerstones to improved student achievement (*Breaking Ranks II* 2004). The system must be expanded to include more ideas from multiple sources.

The power and drawback of effective consensus decision making is that the organization needs to go slow in order to go fast. The more a topic is discussed, the more refined it gets and the more voices are heard in the process. However, this process takes a lot of time and often becomes frustrating for participants who seek immediate, quick fixes for issues. Comments sometimes become disingenuous, people stop listening to others, or participants anticipate what will be said because they have heard it all before. Such a process, unchecked by specifically designed procedures, creates an atmosphere of distrust and disrespect, causing some people to withdraw from conversations, to become clock-watchers, or worse yet, feel "unsafe" sharing feelings and ideas in a general dialogue with others.

Finally, when participants in the program are engaged in the change process, the leader needs to create and post a change model so that everyone engaged in the activity knows where they are in the process, what steps to anticipate, and how to maneuver through the change. Too often, organizations move into the change process without clear direction or steps to follow. People need to know the rules of the game and how the suggested changes interact and mesh with the decision-making process and decision makers.

Reflection #4: Become a Political Buffer

One of the characteristics a principal is most appreciated for is the ability to protect the school staff from district politics. Usually, principals are scheduled to attend high school principals' and leadership meetings on a monthly basis. Often, both meetings host a series of "talking heads" and include a variety of topics related to many items of minimal interest to building staff.

Sometimes, especially during troubled economic periods, the news about budget woes or staff cuts is designed to prepare leaders to address upcoming events. The principal must become an effective political buffer in sifting through a host of these items to determine which ones need to be shared with staff and which can be placed in the principal's personal FYI file and left untouched. Determine which ones have an immediate impact on your program, students, and vision/mission and share them at appropriate times or with appropriate individuals. Hesitate to share speculations or hints of major policy or program changes until the decision-making process is complete.

Speculation and rumors needlessly get in the way of effective instruction and have a negative impact on the learning culture for students. If staff members hear rumors from colleagues in other buildings, these messages need to be addressed. However, make the personal commitment to not be the bearer of speculation or rumor after attending a central office meeting. Your staff will appreciate this courtesy.

Reflection #5: New Kids on the Block

The principal faces a huge challenge whenever a new staff member is hired. The problem is, how will the new employee be acculturated into the program? For new kids on the block, their biggest challenge is to identify how to fit into an established system and still initiate new ideas, delivered with exuberance, while remaining filled with the desire to contribute to the school. Veteran teachers, who have taken great pride in establishing tradition and cultural components that work, often resent interlopers, who do not have a sense of history with the program. If not properly handled, the integration of new teachers will be fraught with tension and power struggles, and will create a "war of resistance" among veteran staff that will have a negative impact on the building culture and students.

In some cases, acculturation into the school is assisted by creating a buddy system in order for individuals in similar departments to learn norms and culture protocols. However, this may have limited value if the veteran "buddy" happens to be on the fringe of the school's culture and uses the mentoring opportunity to recruit an ally in a culture war. It also has limited value if the mentor is a teacher with only one or two years of experience in the current building, because he or she is still learning the subtle nuances embedded in the existing atmosphere.

Another, more successful, approach is to designate a veteran staff member to be the resident building mentor. Such a building coach can convene bimonthly meetings, review written policies and staff protocols, invite former students to address the group, and ask veteran staff members and former graduates to talk about their experiences in the school. The meetings may be held without the principal so people can be candid and insightful, not measuring words in the presence of an administrator.

Due to the increasing numbers of babyboomer retirements, it may be wise to consider providing financial compensation for the building's mentor coordinator. If the district cannot support such efforts, the principal may want to find discretionary dollars to compensate a designated mentor in his or her building. No matter what approach is used, the acculturation process for new staff members should never be slighted, minimized, or neglected.

Reflection #6: Working with Gen X Teachers

As retirement possibilities capture the attention of more and more seasoned teachers throughout the nation, the culture of school, like the business world, will dramatically change. Nicely summarized in the pages of the Center for Generational Studies newsletters, various authors emphasize that baby boomers, who entered education as a lifetime career, most often thrived on rewards and validation that flowed for a job well done. As salaried employees, boomers made a commitment to work long hours to complete tasks, often to the detriment and sacrifice of family and personal life. Driven by a strong work ethic modeled by many parents, boomers were results oriented and took time to build relationships that led to team approaches in problem solving and task completion. The baby boomers experienced careers filled with opportunity and many personal rewards.

Now, Generation X teachers, born between 1970 and 1990, are graduating from colleges and universities and moving into the teaching field. Their approach to education as a profession differs significantly from that of the boomers, who have been around for thirty years or more. Their approach to life and career often presents the seasoned principal with several challenges. According to the Center for Generational Studies, in Aurora, Colorado, Generation X teachers need to feel a sense of appreciation from their bosses and colleagues. They thrive on personalized feedback and recognition for unique projects or lessons taught in class.

Much to the chagrin of the previous generation of educators, Gen X instructors do not typically view teaching as a lifelong career, with a loyalty to a particular building or program. They consider teaching a job, not a career, and often view themselves as free agents with specialized skills to attract offers from other school districts that can offer them more. They have strong personal interests and hobbies, and enjoy lives outside of school, causing many to leave the building when their students do. Baby boomers who are often loaded down with papers to grade or leave school long after closing hours resent this behavior but may secretly admire it. Many Gen X people grew up as latchkey kids; they want to work as independent members of a team, take ownership in projects they choose, and have fun in the process.

A principal's challenge is to create a working environment that will strike a balance between the remaining baby boomers, quickly transitioning into retirement, and the new Gen X teachers who are flooding personnel departments with applications. If the principal takes time to respond to the needs and attributes of the Gen X teachers, he or she can forge a building culture that adds value to the program. For example, with massive retirements occurring yearly, it is reassuring to realize that Gen X replacements thrive on change and can easily adapt to new faces and teaching assignments from year to year. Because many have lived with divorced and blended families, they can move from room to room or program to program with minimal stress. The baby-boomer teacher, however, often takes possession of a room, "owns" it until retirement, and is greatly stressed when asked to move or change instructional assignments.

Gen X teachers are comfortable with technology, because they grew up surrounded by Game Boys and a multitude of software programs.

They establish innovative ways to use the expensive technology schools are purchasing. They are independent and, if the principal's instructions and parameters are clearly communicated, take responsibility to complete any task. These younger teachers are not intimidated by authority and proceed without seeking approval for completing projects. If the principal requires personal input on projects assigned to Gen Xers, he or she must establish review dates and benchmarks as assigned projects unfold. Given freedom within specific guidelines, these younger teachers tend to add a creative flair to a given project and turn it into something special and uniquely theirs.

As principal, you can establish a working balance between boomers and Gen Xers by applying some creative management techniques. In order to establish a unified connection between both generations, it is necessary to establish a clear vision and a set of goals to achieve. This fact offers the principal a cultural glue to provide a common bond between the two groups. Therefore, the key to success returns to that "vision thing."

Robert Wendover, director of the Center for Generational Studies, has compiled the following list of what each generation is looking for in the professional setting.

Baby boomers Want:

Leadership opportunities
A team environment
A warm friendly atmosphere
Opportunities to prove themselves
A career track
$$$.

Generation Xers Want:

Fun and informality
Opportunity for development
Flexibility
Quality products and service
Efficiency and functionality
$$$.

Whether you chose to work individually and/or collectively with the last of the boomer teachers and the new Gen X staff members, it is important to respond to their individual needs as educators and people. Knowing an employee's learning style assists in communication issues and thinking processes. Similarly, becoming familiar with the specific generational differences and preferences will also benefit the entire organization.

Apart from the day-to-day interactions with each generation of staff members, the principal may want to consider structuring collaborative work responsibilities in the following manner. Boomers want leadership opportunities within a team environment, punctuated by a warm and friendly atmosphere, and Gen Xers want opportunities for personal development, flexibility, fun, and efficiency. The principal can create committees that respond to the needs of each group.

To respond to the preferences of each generational group, the principal may want to establish a working committee, for example, that is cochaired by a boomer and a Gen Xer. The Gen Xer's task would be to create grounding activities (icebreakers) for committee members to develop a way of bonding and becoming friendly with each other. The assignment would permit the Gen Xer to have fun and foster informality in the process. In similar fashion, charge the boomer cochair with a given criteria that requires the committee to stay on task, demonstrate efficiency, and produce a quality product that blends the experience of the boomer with the focus of the Gen Xer. The parameters would encourage creativity and multiple options that both groups support.

After such blending is accomplished as a cultural norm, both groups may be interested in discussing the generational research related to the students they are currently serving. The Center for Generational Studies describes children born between 1982 and 1999 as the "millennial generation," sometimes referred to as the digital generation, Generation Y, or the Echo Boomers. This group makes up the population of students now sitting in elementary, junior high, and senior high schools. Some are even seeking positions as teachers in your community.

According to the center's research, this generation was born into a world of cell phones, pagers, voice-recognition software, and the Internet. These youngsters have learned to question everything, including authority both in the school and the classroom. One in three millennial kids is classified as a minority, and one in four has grown up in a single-parent home. They live "in the moment" and expect immediate gratification, especially with technology. They require consistency and will demonstrate respect for others only after they have been treated with respect first.

To a school principal and staff, dominated by a mixture of boomers and Gen Xers, this established generation of students challenges current teaching strategies, traditional approaches to information acquisition, and classroom-management techniques. These learners expect classroom consistency and efficiency with every lesson, and they question statements professed to be the truth with "what if" exceptions and scenarios. Millennial students are not patient or reflective about philosophical issues or lessons that require time to develop.

This generation requires teachers to present ideas that permit and encourage multiple answers and creative, unconventional thinking. Teachers will need to keep their egos intact, present and implement classroom rules that students believe are both fair and consistent, and handle justice and accountability quickly. The future of education offers the school leader many challenges. The most interesting will be working with two diverse generations of educators and coping with a demanding group of Generation Y students.

Reflection #7: Lonely at the Top

When you become the principal of a school, all final responsibility rests on your shoulders. Even if you are fortunate enough to have a host of assistant principals or a counseling staff that offers advice, the reality is that they go home at night and return in the morning anticipating your decisions. Principals who are married often turn to their spouses for support and comfort when discussing school issues over the dinner table. Therefore, it is helpful to be married to an educator who has an understanding of the culture of schools and can relate to the issues facing you as a school administrator.

However, some individuals are not so fortunate. If married, they may have spouses who do not relate to or care about "what happened at school today." The school district often tries to provide a support network, but principals often fail to use colleagues as sounding boards for problem solving. They tend to feel embarrassed about sharing concerns and problems with others, fearing they may be viewed as weak or indecisive. Therefore, as the pressures of administrating schools in the twenty-first century become more complex and time consuming, new principals should avail themselves of the services of a personal "life coach."

This relatively new discipline establishes a personal relationship between an organizational leader and a professional life coach, trained in

Energy Management

Managing energy, not time, is the fundamental currency of high performance. Performance is grounded on the skillful management of energy. . . . To be fully engaged, we must be physically energized, emotionally connected, mentally focused and spiritually aligned with a purpose beyond our immediate self-interest.

—Jim Loehr and Tony Schwartz,
The Power of Full Engagement (2003), 17 and 5

the skills of assisting the client to stay focused on goals, organizational skills, day-to-day job performance, or personal life issues in order to seek a balance between various aspects of healthy human behavior.

In an effort to address the issue of principal isolation and to help new principals learn the culture of the learning community, the Fort Collins School District asked the staff development team to create a large loose-leaf binder filled with various aspects of the inner workings of the district's culture. The staff development department organized regularly scheduled meetings for the district's new principals where panels of veteran principals discussed many district and building protocols, procedures, and organizational topics. These meetings assisted the new principals in learning about the parameters and flexibility of the district's norms.

Taking this concept one step farther, the assistant superintendent for elementary schools restructured monthly principal's meetings so that the "sit and get" agenda played a minimal part in the time spent together. Most of the meeting engaged principals in dialogues about specific topics of interest. For example, for one assignment the assistant superintendent e-mailed the principals a series of questions about "How do you most effectively organize a schoolwide writing program?" During the meeting, principals came with prepared notes, experiences, and ideas to share with colleagues in small groups. In this way, novice and veteran principals engaged in collaborative communication.

PARTICIPATING IN THE CHANGE PROCESS

Reflection #1: Creating a Vision for the School

If you choose to be a leader and change agent, you need to know that you and the school staff are a good fit before you take the job as principal. Organizational managers can survive in any position as long as they follow procedure, policy, and protocol. However, leaders who enter positions as change agents are doomed to a tenure filled with frustration if a match between the leader's and staff's visions cannot be achieved. If no match exists, the change agent's efforts will only create protectionist walls for the status quo. After the interview process is complete and the environment analyzed, the candidate must assessed what transpired in the interview and also listen to the inner voice of conscience or intuition to determine if he or she can make a difference. The following ideas offer several approaches to maximize the leader's capacity to become an effective change agent.

First, the principal must be clear about his or her personal beliefs and share them with everyone concerned. People will judge you by the way you "walk your talk." Therefore, be sure your beliefs are grounded in solid research, effective experiences, and the silent messages provided by your inner voice. It is perfectly all right to change your mind about what you believe, because you are also an evolving human being, but be sure to share those changes, apologize for errors as necessary, and then move on with revised beliefs and the actions that follow.

Second, create a sense of urgency for change and then go slow to go fast. Staff members need to know the *why* of change and buy into the *need* for change before they make a commitment to any change process. If they do not know the reasons for the change, they will feel as if the change is a top-down decision, resent being told what to do, and sabotage the process. Nurturing an environment for change may take as long as six months before the staff endorses the process. After that, the change process gains momentum, and restructuring ideas or programs will occur very quickly.

Remember, there is always a spectrum of positions, beliefs, and traditions that must be reviewed, discussed, and modified. Some of your more impatient staff members will press you to act immediately, while others will be reluctant to make any changes at all. Do not yield to either pressure. Delayed decision making offers an opportunity to gather more information or to let proposed ideas take root and mature. In the change process, time can be your most important ally. It is imperative to keep the pressure to change on the entire system, but the pace of change can be accelerated or slowed based on your understanding of the participants' needs and readiness.

Do not promise your supervisor that a given change will occur by a specific date unless you have lots of alternative job offers. Most educational restructuring takes at least five years to complete. Be patient with progress and make a commitment to be the school's leader until the vision is completed. There is nothing more frustrating and disappointing to a staff than to work toward a long-term goal only to see the leader abandon the group before the work and the vision are accomplished.

Third, organize your staff into meaningful committees with short-term tasks to perform so that the progress of change is on the front burner of the school's business agenda and a consistent, visible part of the building's culture. Establish regular times to meet and share information. Find and share relevant research information on a weekly basis. Whenever possible, encourage all staff members to read current books and articles on various educational themes so that a culture of change is driven by research or the most promising practices being implemented in schools.

Chinese Proverb

Those who want to leave an impression for one year should plant corn; those who want to leave an impression for ten years should plant a tree; but those who want to leave an impression for one hundred years should educate a human being

—Excerpt from Chris Gillespie's
graduation speech, June 1993

Finally, create pilot and/or all-school projects that are guided by specific timelines and evaluated by authentic and credible assessment instruments. Share the results in a timely fashion so that no hint of pressure or "conspiracy" can emerge. If the experiment does not work to the staff's satisfaction, do not let egos get attached to the idea. Honestly examine the data to determine if the idea can be saved, modified, or totally scrapped. Scrapping a bad idea preserves credibility and promotes authentic actions.

Reflection #2: Size Makes a Difference

Students continually indicate they need to have a positive relationship with meaningful adults, their peers, and their learning environment. Currently, based on the economy of scale, many school buildings are constructed to house between 1,800 and 2,000-plus students. This size creates an impersonal, often hostile, environment that fosters the development of a toxic relationship between students and all forms of authority.

The larger the school setting, the greater the distancing factor between students and teachers, and students and their peers. If you walk the halls of most large high schools, you can observe the territoriality established by identifiable groups of students. You will wander through "jock hall," visit a "geek" computer lab at lunch, or stroll outside to find clusters of "Goths" or outcasts smoking across the street or just beyond school boundaries. One aspect of a successful educational program is based on relationship, relationship, and relationship. According to *Breaking Ranks* and research surrounding the small learning-community movement, the largest school should be limited to between four hundred to five hundred students. This may be an impossible financial task for any community to realize, but a creative principal and staff can design a smaller learning community within the confines of the larger school to minimize the distancing phenomenon created by school populations that resemble the size of small midwestern towns.

In the Fort Collins school system, the issues of relationship and school size captured the attention of the school board and planners when they secured bond money for the construction of a fifth high school. The building design will house up to 1,800 students, but the school is physically divided into three schools-within-a-school. Each wing of the building will have its own administrative offices, led by an

Back Alternative High Schools

In the past, alternative education has been looked down upon and viewed as a place where "bad" kids go. As a graduate of Centennial High School, an alternative school in Fort Collins, I can tell you this is no longer true.

The smaller school environment was exactly what I needed. Many students have difficulty in classes that have thirty-five kids or more crammed into a class with one teacher. When I changed schools, I found that my success rate improved, and so did my desire to be in class. My social skills improved, and I slowly changed from the quiet girl who always sat in the back to a student who was genuinely interested in learning. Not only that, but since I was interested in learning, I was able to graduate half a year early and enroll at Front Range Community College. The alternative education system has changed my life. . . . If it weren't for schools like Centennial, I might have been another high school dropout.

—Tara Clarkin, excerpts from letter to the editor,
Fort Collins *Coloradoan*, May 14, 2003

assistant principal and two counselors. In this way, each mini–high school will house a manageable number of students, who will enjoy a more positive relationship with peers and adults. The new school is scheduled to open in the fall of 2005.

The small learning-community movement fosters high relationships between adults and students. The introduction of community mentoring or a staff advisory program is an attempt to foster the relationship between a significant adult and a changing adolescent. Many schools are creating academic "looping" programs so all students can learn at their own rate and work with the same teachers for longer periods of time. Smaller learning communities can be designed to operate in large schools and take many forms to meet a variety of needs. Some of these include academies, magnet schools, houses, and transition programs. Each merits a separate examination.

Reflection #3: Big-Picture Thinking

Whether you are a principal who is a manager of change, a leader of change, or a combination of both, you must train yourself to be a "big-picture" thinker. Establish yearly personal goals as principal that implement and reinforce the program's long-range vision. Professionals often get caught up in doing things the right way for their supervisor or in response to the changing whims of the staff, and they lose sight of the big picture. They consume a lot of time and energy staying busy but miss opportunities to take the program to the next level or closer to the vision.

In order to keep your eyes on the big picture, create a chart or diagram that outlines the ideal school you want to lead. In this diagram, identify programs, positions, people, finances, and a time line that clarifies the dream. Hang this chart in your office so that visitors, community members, and school personnel can see your vision and the big picture of the program. Include some of these items on business meeting agendas for discussion. Become a "Johnny Appleseed" and drop ideas on interested staff members to see if proposals will take root and grow. Find research books and articles that address these ideas and distribute them to staff members.

As principal, your responsibility is not only to lead but also to nurture change, even when staff members are too entrapped in the day-to-day routines to look at any pictures, let alone the big one. As change occurs, craft action-research questions to measure the impact of pilot programs or experiments the school implements. Contact professional organizations to determine if an idea or concept has been implemented in any other setting and whether it has been successful. If possible, use staff development funds to send staff members to visit such programs in operation and have them report to their colleagues upon their return. Whenever possible, send school representatives to national or regional conferences, with specific directives to attend sessions where big-picture ideas are shared. The best way to keep the fires of change smoldering and ready to burst into flame is to make sure the big picture provides the fuel.

Reflection #4: Take Nothing for Granted

Every three or four years the entire student population of a high school changes. During that time, there is often a subtle shift in the

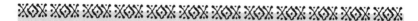

Addressed Self-Doubt

Centennial High School has given me the opportunity, rather, a second chance, to not only validate the last seventeen years of my life, but also to once again find direction for my future aspirations. A college education was always a of dream of mine ever since I was a little girl, but it was not until I enrolled at Centennial that I discovered this dream was obtainable. . . .

The realization that my high school graduation was only a year away evoked an unsettling fear. Although I knew that I had garnered the required credits for graduation, I realized that I had neither the confidence nor the self-awareness that merited a high school diploma. It is my belief that a high school diploma is more than just the spectacle of caps and gowns, proms and inspirational speeches; it is a rite of passage that must be founded in one's character and personal sense of accomplishment. I did not want to just receive a diploma; I wanted to feel as though I was truly a symbol of this passage, thus, my decision to transfer to Centennial High School.

Centennial High School is not an ordinary high school; it is a school with a caring, family atmosphere. This unique atmosphere was in many ways more challenging and demanding than the high school I had previously attended because it encouraged me to not only incur risks, but also to face my self-doubt and uncertainty, both of which I had struggled with for several years. With the unconditional support of fellow classmates and the patience of the Centennial staff, I was able to overcome the fears that prevented me from reaching my full potential in the past.

—Excerpts from Melanie Pierz's
college application essay, 1994

needs and profile of students. Make it a practice to administer a student-profile survey every two to three years to determine if the goals and purpose of your school site match the needs of the current school's population. From 1990 to 2000, the population of Centennial changed three times. The profile of its students changed, and, as a result, the staff's instructional emphasis and programs had to change to meet their needs.

In 1990, more than one-third of Centennial's students lived by themselves, and another third lived with friends. By 2000, more than 50 percent of the students lived with both parents. In 1990, the average age of students enrolled in Centennial was 18.2, but by 2000 the average age was 16.2. This was a significant shift in a decade and greatly impacted Centennial's instructional format, behavioral protocols, and its working relationship with parents.

In addition to conducting a tri-year survey, keep an updated database to track changes in the school's history, population shifts, and needs. Staff members and school leadership often change, and such a database provides a valuable asset for new staff members or a new principal to grasp a sense of the building and program history and to plan future visions.

Finally, identify the official school grant writer, someone in your building who has a flair for writing, number crunching, and organization. No matter how much money the state provides the school district or its sites, there is never enough money for the institution to experiment with change. As new visions and goals unfold, there is a constant need for site-based research and development dollars that rarely come from the district. Therefore, find an individual or team of people to write for the variety of grants that are available every year. Having an accessible database available for this individual or group will make the tedious job of filling out grant applications much easier.

COMMUNITY PARTICIPANT

Reflection #1: Become a Visible Symbol

Some principals limit their focus and energy to the school site. View yourself as a beacon in the community, one of those individuals who uphold its standards, traditions, and culture. Become a member of a community service club. Within a short time, you will be able to nurture support and enjoy a visible relationship with a variety of prominent, interested civic leaders in the community. Membership in these organizations offers you another public forum to add luster to the school's program.

Service clubs are always looking for programs to present and, if you have created a vision for the future and a captivating program to share, volunteer to become a speaker for the organizations you belong to and others that show an interest. Use every opportunity to share your school's vision and to market its purpose with people who will spread the word to others.

In addition, it would be helpful to dust off your writing talents and pen an article or two for publication in the local newspaper, magazines, or other outlets distributed throughout the community. Short articles about the nature of adolescents, parenting advice, or various aspects of unique curriculum offerings foster great public relations.

Reflection #2: Open Doors and Open House

In another public relations move, hold monthly open-house days for various sectors of the community. If you want to impress the community with the nature and success of your program, hold these special events from 11 a.m. to 1 p.m., offering lunch or snacks, and provide guided tours led by students who have a passion for and commitment to the school's program. This kind of event impresses everyone.

Realtors are one of the most important groups in the community to invite to an open house. Clients constantly ask selling agents what the city schools are like and which would they recommend. Other groups who have a huge communication networks throughout the city include hair stylists, medical professionals, dentists, and government officials. If they visit the school and are welcome by enthusiastic student guides who explain the unique features of the program, the reputation of the school will soar.

Reflection #3: Take the Time to Shake Hands

No matter who walks into your building, get out of your office, introduce yourself and shake the visitor's hand. Make it a ritual to stop what you are doing, even if you have a busy schedule, and greet each visitor. Establish this protocol with staff members, the receptionist, and your secretary so all visitors feel special when they enter the building. Encourage students to extend a greeting to any visitor who enters the building as well. They become excellent ambassadors for the program. If students spend five to ten minutes chatting with visitors, guests will learn more about the school's culture than in an hour's visit in the principal's office.

TRANSITIONS

Reflection #1: Future Leadership Challenges

With building bonds approved by the citizens of Fort Collins, the place of Centennial High School as the district's alternative program was assured. The architectural plans called for the construction of classrooms, administrative area, computer labs, a new science lab, art room, gymnasium/multipurpose room, and the creation of a building trades facility. By the fall of 2005, Centennial will become a state-of-the-art school, and the "visioning process" will begin again. After the construction dust settles, it will be time to create a new five-year vision to take the program to the next level. The principal, staff, parents, and students have the opportunity to create a vision that will take the program to the next level of excellence. We know that change is constant and nothing ever stays the same. Programs improve or decline based on the passion and vision of participants.

Even though the future of Centennial High School is guaranteed, an even greater challenge awaits current and future principals in public education. Principals continue to face ever-increasing expectations from the public. Parents now seem to be more concerned with what is best for their own children and less on education for the common good. In other words, parents want schools to develop programs that specifically address the needs of *their* sons and daughters and want less discussion about the needs of the greater community of learners. This attitude may be the result of the continuous attacks on public education or the realization that public schools cannot adequately address the needs of all people. Dwindling financial resources and the belief that the school needs to do it all may have reached a critical mass.

No matter what the reasoning, parents exhibit discontent and impatience with schools and show these feelings by either becoming more passionately active in school politics or by abandoning support for the local school. They voice complaints to the principal and withdraw their children if the solution does not meet their specific needs. There seems to be little "middle ground" or patience to negotiate. The rapid growth and government sanction of charter schools offers parents a full menu of educational choices. In order to preserve public education, the principal is required to become more adept at problem solving, conflict management, and negotiation to retain student enrollment.

The emergence of No Child Left Behind legislation, annual yearly progress requirements, mandated testing by states, and the voucher system has also created more concern for the principal. The principal must function as a statistician, staff morale booster, data interpreter, and public reporter. Schools have been pressured to perform or be labeled "underachieving" schools or, worse yet, be ridiculed in public as a school on probation or slated for closing.

By necessity, the principal is forced to become a marketing expert, driven by data and test results in an attempt to prove that his or her school is better than others. Since many schools have open-enrollment options, the principal may be faced with an ethical dilemma of seeking preferred students who excel in standardized testing rather than accepting the more needy groups of students who are challenged by lower reading, math, and writing skills. Even though these students may need a quality school setting, they may not be enrolled as preferred customers. By necessity, alternative schools will be required to fill the educational gaps of a district's most academically challenged students.

Although principal licensure programs do not emphasize marketing strategies, public relations skills, grant writing, and statistical information analysis, today's principal must learn to wear these hats in order to survive. Based on budget cuts in difficult economic times, many school districts are beginning to embrace the notion of "principal-centered leadership"—that is, reducing the central office's role in providing curriculum and other services and empowering the building principal with the authority to accomplish these tasks, thus adding more responsibility and stress to the leader of the school site.

In his book *Schools That Learn* (2000), Peter Senge suggests that the new principal will have to master four key competencies: engagement, systems thinking, leading learning, and self-awareness. The effective principal can no longer lead from institutional power derived from the position and authority once bestowed upon the school leader. The modern principal must have the people skills and ambiguity tolerance to mobilize people to converse about problems or situations that may have no clear definition or recognizable solutions. He or she must become skilled at orchestrating divergent thinking, recognizing and resolving conflicts between players, and moving various groups toward problem resolution.

The principal must become an effective systems thinker. The building leader needs to have the big-picture view of situations or problems being discussed. With the complexity of large school systems and the tendency to be loosely coupled organizations, the principal will not only have to think outside of his or her box but also be aware of what opportunities and challenges lie in other boxes. In spite of passion and loyalty, a particular school is not the center of the universe, and its staff must adjust to the realities of the system and community in which it resides.

As a collaborative leader, the new principal cannot hope to be the self-appointed, knowledgeable authority for every problem or dilemma facing the school. As the "leading learner," the principal must model behavior that demonstrates a willingness to learn and discover solutions along with the rest of the staff and community. Based on the pace of life and the information explosion created by technology, the concept of the all-knowing sage as principal is obsolete. Access to a computer and multiple websites makes an "informational expert" of anyone who cares about an issue and has time to explore it.

Finally, Senge indicates that the principal will live with ever-increasing stress and tension and must seek time for personal reflection and renewal. To be an effective principal, one must have a solid handle on his or her motivations, personal sense of self-worth, and life goals. This requires taking time away from the office for self-renewal and seeking professional consultations with either a psychotherapist or personal coach. Inevitably, the principal must ask the personal question, "Do I continue to offer the system, my staff, my family, and myself the value I believe we deserve?" If the answer is no, it's time for a change.

THE MODERN PRINCIPAL

The twenty-first-century principal is asked to play many roles in the community and at school. The principal needs to become an architect of change and, at the same time, a protector of community traditions and school culture. The principal is required to be a statistician and accountant and still maintain a humane relationship with staff, parents, students, and community members. The principal is expected to be a kind, caring, sensitive person, responding to everyone's needs, but also to enforce state mandates, safety regulations, and school laws, and implement standardized tests. The principal needs to be a leader who empowers collaborative groups to share decision making, set policy, and govern the system, while still maintaining the vestiges of the power and authority that come with the institutionalized role.

The next few decades will try the patience, will, and stamina of the new principal as he or she tries to meet the needs of multiple stakeholders and constituents. The ideas, observations, and suggestions presented in this book offer ways to more effectively organize the process of change, and drive a school with a clear vision. The process presents a continual challenge to establish and maintain credibility and trust with staff, students, parents, supervisors, and the community while attacking the status quo and causing discomfort to employees

In spite of all the pressures and responsibilities facing the modern principal, one must always keep in mind the important work being accomplished. Julie Baxter, a former Centennial High School graduate and now an assistant city editor for the Fort Collins *Coloradoan*, remembered her time as a student at Centennial and wrote a column about the school.

In part, she said,

> Centennial was the first place where I realized no one but me would dictate my future success. And as I looked around the crowd of past and present students gathered last week, I was convinced it was the same for them. Among the alumni were police detectives, business leaders, stay-at-home moms. Among the students were dreamers, confident that their opportunities were as endless as their imagination and drive. And I was proud to be among them. Centennial is the place where hope lives, where past mistakes don't count against future success, where students can be anything and everything they are willing to be.
>
> Having a safe haven for such self-discovery is only a start, though, for that discovery is no small act. As the e. e. cummings quote on my invitation so eloquently stated, "It takes courage to grow up and turn out to be who you really are."

In spite of the challenges and energy needed to model effective leadership and to shape dreams into attainable visions, isn't that what it's all about?

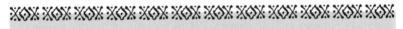

Centennial High School's Official Poem

The Road Not Taken,
by Robert Frost

Two roads diverged in a yellow wood,
And sorry I could not travel both
And be one traveler, long I stood
And looked down one as far as I could
To where it bent in the undergrowth;
Then took the other, as just as fair,
And having perhaps the better claim,
Because it was grassy and wanted wear;
Though as for that the passing there
Had worn them really about the same,
And both that morning equally lay
In leaves no step had trodden black.
Oh, I kept the first for another day!
Yet knowing how way leads on to way,
I doubted if I should ever come back.
I shall be telling this with a sigh
Somewhere ages and ages hence:
Two roads diverged in the wood, and I—
I took the road less traveled by,
And that has made all the difference.

BIBLIOGRAPHY

BOOKS

Blanchard, K., and S. Johnson. 1982. *The One-Minute Manager*. New York: Harper and Row.

Breaking Ranks: Changing an American Institution: A Report of the National Association of Secondary School Principals on the High School of the 21st Century. 1996. Reston, Va.: National Association of Secondary School Principals.

Breaking Ranks II: Strategies for Leading High School Reform. 2004. Reston, Va.: National Association of Secondary School Principals.

Butler, K. 1986. *Learning Styles and Teaching Styles in Theory and Practice*. Columbia, Conn.: Learner's Dimension.

Coelho, P. 1994. *The Alchemist*. San Francisco: Harper.

Collins, J. 2001. *Good to Great: Why Some Companies Make the Leap . . . While Others Don't*. New York: HarperCollins.

Fullan, M. 1993. *Change Forces*. Bristol, Pa.: Falmer.

———. 2001. *Leading in a Culture of Change*. San Francisco: Jossey-Bass

Glasser, W. 1990. *The Quality School: Managing Students without Coercion*. New York: Harper and Row.

———. 1993. *The Quality School Teacher*. New York: HarperCollins.

Goldstein, A. 1988. *The Prepare Curriculum: Teaching Prosocial Competencies*. Champaign, Ill.: Research.

Goodlad, J. 1990. *Teachers for Our Nation's Schools*. San Francisco: Jossey-Bass.

Hansen, J., and E. Liftin. 1991. *School Restructuring: A Practitioner's Guide*. Swampscott, Mass.: Watersun.

Harris, T. 1969. *I'm O.K., You're O.K.* New York: Avon Books.

Loehr, J., and T. Schwartz. 2003. *The Power of Full Engagement: Managing Energy Not Time Is the Key to High Performance and Personal Renewal*. New York: Free Press.

McEwan, E. 1997. *Leading Your Team to Excellence*. Thousand Oaks, Calif.: Corwin.

Meier, D. 1995. *The Power of Their Ideas: Lessons for America from a Small School in Harlem*. Boston: Beacon.

Pascale, R., M. Millemann, and L. Gioja. 2000. *Surfing the Edge of Chaos*. New York: Crown Business.

Schrumpf, F., D. Crawford, and R. Bodine. 1997. *Peer Mediation: Conflict Resolution in Schools*. Campaign, Ill.: Research.

Senge, P. 1999. *A Fifth Discipline: The Dance of Change*. New York: Doubleday.

———. 2000. *A Fifth Discipline: Schools That Learn*. New York: Doubleday.

Sergiovanni, T. 1992. *Moral Leadership*. San Francisco: Jossey-Bass.

Sizer, T. 1984. *Horace's Compromise: The Dilemma of the American High School*. Boston: Houghton Mifflin.

———. 1996. *Horace's Hope: What Works for the American High School*. Boston: Houghton Mifflin.

Steinbeck, J. 1962. *Travels with Charlie*. New York: Penguin Books.

Villeneuve, P. 2002. *Want to Be a Millionaire? Investing Strategies for Young Investors*. Fort Collins, Colo.: Academy of Young Investors.

Williams, P., and D. Davis. 2002. *Therapist as Life Coach: Transforming Your Practice*. New York: W. W. Norton.

ARTICLES

Alderman, M. K. 1990. Motivation for At-Risk Students. *Educational Leadership* 48 (1): 27–30.

Bauman, S., and P. Sachs-Kapp. 1998. A School Takes a Stand: Promotion of Sexual Orientation Workshops by Counselors. *Professional School Counseling* 1 (3): 42–45.

Berman, S. 1990.Educating for Social Responsibility. *Educational Leadership* 48 (3): 75–80.

Carroll, J. 1990. The Copernican Plan: Restructuring the American High School. *Phi Delta Kappan* 75 (5): 358–65.

Clifford, M. 1990. Students Need Challenge, Not Easy Success. *Educational Leadership* 48 (1): 22–26.

Deal, T. 1990. Reframing Reform. *Educational Leadership* 47 (8): 6–12.

Edwards, J. 1991. To Teach Responsibility, Bring Back the Dalton Plan. *Phi Delta Kappan* 72 (5): 398–401.

Goodlad, J. 1990. Studying the Education of Educators: From Conception to Findings. *Phi Delta Kappan* 71 (9): 698–701.

———. 1992. On Taking School Reform Seriously. *Phi Delta Kappan* 74 (3): 4–10.

Hodgkinson, H. 1991. Reform Versus Reality. *Phi Delta Kappan* 72 (1): 9–16.

Holmes Group. 1990. *Tomorrow's School's*. East Lansing, Mich.

Lamperes, B. 1994. Empowering At-Risk Students to Succeed. *Educational Leadership* 52 (3): 67–70.

———. 1996. Building a Culture of Success. Proceedings of the 8th annual National Dropout Prevention Conference, Tampa, Fla., March.

———. 1997. Count to Five . . . Tools Help Teens Deal with Problems without the Skills and Experience of Adulthood. 2, 3, *Fort Collins-Loveland Parent Magazine*, p. 16.

———. 1999. The Roads Scholar Program: Personalizing Learning through School, Travel and Service. *Classroom Leadership Newsletter* (September). Alexandria, Va.: Association for Supervision and Curriculum Development.

———. 2004. Ten Strategies for Staff Empowerment. *Principal Leadership* 4 (6): 32–37.

Landfried, S. 1989. Enabling Undermines Responsibility in Students. *Educational Leadership* 47 (3): 79–83.

Newmann, F. 1991. Linking Restructuring to Authentic Student Achievement. *Phi Delta Kappan* 72 (6): 458–63.

Nickle, M., F. Flynt, D. Poynter, and J. Rees. 1990. Does It Make a Difference If You Change the Structure? School-within-a-School. *Phi Delta Kappan* 72 (2): 148–52.

Sternberg, R. 1990. Thinking Styles: Keys to Understanding Student Performance. *Phi Delta Kappan* 71 (5): 366–72.

Wendover, R. 1966. Generation X. *Generations Newsletter* 1 (winter). Aurora, Colo.: Center for Generational Studies.

———. 1997. Generation X's Preferred Working Environment. *Generations Newsletter* 4 (fall). Aurora, Colo.: Center for Generational Studies.

———. 1999a. Millennial Generation: From Beanie Babies to Beepers. *Generations Newsletter* 7 (fall). Aurora, Colo.: Center for Generational Studies.

———. 1999b. Showdown at Generation Gap: The Boomers vs. the Busters. *Generations Newsletter* 6 (winter). Aurora, Colo.: Center for Generational Studies.

———. 1999c. The Experts Are Saying the Millennials Are . . . *Generations Newsletter* 7 (fall). Aurora, Colo.: Center for Generational Studies.

———. 2000. The Xers and the Boomers: Ten Delineators. *Generations Newsletter* 8 (fall). Aurora, Colo.: Center for Generational Studies.

NEWSPAPERS

Baxter, J. 1996. Hands-on Learning. Fort Collins *Coloradoan*, February 15, p. 1, Choice Section.

———. 2003. Centennial Defined by Spirit, Not Stereotype. Fort Collins *Coloradoan*, April 16, p. 1, local section.

Fort Collins, Colorado. 1997. "News from Every State," *USA Today*, April 3 p. 13A.

Ward, S. 1991. Fourth High School Has Personal Touch. Rocky Mountain *Highlighter* 18 (4), p. 6.

CORRESPONDENCE

Anonymous Parent. Letter to Bill Liskey, December 12, 1997.

Bauman, S., et al. Letter Centennial staff to Interim Superintendent of Schools, Armon Johannsen, June 7, 1991.

Bonnette, R., and P. Letter to Bill Lamperes, May 5, 1994.

Burleson, R., principal of Freemont School, Florence, Colo., to Bill Lamperes, February, 5, 1999.

Daniels, M., and B. Anderson, Centennial High School, Peoria, Ariz., to Bill Lamperes, January 12, 2001.

Evans, J. Letter to Bill Lamperes, June 12, 1994.

Foster, A. Letter to Bill Lamperes, April 25, 1999.

Jacobsen, J. Letter to Bill Lamperes, May 26, 1993.

Kellemeyer, K. Letter to anonymous donor, August 31, 1998.

Kellemeyer, R. Letter to anonymous donor, August 25, 1998.

Lachman, L. Letter to Bill Lamperes, March 24, 1997.

Lamperes, B. Letter to Thornton Charitable Foundation, August 20, 2000.

Martinez, R. Letter to Bill Lamperes, March 21, 2002.

Mathews Street Students, Letter to Joe Hendrickson, director of Special Education, Poudre School District, November, 1993.

Mills, K. Letter to Bill Lamperes, June 6, 1998.

Sandoval, J. Memo to Bill Lamperes, September 13, 1990.

Schumacher, M. Letter to Bill Lamperes, November 5, 1994.

Theimer, L. Letter to Bill Lamperes, January 31, 1999.

Tobin, D, V. Nastav, and K. Mass. Letter to Bill Lamperes, September 1, 1997.

Wilkerson, D. Letter to Dr. Davis Hendrix from Don Wilkerson, May 7, 1992.

INTERVIEWS

Bamford, G. Interview conducted April 24, 2003, by Bill Lamperes, author.

Cook, D. Interview conducted April 27, 2003. by Bill Lamperes, author.

Hendrickson, J. Interview conducted April 24, 2003, by Bill Lamperes, author.

MISCELLANEOUS DOCUMENTS, BOOKLETS, AND PRESENTATIONS

Centennial High School "Catch the Vision" pamphlet. 1991 Unpublished student brochure distributed to visitors of Centennial High School.

Concerns-Based Adoption Model. 1974. Research and Development Center for Teacher Education, University of Texas at Austin.

Deal, T. 1991. Assessing and Changing Cultures. Presentation made at an in-district leadership conference on February 19, Marriott Hotel, Fort Collins, Colo.

Deniston, T. 1997. Authentic Inquiry and Collaboration at a Non-Traditional Professional Development High School. Unpublished Ph.D. diss., Fort Collins, Colo.: Colorado State University.

National Commission on Excellence in Education, A Nation at Risk. 1983. Washington, D.C.: Government Printing Office.

Shiola, S., and M. Hazel. 2002 Poudre School District Administrator Resources, Fort Collins, Colo., Office of Staff Development.

Sopris West Educational Services, 4903 Specialty Place, Longmont, Colorado, 80524, (303) 651-2829.

Substance Abuse Subtle Screening Inventory. 1985. Springville, Ind.: SASSI Institute.

Tiberio, M. 1995. Centennial Writing Guidelines. Unpublished booklet produced at Centennial High School, Fort Collins, Colo.

Wendover, R. 2001. From Ricky and Lucy to Beavis and Butthead. Aurora,
    Colo.: Center of Generational Studies, 2001.
Wilson, T. 1995. Report of the Visit of the North Central Association Evalua-
    tion Team on April 3 through 7, 1995. (May 15).
———. 1996. Report of the Follow-up Visit of the North Central Evaluation
    Team Chair. October 17.

INDEX

action research, 206–7
assessment data: American College Test (ACT), 177, 179, 180; Colorado Student Assessment Program (CSAP), 177; graduate plans survey, 180–82; Iowa Test of Basic Skills, 179; North Central assessment, 147, 150–51, 167; questions used to generate data, 23–24, 44; Test of Basic Education (TABE), 78–79, 176

belief statements: of the leader, 3–4, 226; of the organization, 61, 155
Breaking Ranks, recommendations of, vii, 127, 129, 156, 211, 225, 230, 240
budget process, 35–37
building trades program, 171–73

campus beautification project, 134–37, 160
Centennial High School: description of campus, xv–xvi, 157–58; in transition, 244
Centennial West High School, 159–62
change process: analysis of North Central Report, 147–53; asset model, 20–23; hearing the critics, 53–55; initiating change, 47–73, 230; preparation for, 27–45; profile of customers, 55–57, 242–44; shared decision-making model, 32–38; staff reading seminars, 42; stepping into the circle, 66–71; using the CBAM survey to measure change, 72–73; war room strategies, 58–60
Colorado State University: Bridges program, 173; Center for

ABOUT THE AUTHOR

Bill Lamperes received his doctor of arts degree from Carnegie-Mellon University, Pittsburgh, Pennsylvania, in 1985. He has taught social studies in elementary, junior, and senior high schools. He worked for the Fort Collins (Colorado) School District as a social studies curriculum specialist for ten years. For twelve years, Bill also served as the principal of Centennial High School, an alternative school in Fort Collins.

Currently, Bill is the director of transitional services in the Peoria Unified School District #11, in Glendale, Arizona. He is engaged in the process of inventing several alternative programs for the district, including redesigning summer school, community education, alternative schools, and the creation of a high-tech high school. He has published several articles on innovative educational programs and has made presentations on developing and implementing effective alternative programs at various regional and national conferences.

Bill Lamperes may be contacted at the Peoria Unified School District #11, 6330 W. Thunderbird Road, Glendale, Arizona 85306, 623-486-6011, or by e-mail at blamperes@peoriaud.k12.az.us.